Pathology and Law

Springer
New York
Berlin
Heidelberg
Hong Kong
London
Milan
Paris
Tokyo

Pathology and Law

A Practical Guide for the Pathologist

Gregory G. Davis, MD, MSPH,
Department of Pathology
University of Alabama at Birmingham
Birmingham, Alabama

 Springer

Gregory G. Davis, MD
Associate Professor
Department of Pathology
University of Alabama at Birmingham
and
Associate Medical Examiner
Jefferson County
1515 Sixth Avenue South, Room 611
Birmingham, AL 35233
USA

Library of Congress Cataloging-in-Publication Data
Davis, Gregory G.
　　Pathology and law : a practical guide for the pathologist / Gregory G. Davis.
　　　p.　; cm.
　　Includes index.
　　1.　Forensic pathology.　2. Evidence, Expert.　I. Title.
　　[DNLM: 1. Pathology—legislation & jurisprudence.　2. Expert Testimony—legislation &
jurisprudence.　3. Forensic Medicine—legislation & jurisprudence.　4.
Malpractice—legislation & jurisprudence. QZ 32.4 D261p 2003]
　　RA1063.4.D385　2003
　　614'.1—dc22　　　　　　　　　　　　　　　　　　　　　　　　2003058442

ISBN 0-387-20035-5　　　　　Printed on acid-free paper.

Printed in the United States of America.　　(RW/EB)

9 8 7 6 5 4 3 2 1　　　　SPIN 10938577

Springer-Verlag is a part of *Springer Science+Business Media*

springeronline.com

To Sue
who encourages

Acknowledgments

My debt to my contributors, Drs. Margie Scott and Gregory J. Davis, is obvious. A conversation with Drs. Stephen Vogel and Bruce Alexander was the germ for this work, which first appeared in an abbreviated form as a short course at the United States and Canadian Academy of Pathology. I am grateful to Springer for giving the seed the opportunity to grow into a book. Carol Wang of Springer has been unfailingly helpful and cheerful. Margaret Dotzler and Dr. John Smith shared their enthusiasm and experience in writing books, easing my task. Bob Goodwin, J.D., Jonathan Briskin, J.D, M.D, and Greg Skipper, M.D. provided their unique insight, and the book is better for it.

Gregory G. Davis, M.D.

Preface

This book has been written by physicians for physicians. Each contributor is a board certified pathologist who is licensed to practice medicine. Two practice as forensic pathologists, and one practices as a director of laboratory medicine. Each has testified as an expert witness in court many times. None has formal training as an attorney. The information in this book is a product of our experience as pathologists interacting with the American legal system. Some of the information comes from reading and some from talking with attorneys, but mostly it comes from the school of hard knocks that we have attended while dealing with attorneys and testifying in court. Our purpose is to present a physician's-eye view of court to physicians so that if you as a physician are ever called to court, the judicial process will not seem so alien.

Gregory G. Davis, M.D.

Contributors

Gregory G. Davis, M.D., Associate Professor, Forensic Division, Department of Pathology, University of Alabama at Birmingham, and Associate Coroner/Medical Examiner, Jefferson County, Alabama 35233 USA

Gregory J. Davis, M.D., Professor, Associate Director, Residency Training Program, Department of Pathology and Laboratory Medicine, University of Kentucky College of Medicine, Lexington, and Associate Chief Medical Examiner, Commonwealth of Kentucky, Frankfort, Kentucky 40601 USA.

Margie A. Scott, M.D., Chief, Pathology and Laboratory Medicine Service, Central Arkansas Veterans Healthcare Systems, and Associate Professor of Pathology, Department of Pathology, University of Arkansas Medical School, Little Rock, Arkansas 72205 USA

Contents

1
Introduction

On Medicine and Law

The profession of law has a history as old and rich as that of medicine, for there have always been disputes that needed settling just as there has always been illness that needed curing. The disciplines of medicine and law have similarities and differences, and a physician will come to understand the workings of the legal field most effectively if he reflects on the similarities and differences between the two professions.

Similarities

In many ways, the legal system is similar to the medical system. Both professions require training at the graduate level. Each profession is practiced in its own special setting, using a specialized vocabulary unique to its practitioners and incomprehensible to laymen. Medicine and law can both be divided into two great camps—surgery and internal medicine, and civil and criminal law. Both fields have general practitioners, who provide a broad range of services to all who come, and both fields have specialists, who concentrate in a particular discipline such as neuropathology or tort law and provide services to those individuals who need such specialized consideration. A person requiring a physician's care will enter as a patient at some designated access point, whether by referral to a physician's office or as an emergency admission to a hospital. In like manner, a person in need of an attorney's services will enter as a client at some designated access point within the legal profession, whether by referral to the attorney's office or by court appointment after being arrested for allegedly committing a crime. Some legal clients have simple needs that are cared for as quickly and easily as a mildly sprained ankle, while others have an extremely complicated case that seems to take on a life of its own, much like a malignant tumor. In evaluating a case, both attorneys and physicians must prove or satisfy a list of elements in order to verify a position, whether that position is a diagnosis (in medicine) or a point of view in a dispute (in law). In the United States, both professions have solo practitioners, but most professionals, whether practicing medicine or law, join together into group practices. No single attorney is interchangeable with any other attorney, just as no one physician is interchangeable with any other in his specialty, or even within his group. The most important similarity perhaps is that there are capable attorneys and incompetent attorneys just as there are capable physicians and incompetent physicians.

Differences

On the other hand, medicine and law differ in fundamental ways. Even though physicians may be divided roughly into two camps, medicine and surgery, and even though there is sparring now and then between the camps, physicians still acknowledge one common enemy—disease. When necessary, even physicians of different temperaments will work together to combat the common enemy of disease. It would appear to be different for attorneys, however. A perfectly good attorney may begin practice on the side of criminal prosecution, then switch to a job in criminal defense, then later switch back to prosecution or else over to the practice of civil law. The way in which attorneys practice on both sides of the law makes little sense when viewed from a medical perspective; it seems as though attorneys try to fight disease, then try to spread disease, then repent and fight disease until a better offer to spread disease comes along.

Another distinction between medicine and law is science. Medicine is both an art and a science, but science holds sway in the training of physicians in the United States. Attorneys tend to dislike science. The distinction between physicians and attorneys begins to grow clear in college, where prelaw students concentrate on courses such as political science and economics, while their premedical classmates study chemistry and molecular biology. Since attorneys dislike science, they typically respect physicians and the discipline that physicians demonstrate by learning the science of medicine. (As we will discuss later, this respect may prove beneficial to a physician in court.) What attorneys lack in science, they make up for in social skills. Attorneys are far more attentive to points of social grace and etiquette than is the average physician. Outside of a courtroom (their arena of battle), attorneys tend to be polite, and they are very careful to remember names and faces in a way that most physicians are not. In fact, the ability of an attorney to remember your particular name and face months or even years following a chance meeting in a restaurant can be startling, not to mention disconcerting, for a physician. Upon reflection, though, the ability of an attorney to remember your face and name after years is probably a skill akin to being able to recall the major points of someone's medical history months or years after last seeing the patient.

The most important difference between physicians and attorneys is the way in which each one is taught to approach problems, because the approach of a physician is fundamentally different from that of an attorney. Physicians are taught to approach a case empirically, considering the history, physical evidence, and laboratory results in a particular case, applying those facts and their deductions to their general fund of medical knowledge but always remembering that each case is unique. The medical approach to problem solving is reproducible in a scientific way; that is, in most cases two physicians will come to the same conclusion about the proper diagnosis for a given patient. Attorneys approach a case the other way around. Every legal case that arises has unique features, to be sure, but the laws that will govern the case were not written to address that specific case. Instead, laws are general principles that attorneys must keep in mind in order to accomplish their purpose in a given case. Each attorney in a case starts with the same law and the same facts, but their deductive reasoning based on the law and facts will end in two divergent opinions of how the legal case is to be properly interpreted. There you have the profound difference between physicians and attorneys. Physicians use a scientific approach to try to come to a single correct diagnosis, whereas attorneys always use the one set of laws that they have to come to entirely different conclusions. These different approaches that physicians and attorneys take to a problem make it difficult for either profession to understand the other without an effort of will.

The differences between what is important to attorneys and physicians are probably inherent in the personality traits of the individuals who choose one career over the other. The individual differences are then refined by the distinctions that separate the practices of medicine and law.

The King in His Court

Physicians are comfortable in medical and hospital settings, but it was not always so. However much an individual wants to be a physician, most second-year students feel intimidated by the wards and patients as they begin to practice physical diagnosis. As a second-year student, you are sharply aware of your lack of knowledge. You do not know your way around the wards, all the acronyms at the nurses' station and in the charts are a new language that you hardly comprehend, and the protocols for proper behavior on the wards are a mystery. During the third and fourth years of medical school, a medical student becomes accustomed to the medical setting, and as the years go by it is hard to remember a time when you, the practicing physician, did not enjoy being in the medical setting where you are, after all, the boss. It is enjoyable to speak of cases with your colleagues in the lunchroom, enjoyable to share a body of special knowledge. When admitted as a patient, most laymen, including attorneys, are intimidated by the medical setting that has come to be so familiar to you the physician. Some of a clinician's medical art lies in putting an anxious patient at ease in the unfamiliar surroundings of a hospital.

Court, on the other hand, is the familiar playing field of attorneys. It is only natural that any physician forced onto the playing field of attorneys would be bewildered by a setting where he does not know his way around, where the usual players sometimes speak in a foreign language, and where the protocols for proper behavior are a mystery to the uninitiated. Matters are made worse for the physician new to court because it is likely that he has been coerced into coming by a summons or subpoena to appear at a trial where his professional reputation may be on the line. It is uncomfortable to be in a new and confusing setting when the stakes are so high, just as it is hard for an attorney admitted to the hospital for evaluation of a lung mass to relax. The premise of this book is that if you as a physician already know some of what court is about and how it is conducted, then you will not be so confused, and you will probably make a better impression, whether you are on trial for malpractice or testifying as an expert witness.

2
Theory and Operation of the American Legal System

American Legal Theory

Both law and medicine are dramatic. Many radio dramas, television shows, and movies are based upon either medicine or law because what physicians and attorneys do is sometimes the stuff of high drama. Court is especially dramatic because a trial is, in a very real sense, a piece of theatre. A trial occurs when two parties who disagree over some matter present themselves before an independent party for a judgment that is binding upon the parties that disagree. The American judicial system arrives at that judgment, called the verdict, through an adversarial trial system. You may think of an adversarial trial system as a civilized version of trial by combat. In order to understand the legal proceedings in a courtroom, it is critically important to understand the theory and practice of the adversarial trial system. The method by which every trial in the United States is conducted hangs on this adversarial approach to justice.

The legal system in the United States is founded on the principle that a dispute is settled most fairly when the following three things occur.

1. Each side presents its evidence publicly.
2. The evidence is presented in the presence of the party that has been accused of wrongdoing.
3. The evidence for each side is presented in a forum where the opposing side can then vigorously challenge the merit, or even truth, of the evidence just presented.

Several points that merit discussion derive from this adversarial approach. Foremost is that the purpose of court is not, as many believe, to find out the truth in a case. This fact often comes as a surprise to those unfamiliar with court, and it echos the point made in Chapter 1 concerning the completely different approaches that physicians and attorneys take toward solving a problem. Physicians try to reach the "correct" diagnosis, whereas attorneys, who are not specifically trying to find truth in a case, are not trying to reach a "correct" anything. What is the purpose of court, if not to establish truth? The purpose of court is to settle a dispute in a civilized way, thus preventing vendetta. (The civilized solution to vendetta is the point of Aeschylus's *Orestia* trilogy.) Do not think that the legal system has no interest in establishing the truth in court, for it does. The legal system considers that the truth in a case is most likely to be determined by an adversarial approach including all three elements listed above. With truth should come a fair verdict. Court is considered civilized and is respected because, in general, the truth is made clear by public review of the evidence, and thus the United States has been largely spared the atrocities of vigilante justice.

The adversarial nature of the legal system also explains why an attorney can practice first on the side of prosecution and then on the side of defense. Whichever side the attorney represents, he is still helping to settle a dispute in the time-honored method of the legal profession.

The adversarial system makes clear why court can be such an unpleasant experience for those individuals who testify concerning evidence that they witnessed. The legal system is designed to allow the attorney representing one side to strive mightily, as if in combat, to reveal errors or flaws in the witness's testimony. Unfortunately, human nature being what it is, the valid testimony of a truthful witness can be rendered useless if that witness flinches in the heat of adversity. Therein lies the germ of what can make testifying unpleasant. No physician is a stranger to having his opinion challenged, whether by his colleagues in a weekly morbidity and mortality conference or in an academic setting. But physicians, like other professionals, chafe at having their opinion challenged publicly by someone who is not a colleague and in a way that allows the truth of the physician's words to be overpowered by a moment's lapse during trial by combat. Perhaps it will take some of the sting out of the experience to remember that when the United States was drawing up its laws governing court, the founders chose the adversarial system to redress what they considered an injustice of the English system. English courts at the time of the American Revolution heard evidence, but any man accused of a crime was excluded from hearing the evidence brought against him at his own trial. The American system sought to correct this injustice against one accused of a crime not only by assuming that a man is innocent until proven guilty but also by allowing the man accused to hear the evidence against him as it came from the lips of the witnesses. Moreover, the accused man's advocate in court—that is, his attorney—could challenge the statements of the witnesses on behalf of the accused. Seen in this light, the adversarial system does not seem such a bad thing, but it can be hard to remember that fact when you are a witness in the hot seat. (Incidentally, the right of the accused to hear all the evidence against him explains why you cannot simply fax the pertinent surgical pathology report to court. You must appear before the accused so that you can be questioned.)

American Legal Theory in Operation

The *Dramatis Personae*

There can be no theatre without players, and in an adversarial trial as described above there are four main types of players. Any trial will have a judge, who presides over the courtroom. One or more attorneys represent each side in the dispute. The witnesses are called one at a time and asked to present their story of what happened before the judge and, in most cases, to the jury, who will render the verdict. The judge, the attorneys, the witnesses, and the jury are the players in a trial.

The Jury

Recall that in an adversarial system the evidence is presented publicly. Since the entire public cannot be present in the room, the jury of citizens represents the public. A jury of your peers is not a jury of your professional peers but rather a jury of your peers as a human being and citizen (this point will be discussed in greater detail below). In a jury trial, it is this corporate body of citizens that will decide the verdict based on the evidence presented in court. The jury is chosen before the trial begins, with input from the attorneys representing each side. The attorneys for each side will interview the prospective jurors, looking to see which individuals might be especially sympathetic to their cause and which individuals might be prejudiced against their cause. The attorneys for each side may challenge a prospective juror with questions designed to bring out the bias that they suspect in that prospective juror. If the prospective juror exhibits sufficient bias, then the attorney will ask the judge to strike that prospective juror from the jury. The judge will decide whether to strike the juror or not. The attorneys for each side also get a certain number of peremptory strikes; that is, the attorney can strike a prospective juror for whatever reason the attorney wishes without recourse by the attorney for the other side or by the judge. Of course, each side in the dispute is granted the same number of peremptory strikes. Three peremptory strikes is a common number, and these trump cards must be played carefully. If you are the one on trial, then you are permitted to sit in the court at the table with your attorney while jury selection takes place. Some attorneys who represent physicians in malpractice cases like for the physician to be present during jury selection. A good physician is skilled in sizing up individuals quickly, as is a good attorney. By having the defendant physician by his side, the attorney gains an extra set of eyes to look for subtle signs that might indicate a prejudiced juror.

In one case, the physician noticed that a potential juror frowned and looked angry whenever "doctor" or "physician" was spoken. After bringing this to the attorney's attention, the attorney used one of his peremptory strikes to remove the individual from the jury pool. In another case, a prominent criminal defense attorney was called to jury duty as a citizen in a criminal trial. The defendant's attorney was certain that the prosecuting attorney would use a peremptory strike to remove the prospective juror who was an attorney. The prosecutor, however, believed that the attorney in the jury pool was fair-minded and that he would judge the case based on the evidence presented. The defense attorney did sit on the jury and was chosen as the foreman. The jury, led by the attorney, found the defendant guilty.

All phases of a trial are important to the outcome, and jury selection is an early round of gamesmanship in the process.

Physicians on trial for malpractice are prone to complain that the jury that will try them is not composed of professional peers. A jury of one's peers stems from the practice in feudal times in England of having serfs and commoners tried in courts that were the sole province of the nobility. Recall that with the Norman conquest the nobility were of French descent while the serfs and commoners were Anglo-Saxons, so the feudal system was a way for those in power to ensure that things stayed that way—a form of apartheid. In time, the concept emerged that commoners should be judged by a jury of other commoners, their peers, rather than by a jury of noblemen. Never was a jury of peers meant to imply that physicians should be judged by physicians any more than that criminals should be judged only by other criminals.

Because a jury that would sit in judgment of a physician will not be a jury of his professional peers, comment is often made that attorneys want naive jurors who are easily led to a conclusion. There is a grain of truth to this, but attorneys know that a jury composed entirely of sheep does neither side any good because sheep cannot lead themselves. Likewise, a jury composed only of leaders will get bogged down. (Imagine a jury composed entirely of departmental chairmen trying to come to an agreement.) A workable jury has one or two leaders on it. A fictional example of a workable jury is Reginald Rose's play "Twelve Angry Men," later made into a movie starring Henry Fonda.

Beware of thinking that the members of a jury are unschooled in medicine. Although unlikely to have formal training, they are Americans who doubtless watch television news or read the paper. When a prominent politician has an operation, there is often a diagram of the procedure in the paper. Important medical articles are commonly reported and discussed in the media on the day they are released in a medical journal, sometimes accompanied by sophisticated medical illustrations. The members of the jury have a degree of medical sophistication not enjoyed by citizens fifty years ago. That is to your benefit as a medical witness—the jury is that much more likely to understand and be interested in the medical matters you will discuss.

The members of a jury may not all be physicians, but they all have a life and it does *not* consist of spending weeks on a bench in a courtroom. Most jurors have jobs and families, and they are eager to fulfill their duty and return to their routine. Establishing facts in a trial is often dry and boring. The members of the jury take a dim view of anyone who wastes their time, so do not waste their time. The attorneys are the ones most likely to make the trial last overly long, so the attorneys have the most to lose by not moving the trial along at a reasonable pace.

The Judge

The judge is in charge of the trial and the courtroom. He is, in fact, the sole authority in the courtroom. The judge sets the tone for the courtroom and thus for the trial. Some judges are grave and formal; some are friendly and relaxed. Regardless of the judge's demeanor, his word is law in the courtroom, and he has armed guards, in the form of bailiffs, to back him up. The role of the judge in the courtroom is much like the role of the head surgeon in an operating room—each has a duty to maintain order, and whatever either one wants, he gets. The judge presides over the trial. Any disagreement between the two attorneys will be settled by the judge. If the judge wishes to do so, then he may interrupt the trial and ask the witness a question. It is not the place of a witness to talk to the judge, so as a witness or defendant you would do well to follow the maxim of "Do not speak unless spoken to." If the judge should choose to talk to you, then he is properly addressed as "Your Honor." If the judge is the sort to make small talk, and he wishes to make small talk with you, then you are welcome to chat, but always with respect and on topics removed from the trial. It is very important that you never alienate, anger, or otherwise cause the judge to become hostile to you. Remember that the judge sets the tone of the courtroom; if he comes to dislike you, the jury will quickly pick up on it, and things will go ill for you, no matter what your role in the trial.

Judges are professionals, and they generally understand that expert witnesses are professionals with demands upon their time in addition to a trial. Judges certainly expect a professional to respect the time of the judge and everyone in the courtroom, but with that in mind, judges usually will try to schedule a trial or organize the expert witness's appearance in trial so that the expert witness will be able to keep other professional commitments, such as scientific meetings or a busy clinical practice. Having said this, however, it remains true that a few judges will demand that they come first no matter what other obligations you may have. Every forensic pathologist knows of a case where a physician scheduled to present at a scientific conference was forced to cancel his presentation so that he could testify in a judge's court at that same time. To best avoid such an unpleasant occurrence, it is important to let an attorney who has called you to testify know your travel obligations as soon as you know of them yourself.

Judges try to protect expert witnesses from unduly harsh questioning or attacks in court, but at the same time a judge realizes that confrontation is the name of the game in trial. In other words, the judge will not strive to protect an expert witness from having his feelings hurt.

In a malpractice trial, some of the evidence that will be presented will undoubtedly come from expert witnesses. The concept of an expert witness will be discussed later in this chapter, but for now it is sufficient to say that expert witnesses will testify about complicated medical matters. In addition to the responsibilities and authority mentioned above, the judge presiding over a malpractice case has the responsibility of deciding whether the testimony of a given expert witness will be admitted into court. This authority stems from a legal ruling, known as the Daubert ruling, concerning unethical expert witness testimony.[1] Some judges consider that the attorneys are responsible for presenting the judge with sufficient evidence that the science their expert witness will discuss is sound, as opposed to quackery. Other judges, however, take a more hands-on approach to evaluating the scientific soundness of witnesses scheduled to testify before them. At present, a malpractice suit will probably be handled with less direct involvement by the judge. Judges hearing complicated class action lawsuits may get more involved in expert witness evaluation, however. Because half of all expert witnesses now testifying in federal court are physicians, the following few paragraphs will discuss the reasons why a judge might choose to actively involve himself in evaluating the science proposed by expert witnesses.

A judge presiding over a civil lawsuit that is expected to last for months and to involve many expert witnesses, such as a class action lawsuit filed for injuries related to silicone breast implants, may call a meeting with the expert witnesses scheduled to testify before him so that the judge can hear what each witness has to say in an unsworn conference prior to trial.[2] Most expert witnesses are professional, reasonable people who can sit together and discuss a matter, each presenting his viewpoint in a professional way without being unduly swayed by the viewpoints of others. By meeting with the expert witnesses, the judge gains a better understanding of the scientific issues involved, which enables the judge to define the issues in the case in his own mind and thus organize the trial to present the science to the jury most effectively. Furthermore, such a meeting allows the expert witnesses and judge to agree on common ground so that time is not wasted in court arguing over something that everyone actually agrees upon. Any conflicting opinions that threaten to erupt into conflict can be handled privately, too, rather than in the courtroom. Unlike the attorneys presenting evidence in a trial, the judge is not on a side, just as the expert witness should not be on a side. The judge is there to organize and maintain order in the trial, and the expert witnesses are there to instruct the jury in what the jury needs to know. Both the judge's objectives and the goals of the expert witnesses can be expedited by a meeting of the judge with the expert witnesses.

By reviewing the reports of expert witnesses that attorneys plan to call, a judge can limit the number and kind of expert witnesses called in a trial if, for example, the judge finds the science spurious or that two experts are essentially saying the same thing for the same side (thus avoiding duplication in the trial). Review of the reports also makes clear to the judge any area in which he needs a little tutoring, such as epidemiology, so the judge can ask the attorneys to provide him with a half-day course pertinent to the topic the judge needs to understand.

A judge has the authority to require an expert witness expected to testify before him in a trial to provide the judge, long before the trial, with a written report summarizing the opinions of the expert witness and the scientific bases for those opinions. The expert witness must sign the report, of course, and along with the report he must also submit a current copy of his curriculum vitae, a list of all the cases he has testified in for the past four years, and a disclosure of his compensation for participating in the case in point. All this information that has been submitted to the judge, and thus to the court, is admissible into court during the trial.

A judge who has gotten as involved as the judge discussed above will be the sort of judge to pay close attention to what is going on in his court. If the judge believes that neither attorney has asked a question that needs to be asked in order for the jury to understand the issue, then the judge can ask the question. Or, if the judge thinks an answer is too complicated, then the judge may gently remind the expert witness to please explain this concept to the court so that anyone can understand it. Either of these occurrences may well happen in a simple malpractice trial as well. It is rare, but not unknown, for the judge to give the members of the jury an opportunity to question the expert witness directly to clarify the jury's understanding of the case.

The Attorneys

Attorneys in a trial are advocates for clients or for entities, such as a corporation or the state. Going back to the concept of trial by combat, if you had to fight hand-to-hand to achieve victory and had the opportunity to choose a representative for you, you would choose the strongest, meanest representative that you could. Strong is not so important in court. In court, you need someone to represent you who knows all the intricate rules of battle. That someone is an attorney. You could represent yourself in court, and occasionally someone does, but it is usually to that person's detriment. Even attorneys do not represent themselves. Just as we say "The physician who treats himself has a fool for a patient," attorneys say "The lawyer who represents himself has a fool for a client."

Most attorneys practice within either civil or criminal law, although some do both sorts of work. It is likely that the attorneys representing each side know each other professionally, and possibly socially. Since the attorneys know each other, it is small wonder that they will enter the court together, joking and laughing. When the trial begins, they go at each other with no holds barred and then, when the day ends, they leave court chatting as amiably as when they entered. To them the battle of words waged in court is all in a day's work, and it is work that they enjoy or else they would not do it. It is as though attorneys are friends who really enjoy playing rough, "no autopsy, no foul" basketball together on a regular basis. To put it in the words of one attorney, "The only thing that I as an attorney enjoy more than really sticking it to an attorney who is an enemy of mine in court is really sticking it to one of my friends."

Because an attorney is the advocate of his client, the attorney must abide by his client's wishes. This can be important because if the client wants to accept an offer made to settle the case, then the attorney must do so.

A young woman reached into a public fountain at a shopping mall to retrieve a pacifier that her baby dropped and was electrocuted. The mall, the city, and the electric company were all sued for wrongful death. As the trial was beginning, the defendants made an offer to the family of five million dollars. The relatives wanted to accept, but their attorney, who was working on a percentage of the money the family would be awarded in damages, tried to discourage the family, saying that they stood to win far more. The family asked was it not also true that they could walk away with nothing, and the attorney was forced to concede that possibility. The family then said that five million dollars was more money than they knew how to count, and it sounded like plenty to them. The attorney was not happy about it, but he had to abide by his client's wishes, and the case was settled for five million dollars.

The Witnesses

Witnesses will be called by means of a subpoena by both sides in a trial. A subpoena is an order that compels a witness to appear in court. Each witness is called to tell what he saw or heard or otherwise sensed that is pertinent to the trial. Each witness is called to the witness stand one at a time to tell his tale. The witness will first be sworn in. Each judge has a different way of having witnesses swear to tell the whole truth and nothing but the truth. Some judges administer the witness's oath themselves, while in other courtrooms the witness is sworn in by a bailiff or by the court reporter. Once a witness is on the stand, he will be the focus of questions from the attorneys representing each side until all the attorneys are finished asking questions. The order in which the attorneys get to ask questions is set and never varies. The witness is first asked questions by the attorney representing the side that called the witness to testify. This phase of the questioning is called direct examination. Since the witness is being questioned by the attorney who wants to hear what the witness has to say, direct examination should be a smooth ride. The attorney representing the other side may or may not object to something done by the attorney questioning the witness, and any objection will be handled by the judge. When the direct examination is completed, the attorney conducting the direct examination will say "No further questions, Your Honor." The attorney advocating the other position may now ask questions of the witness. This second phase of the questioning is called cross-examination. Cross-examination is usually more harrowing than direct examination because the attorney cross-examining the witness will try to discredit, or at least make unimportant, the portions of the witness's testimony that are damaging to the position of the cross-examining attorney's client. The attorney who handled direct questioning may or may not object to something done by the cross-examining attorney while he is questioning the witness, and any objection will again be handled by the judge. When the cross-examination is completed, the attorney conducting it will say "No further questions, Your Honor." It is now possible for the attorney who directly examined the witness to ask more questions (re-direct examination) to clarify matters brought up during cross-examination in a way that is favorable to the direct examiner's client. If the attorney chooses to engage in re-direct examination, then the opposing attorney will be allowed to re-cross-examine the witness. This exchange can go back and forth *ad infinitum*, although it rarely happens more than twice. If, on the other hand, the attorney who began the examining chooses not to ask any questions following cross-examination, he will say "No further questions, Your Honor." When each attorney states that he has no further questions, the witness is excused.

In general, in most states no witness may hear the testimony of any other witness before he himself testifies. If a witness were to hear someone else's testimony, it might cause him to change his own version of what happened. Hearing another witness's testimony is grounds for a mistrial, as is two witnesses talking together out in the lobby of the court while each waits to testify. Form the good habit of not talking about the case with anyone in the courthouse who is a witness or whom you do not know. It is permissible to talk with the attorney who called you concerning what you witnessed prior to testifying, as often occurs during a break, or recess, in the trial. In some instances, it is permissible to talk with the attorney representing the opposing side, too, but check with the attorney who called you first. After the judge excuses a witness from further testimony, the witness may sit and watch the rest of the trial if he desires.

Types of Witnesses—Fact and Expert

There are two types of witnesses—fact witnesses and expert witnesses. Fact (or evidentiary or material) witnesses saw, heard, or were otherwise directly involved in the matter that is being disputed in court. In a medical case, a fact witness is one who actually saw the patient, either as the attending physician, as a consultant, or as part of the support staff. Any procedure done or any notes or reports generated by the physician will likely be the major reason for the testimony. When the physician's opinion about the case is sought to any significant extent, then the physician is testifying as an expert witness. Expert witnesses rarely, if ever, were direct witnesses of the event in question. Nevertheless, because the court (that is, the judge) finds that the expert witness has special training or experience that is not common to all individuals, the expert is allowed to use his special training to help make understandable things that would not be obvious to the jury or judge. Experts are not needed for the obvious. An example should help make the distinction clear.

An oncologist might be sued by the relatives of a deceased patient for failing to disclose a side effect of chemotherapy that hastened the patient's death. In that case, the pathologist who made the diagnosis of malignancy might be called to testify that the patient did have such and such a cancer. Provided that all the pathologist is asked to do is to read his diagnosis from the surgical pathology report and to affirm that the report just read is his own work, with his signature at the bottom, the pathologist would be testifying as a fact witness because he is testifying about something that he did. The pathologist would not be asked about the actions of the oncologist because that would be a matter of speculation for the pathologist. Another oncologist, however, who was never involved in the patient's care, might be brought in by the attorney representing either side in the lawsuit to comment on the care provided by the oncologist who has been sued. The oncologist who never saw the patient would be an expert witness, bringing his special expertise to the case to help the jury better understand the issue.

An expert witness differs from a fact witness in a very important way: the expert witness may offer his opinion on what happened in court, and his opinion has legal worth.

As an example, a man is accused of murder in a criminal trial for shooting the decedent. The attorney representing the accused man offers a plea of self-defense, saying the dead man was coming at his client with a gun. A fact witness might have been around the corner and heard the two men scuffle, then a moment's silence followed by a gunshot. All that the fact witness heard will be admitted into court and is important information. But the fact witness who heard the events will not be asked for his opinion about what happened. If the fact witness were to say "I know the man who is accused of this crime, and I believe he is lying," then such a remark would be stricken from the court record. The forensic pathologist can offer his opinion on the matter, however, since he is an expert witness. In effect, the pathologist could say, "I was not there, I do not know what transpired firsthand, but my examination at autopsy showed a single gunshot entrance wound in the back of the decedent, and in my opinion the decedent was not coming at the accused with a gun."

If you are called to court to testify, be sure that you ask the attorney who called you what sort of questions he is going to ask you. Not only will you be properly prepared, but you will not jump to the wrong conclusion. If all that is required of you in court is to confirm that you did receive a biopsy from Patient X submitted by Dr. Y, then it is a waste of your time to conduct an exhaustive search of the medical literature.

Ancillary Players

The judge, jury, attorneys, and witnesses are the main players in a trial. Less visible roles are played by the bailiff and the court reporter.

The role of the bailiff is to maintain order in the court, by force of arms if necessary. Sometimes it *is* necessary for the bailiffs to stop a fight when the jury makes known its verdict. At least one defendant who smuggled a gun into court in Jefferson County, Alabama was shot and killed by the bailiff when the defendant pulled the gun during the trial.

The court reporter keeps the transcript of what is said in the trial. Reading a transcript reinforces the dramatic nature of a trial, for it looks like the script of a play.

Attorney: What is your name?
Witness: My name is Greg Davis.
Attorney: How are you currently employed?
Witness: As Associate Medical Examiner for this county. *And so on...*

The final players in the courtroom are those people who choose to come and witness the trial as part of the public. Most trials are open to the public. Those who attend are usually relatives of the party on either side and perhaps, if the trial is deemed newsworthy, a reporter for a newspaper and a television cameraman for a local news show.

Types of Trials—Civil and Criminal

We have already mentioned civil and criminal disputes, but we should discuss each in more detail. In a civil dispute, no crime has been committed, instead, one party seeks recompense for harm that he believes the other party caused him. The party who initiates the lawsuit is the plaintiff, and the party against whom the suit is brought is the defendant. The plaintiff bears the burden of proof to establish with evidence that he has been wronged. The standard for establishing proof of a civil wrong is that "the preponderance of the evidence" must indicate that the plaintiff's contention is correct. Presumably as little as 51% of the evidence counts as a preponderance. Malpractice suits are civil suits.

A criminal dispute occurs when a crime has been committed. The party initiating a criminal case is "the people of the state of X." Those "people" are represented by the jury in a criminal trial. That is why the prosecuting attorney at a criminal trial has no client at his table—his "client" is sitting as the jury. The accused in a criminal trial is also a defendant. The standard for establishing proof of the defendant's guilt is that the evidence presented must make it clear to the jury "beyond reasonable doubt" that the defendant committed the crime.

References

1. Daubert v Merrell Dow Pharmaceuticals, Inc, 113 SCt 2786 (1993).
2. Weinstein JB. Expert witness testimony: a trial judge's perspective. Neurol Clinics 1999;17:355-61.

3
Impact of Law on Pathology Practice—Everyday Occurrences

Gregory G. Davis and Margie A. Scott

Medical Practice

Pathologists are physicians, a fact pathologists sometimes remind others of when it suits the pathologist's purpose. Otherwise, pathologists, who have chosen to toil in the wings, are usually content to be overlooked. Nevertheless, the pathologist is a physician first and a pathologist second. Therefore, pathologists have legal obligations that are common to all physicians. Some of those common obligations, however, do take on a special twist in the practice of pathology.

The Duty of a Physician

Many medical graduation ceremonies include a recitation of the Hippocratic Oath. The Hippocratic Oath endures because it affirms ideals of conduct that have remained valid for the past 2,500 years. The very age of the Oath gives it a wonderful mustiness that reinforces the distinguished lineage of physicians that the students are joining as colleagues. Nevertheless, the Hippocratic Oath is not used in the courts of the United States to assess whether a given physician has fulfilled his duty to his patient as a physician. The essence of the standard to which physicians are held in the United States is held within a well-worded opinion from a malpractice case in New York in 1898. It is worthwhile for any physician practicing in the United States to read and consider the opinion, which is quoted below.

A physician and surgeon, by taking charge of a case, impliedly represents that he possesses, and the law places upon him the duty of possessing, that reasonable degree of learning and skill that is ordinarily possessed by physicians and surgeons in the locality where he practices, and which is ordinarily regarded by those conversant with the employment as necessary to qualify him to engage in the business of practicing medicine and surgery. Upon consenting to treat a patient, it becomes his duty to use reasonable care and diligence in the exercise of his skill and the application of his learning to accomplish the purpose for which he was employed. He is under the further obligation to use his best judgment in exercising his skill and applying his knowledge. The law holds him liable for an injury to his patient resulting from want of the requisite knowledge and skill, or the omission to exercise reasonable care, or the failure to use his best judgment. The rule in relation to learning and skill does not require the surgeon to possess that extraordinary learning and skill which belong only to a few men of rare endowments, but such as is possessed by the average member of the medical profession in good standing. Still, he is bound to keep abreast of the times, and a departure from approved methods in general use, if it injures the patient, will render him liable, however good his intentions may have been. The rule of reasonable care and diligence does not require the exercise of the highest possible degree of care; and to render a physician or surgeon liable, it is not enough that there has been a less degree of care than some other medical man might have shown, or less than even he himself might have bestowed, but there must be a want of ordinary and reasonable care, leading to a bad result. This includes not only the diagnosis and treatment, but also the giving of proper instructions to his patient in relation to conduct, exercise and the use of the injured limb. The rule requiring him to use his best judgment does not hold him liable for a mere error of judgment, provided he does what he thinks is best after careful examination. His implied engagement with his patient does not guarantee a good result, but he promises by implication to use the skill and learning of the average physician, to exercise reasonable care and to exert his best judgment in the effort to bring about a good result.[1]

This legal opinion is a succinct outline of the legal obligations and duties that a physician has to his patient in the United States. To this day, judges often use this opinion when instructing a jury on the law governing medical malpractice, albeit in a form rendered into the current speech.[2] A few points from the opinion are worth highlighting.

1. "A physician...represents that he possesses...that reasonable degree of learning and skill that is ordinarily possessed by physicians...in the locality where he practices..." In our age of global travel and telecommunication technology, the "locality where he practices" is the United States. Gone are the days of differing standards for different regions of the country.

2. "The rule in relation to learning and skill does not require the surgeon to possess that extraordinary learning and skill which belong only to a few men of rare endowments, but such as is possessed by the average member of the medical profession in good standing." For specialists, the "rule" requires the learning and skill of an average specialist in the specialist's field.

3. "The rule requiring him to use his best judgment does not hold him liable for a mere error of judgment, provided he does what he thinks is best after careful examination." You may be tempted to laugh a bitter and cynical laugh at this sentence, but it is, in fact, true that you are not supposed to be held liable for a mere error in judgment, and physicians who go the distance in a malpractice trial have been found not guilty of any wrongdoing even when they made an error in judgment. Certainly not all physicians have been excused for an error in judgment, but some have. If you wish, you may think of it in another way, namely that the law does not require that you be right every time, only that you give it your best effort every time. This distinction can have profound ramifications for a physician as a defendant in a malpractice suit.

4. The opinion in Pike v. Honsinger states that the physician, by providing medical care to a patient, "does not guarantee a good result." Some clinicians throw away this protection by guaranteeing a patient a good result. Pathologists, who typically do not see patients personally, and who tend to be cautious in their wording in any case, are unlikely to make such a mistake. Nevertheless, this does bring to mind the importance of effective and honest communication, a point that will be a recurring theme throughout this book.

5. Notice that it is not malpractice for a physician to use a treatment or technique used by a minority of physicians. Malpractice occurs when a physician uses a treatment for which there is *no* respected support and that no one else uses. In other words, the practice of quacks is malpractice. Outright quackery is rarely at issue in a malpractice suit. Most malpractice trials revolve around what happened. (Did the pathologist or someone in his laboratory notify the clinician that the patient had a toxic acetaminophen level? Did the clinician understand what the pathologist said? Did the clinician transmit the pathology results to the patient or to the physician to whom the patient was referred at the tertiary care center?) Knowing that court trials revolve around what happened should reinforce the importance of careful, thorough documentation by the physician of the events that transpire in a patient's care. Unless the call to the clinician about the high acetaminophen level was recorded either on a crisis value call sheet or electronically in the laboratory computer database with date, time, persons involved in the conversation, etc., then proper notification never took place as far as the court and the jury are concerned. As reported by Stephen Mackauf, an attorney who represents patients who sue physicians for malpractice, there is no substitute for a careful, thorough record in the defense of a physician who rendered good care. A physician who rendered bad care can be harmed by a careful record that documents that bad care. A lost record, or worse yet, an altered record, will look guilty to all involved in court.[2]

The opinion from Pike v. Honsinger is recorded here because it is preferable that you as a physician be familiar with your legal obligations now as opposed to first hearing these words while on trial for malpractice. A few moments spent in reflection upon the opinion's implications for your daily practice is time well spent. The opinion in Pike v. Honsinger makes explicit that an individual physician need not be the best in his field, but he does need to possess normally accepted practice skills and strive to make the best-informed decisions and judgments for each patient.

Pathologist–Patient Relationship

Pathologists are sometimes called "the physician's physician," and, with a few specific exceptions, pathologists generally do not see patients. Do not think, however, that if sued for malpractice it is possible to avoid responsibility by claiming that you, the pathologist, never had a personal doctor–patient relationship with the patient. Courts have thoroughly established that a pathologist has a clear doctor–patient relationship by extension of the relationship the patient has with the primary clinician of record. A pathologist is neither more nor less of a consultant than any other clinical physician.

Abandonment

What does the law see as the responsibility of a physician who comes across an individual in dire need of medical help? What will happen to the physician who ignores such dire need? What responsibility does the physician incur who does administer medical aid? What sort of liability does the physician helping in an emergency assume? A person who gives help in a dire situation is often described as "a Good Samaritan," and some of the laws that apply to this situation are nicknamed "Good Samaritan laws" in reference to the biblical parable of the Good Samaritan.[3]

What if, as the priest and Levite did, a physician chooses not to get involved? In the United States, there is no provision for legally punishing an individual for failing to help someone who needs help. In other words, when a wreck occurs during rush hour, anyone who chooses to drive on by the wrecked car cannot be punished for failing to stop and help the injured driver, even if the driver were to die as a result of the wreck. Therefore, as a physician, you incur no liability by choosing not to get involved when an individual is in dire medical need. The point of the story of the Good Samaritan, however, is that being technically correct does not necessarily help someone in desperate need, whereas compassion does.

Assuming that you as a physician do choose to render aid to someone who is injured or desperately ill, you have taken upon yourself the doctor–patient relationship. By assuming a doctor–patient relationship, you have assumed all the duties discussed in the opinion of Pike v. Honsinger. To paraphrase the opinion, by "consenting to treat a patient it becomes your duty to use reasonable care and diligence in the exercise of your skill and the application of your learning," and you must continue to give that patient care until you turn the patient over to the care of another *physician*. In some areas, you can be held liable for abandoning your patient if you begin emergency treatment at an accident scene and then, when the paramedics arrive, let the patient go in the ambulance *without a physician in attendance*. Should the patient die en route, you could be sued for abandonment. In other areas, a "Good Samaritan law" offers some protection from liability in an emergency. To find out at what point you have fulfilled your responsibility as a physician to such an emergency patient in your community, check with a hospital attorney or the attorney who represents your group. Otherwise, if no physician comes with the paramedics, it would be prudent to accompany the patient to the hospital.

The pathologist as a physician is in a tight spot when coming upon someone who needs medical care. We as pathologists are acutely aware of our limited experience in caring for living patients. Nevertheless, even pathologists remember the ABCs (airway, breathing, and circulation) and know to apply direct pressure to stop bleeding. If you as a pathologist find it necessary to treat someone in a dire emergency, then treat that person as you would a member of your own family and stay with them until their care is turned over to some other physician.

Surgical Specimens with Forensic Worth

Surgical pathologists frequently encounter specimens that have forensic implications or importance. Although surgical specimens receive a gross description, the meat of surgical pathology is in the microscopic appearance of the specimen, and thus the emphasis of surgical pathology is on the microscopic examination of tissue. There are a few exceptions to this general rule, for example, focal nodular hyperplasia of the liver. Focal nodular hyperplasia of the liver can be diagnosed grossly with confidence in a consultation from the operating room without performing a frozen section. A permanent section will be submitted, of course, but the gross appearance of focal nodular hyperplasia of the liver is characteristic.

Gross Pathology and the Traumatic Spleen

In forensic pathology, the relative importance of gross and microscopic examination is the reverse of their importance in surgical pathology. It is the gross appearance that holds the diagnostic clues to the questions of forensic interest in most cases. This point about the importance of the gross appearance and description of a specimen has some bearing on the practice of surgical pathology because surgical specimens are sometimes derived from cases that are forensic in nature (such as wounds) rather than from cases caused by natural disease (such as infections or neoplasms). An example of a specimen with forensic implications is the lowly traumatic spleen, which never seems to get the attention that a neoplasm does in the surgical pathology lab. Nevertheless, the event that caused the injury that caused the spleen to rupture was important enough to warrant emergent surgery, and it may become the focus of a lawsuit or trial. The best way to document the pathophysiologic derangement that led to splenectomy is a gross photograph and a description of the extent of the rupture. Because surgical pathologists are so accustomed to concentrating on the microscopic appearance of the specimens they receive, they sometimes forget to doff their microscopic hat and don their gross hat when a gross description better serves to document the pathological findings. Forensic pathologists regularly seek out surgical pathology reports pertinent to their cases. Too often the surgical pathology report reads something like the following:

Specimen: Spleen
Reason for resection: Trauma (motor vehicle accident)
Gross: Received fresh is a 110 gram spleen with evidence of trauma. A representative microscopic section is submitted.
Microscopic description: Normal spleen.
Diagnosis: Traumatic spleen.

In contrast to the description above, the following sample contains more information and, with practice, is no more difficult.

Specimen: Spleen
Reason for resection: Trauma (motor vehicle accident)
Gross: Received fresh is a 110 gram spleen. On the antehilar surface is a network of intersecting lacerations that extend through the capsule, covering a 7 x 4 cm area. The lacerations extend up to 0.8 cm into the splenic parenchyma, and the parenchyma exposed by the lacerations shows pulpefaction. A representative microscopic section is submitted after the gross appearance is recorded with a photograph.
Microscopic description: A section through a capsular laceration shows no inflammatory response. With the exception of pools of extravasated red blood cells along the edge of the lacerated parenchyma, the red and white pulps in the section are free of histopathologic change.
Diagnosis: Traumatic spleen.

The second description gives much more information, especially the impression that the pathologist who examined the spleen actually looked at the organ and thought about how best to describe and record the pathologic changes that led to splenectomy. A photograph is nice, but if time and resources are considered too short, at least provide a gross description that will bring to the mind of a reader familiar with pathology an accurate mental image of what the spleen looked like in your hands. A traumatic spleen may seem less important than a radical neck specimen, but that is untrue. A young person who has lost a spleen faces clinical implications different from, but no less important than, the patient who has undergone a radical neck dissection.

The traumatic spleen serves as a good example of a surgical specimen with forensic implications, and taking the care to describe the injury accurately and succinctly is part of being a good pathologist. In truth, however, the traumatic spleen is unlikely to receive individual attention in court in a civil suit filed for damages caused by reckless driving. A surgical specimen that *may* later become important in a trial is a bullet removed during repair of a gunshot wound. There are two important points in proper evaluation of a bullet received as a surgical specimen. One is the proper handling and description of the bullet. The other is the establishment of a chain of custody for the bullet.

Bullets

Bullets received in surgical pathology are described, just as any specimen is described. Many individuals have great interest in firearms and bullets and can describe bullets in astonishing detail. If you as a pathologist do not happen to have a vast knowledge of bullets, you may be heartened to learn that a sufficiently accurate description for a bullet from a pathological point of view need not be exhaustive nor even complicated. Exhaustive accuracy in describing bullets will be the responsibility of the expert firearms examiner should the district attorney decide to ask the police to retrieve the bullet from your laboratory.

A pathological description of a bullet sufficiently accurate for legal use will include the size of the bullet. This size estimation can be done by careful measurement with a ruler or by rough estimation. Bullets may be small (.22–.25 caliber), medium (.32, .357, .38, 9mm), or large (.45), and that sort of rough detail is what the author (G.G.D.) uses to describe the size of his bullet specimens.[*] Bullets may be unjacketed (made entirely of lead), partially jacketed (a copper or brass coating at the blunt end with an exposed lead nose), or fully jacketed (the entire lead core is covered by a sheath of copper or brass, although the lead base may be exposed). Brief mention may be made of the bullet's condition (dented on one side, undeformed), and that should suffice. In handling the bullet, use gloved hands rather than forceps. Forceps can destroy crucial evidence used to match a bullet to the gun that fired it. Ballistic matches are made by examining the scratches made on the bullet as it traveled down the barrel of the gun that

---

[*]A note to those readers who have more detailed knowledge of bullets than is displayed by the author: Describing bullets as small, medium, or large has never proved an impediment to the author in testifying in court because the author makes no claim in court that he possesses sufficient knowledge of bullets to qualify as an expert witness regarding bullet caliber. Testimony concerning the caliber of a bullet is left to the ballistics expert who examined the bullet recovered at autopsy.

fired it. The scratches made by the gun on the bullet are called tool marks, and metal forceps can destroy those tool marks, rendering a match impossible.

It is important not to use forceps to examine a bullet, but more important still is that the bullet be examined and stored in a way that allows the bullet to be transferred to a firearms examiner for study. In the practice of surgical pathology, should resources permit, it is recommended to take a single photograph of projectiles and to designate a secure, locked location for long-term storage of these unique specimens. (How long will be defined by your practice needs, and this will be discussed further below.) The more standardized the process for handling specimens such as bullets and other foreign bodies removed in the operating room, the more you have safeguarded the items for potential use in the legal system. Another important consideration is the process by which stored bullets are released to various authorities, such as the police. Work with your hospital risk managers to develop a standardized process for the final release of stored bullets. In other words, in order for the bullet to be useful as evidence in court, there must exist a legal chain of custody for the bullet.

Chain of Custody

If you were to ask attorneys for a definition of chain of custody, you will find that chain of custody is an elusive concept because there is no formal definition. (Attorneys find it useful to have as part of their armamentarium an elusive concept that has no formal definition.) Chain of custody, or chain of evidence, is a written record of where an item, such as a bullet, has been since it was removed from the patient. In a homicide case, the bullet may be recovered from the body by the forensic pathologist, who then turns the bullet over to a police evidence technician, who in turn takes the bullet to the ballistics examiner, who later returns the bullet to the police evidence technician after completing the ballistics comparison. The chain of custody will be a sheet of paper that accompanies the bullet and that is signed and dated by both individuals whenever the bullet is transferred from one to another. Four principles should allow for a proper chain of custody that will make the evidence admissible in court.

1. The item must be properly identified, that is, the patient name and hospital number must be associated with the item in an obvious way.
2. The item must be stored in a manner that makes it unlikely that the item will be tampered with (e.g., a locked drawer).
3. The item must be stored so that there would be evidence of any tampering if tampering should occur (sealed envelope with signature or initials over seal).
4. There must be a record of what was done with the object, and by whom, every time the item changes hands or location. (This record may be made a part of the surgical pathology report, as shown below. If bullets and chain of custody are of special interest to you, it might best

be done by retrieving the bullet personally from the operating room as though you were picking up a frozen section specimen.)

Below is a sample of a surgical pathology report that should satisfy the legal requirements for chain of custody.

Received from Operating Room ___ is a medium caliber bullet that has a soft, grey metal core partially encased by a sheath of copper-colored metal. Dr. X personally retrieved the bullet from Operating Room ___. Following completion of examination of this specimen, the bullet is placed in a clean envelope labeled with the patient's name and hospital number. The bullet is sealed in the envelope with tape and then initialed over the tape by Dr. X. The envelope is then secured in the specimen drawer reserved for bullets.

An example of an envelope used to store a bullet is shown in Figure 3-1.

If you receive bullets from the operating room in a labeled specimen cup, then a single photograph of the bullet and specimen cup (with the label showing the patient's name and hospital number visible in the photograph) would show

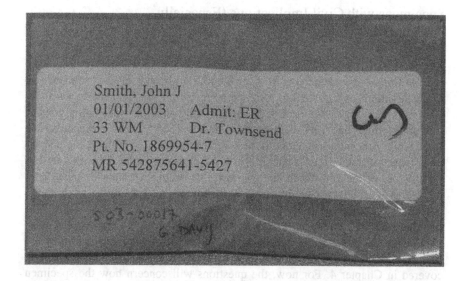

Figure 3-1. An envelope of the sort appropriate for storing bullets received as surgical specimens. The envelope should be labeled with the patient's name, hospital number, date, surgical specimen number, and the name of the pathologist. The name of the surgeon would be useful, too. If the label attached to the specimen cup containing the bullet can be transferred to the envelope, then only the surgical accession number and the pathologist's name need be added, as shown. Note that mailing tape has been used to seal the envelope and that the edges of the seal have been initialed by the pathologist. The envelope in this example is 4.25 x 2.5 inches. The bullet should be dried gently with a clean, absorbent cloth before it is put into the envelope.

what the bullet looked like when you received it and should make clear that the bullet came from the patient in question. If someone official (police or attorney) later comes asking for the bullet, you can give them the bullet and a photocopy of the surgical pathology report in exchange for a signed receipt. If you took a gross photograph of the bullet and specimen jar, then you will likely be asked to provide a copy of your photograph. Do not give away your original photograph, which is part of the medical record.

It is appropriate to discard old bullets periodically just as you regularly discard gross specimens after several weeks. The size of the drawer in which you store bullets may be the factor that determines when you discard the oldest specimens. Bullets stored in small manila envelopes as shown in Figure 3-1 take up little space, and you can store many in a drawer. A helpful hint is to put all the bullets from one calendar year within a single box. If you can fit four such boxes in your drawer, then you will always have at least the last three years worth of cases. As you might expect, if no one has asked you for the bullet in three years, then probably no one will, so you may discard the contents of the oldest box of bullets each January and start anew.

Specimens with Civil Implications (Especially Potential Malpractice)

As pathologists working in the anatomic arena, it is not possible (nor is it desirable) to foresee the potential civil medicolegal significance of each specimen as it reaches the grossing station, intraoperative frozen section station, cytology laboratory, or autopsy table. A pathologist's daily activities focus upon patient care and optimal handling of those specimens and body parts entrusted to his care. While concentrating upon the best approach to specimen handling and diagnosis, we as pathologists happen also to be engaging in the steps required to keep us out of the courtroom and to protect us should we later be called as a witness. After all, the practicing surgical pathologist belongs in the gross room, not the courtroom.

Questions that tend to arise when a pathologist does become involved in a civil lawsuit as either a material or expert witness are predictable, and they are based on the legal foundation necessary to prove malpractice, a topic that will be covered in Chapter 4. For now, the questions will concern how the specimen was handled, the accuracy of diagnosis, and the ill effect (if any) that the patient suffered.

Was the Specimen Handled Properly?

Proper specimen handling includes proper identification, specimen tracking, processing in the gross room, and performance of appropriate ancillary studies beginning from the time the specimen arrives in the laboratory. When ancillary studies are not performed, there should be reasons for such omissions, and these decisions should be documented. Ancillary studies to consider while the specimen is fresh include cultures (ideally the patient is still in the operating room, where additional tissues can be obtained from the sterile surgical field if necessary), cytogenetic studies, polymerase chain reaction studies, fluorescent *in situ* hybridization studies, toxicology studies, and cell culture techniques for identification of metabolic defects. In our current age of technology driven prognostic indicators, it is imperative for the practicing surgical pathologist to stay abreast of new technologies and their impact on guiding therapeutic decisions. On the other hand, hospital administration expects pathologists to serve as guardians of financial resources as we monitor those expensive send-out tests, ensuring that the tests are clinically indicated (not just curiosity-based) and financially justified as a component of patient care (not a research-directed order being shifted to a convenient clinical care financial bottom line). This delicate balance is expected of pathologists. When a pathologist fails to maintain the proper balance, the consequences can be disastrous. Consider the example below.

During the course of a cardiovascular surgical procedure, the surgeon discovers an enlarged lymph node, performs an excisional biopsy of the node, and forwards it to pathology in the fresh state. The surgical pathology requisition states "lymphadenopathy; probable reactive adenopathy," and there is no request for a frozen section or immediate feedback to the surgical team. The pathology assistant reviews the case, noting that no frozen section is requested, and immediately grosses-in the sample, submitting a section for microscopic review and placing the remaining tissue in formalin. At signout the next day, the pathologist discovers that the lymph node shows effacement of nodal architecture due to an infiltrate of monomorphic discohesive cells, probably malignant lymphoma.

Complete evaluation and the best final diagnosis in this case depend upon flow cytometry, immunohistochemistry, and possibly cytogenetic studies. Unfortunately, the window of opportunity for flow cytometry and cytogenetic studies closed irrevocably the moment this node was placed in formalin. This mistake in specimen handling may directly impact patient care. It is true that the decision was made by the pathology assistant (PA); however, the PA operates under a scope of practice defined by the pathologist and as such the pathologist is legally responsible for the way in which this node was handled. The first rule is to forget blame and remember patient care. The pathologist should immediately contact the health care provider for this patient and explain to them that the initial diagnostic impression is "probable malignant lymphoma" and immunocytochemistry studies are under way to classify the type of lymphoma this represents. The pathologist should explain that no flow cytometry or cytogenetics were obtained in this case and should find out which hematology/oncology specialist this patient will be referred to for further work-up so that the pathologist may communicate directly with him as well. Ideally, in cases of unexplained lymphadenopathy, the pathologist must consider all possibilities: infectious, reactive, and malignant (hematopoietic versus metastatic). Whether requested or not, the appropriate step in evaluating a lymph node is to perform a touch-prep or frozen section in order to guide the gross room evaluation. Many a pathologist has been led astray by relying too heavily upon the preoperative impression. Our job is to focus on the breadth of possibilities and guide the tissue studies appropriately based on these possibilities.

Was the Diagnosis Correct?

The second legal question that will predictably be raised relates to diagnostic skill and judgment. Was the correct diagnosis rendered with appropriate follow-up? This is where report documentation is essential. In addition to the final diagnosis, pathologists should document provider notification, any ancillary studies performed on the fixed tissues (even when such studies are negative or noncontributory), concurrence of a second pathologist for first-time malignancies, and consultations in the diagnostically difficult cases. These activities are all part of the pathologist's daily routine. However, for the full benefit of all parties involved in the patient case (including your own), pathologists must strive to document, document, document. Malpractice defense is often weakened due to lack of documentation. It is not just attorneys who know this truth. Hospital surveyors for corporate bodies such as the Joint Commission for Accreditation of Healthcare Organizations (JCAHO) will tell you without blinking: "If it wasn't documented, it wasn't done."

Did the Patient Suffer an Adverse Outcome?

The third predictable question attempts to establish that injury (mental, physical, or emotional) resulted from the level of care provided. That is: Was harm done? In considering this question, we pathologists must review the obvious question of "Was the diagnosis appropriately rendered?" a question that most pathologists can handle with relative ease. In addition, we must consider the timeliness of the diagnosis, especially in the difficult case that may require complex ancillary studies or review by outside consultants. Pathologists sometimes feel pressured by their clinical counterparts to provide some form of "final report" pending outside consultation in a difficult case. Of course the clinician needs some sort of commitment to begin treatment. But giving that commitment prematurely puts the burden of being wrong entirely upon you, the pathologist. In these situations, communication is once again paramount. Say what you know to be true and no more. Summarize (and document by writing down) the difficulties of the case and the reasons outside consultation is necessary. Assume nothing, lest an unaware provider (such as the surgical consultant involved in the case) take definitive action based on your "not quite final report."

Cytology

Cytology is an important diagnostic tool, with expectations and limitations that differ from surgical pathology specimens. Cytology can be divided into the fields of gynecologic pathology via cervical specimens obtained as part of a routine pelvic examination, often referred to as Pap smears, and specimens obtained by fine needle aspiration of suspicious nodules.

Cervical Preparations

In order to understand the liability inherent in the cytologic diagnosis of cervical dysplasia and carcinoma, it is necessary to know a little history. George N. Papanicolaou was a Greek physician whose study of the cellular changes associated with estrus led to a serendipitous finding of exfoliating tumor cells in women with uterine cancer. Dr. Papanicolaou's studies made possible a simple, cost-effective tool for early cancer diagnosis, which essentially formed the world of cancer screening as we know it today. As with any screening test, the goal is to discover and diagnose as early as possible while fully understanding that false negatives and false positives are inherent in any screening test. A single negative Pap smear has never implied that cancer is definitively absent, even if collected using perfect technique and interpreted by the foremost expert in the field of cytopathology. The strength of the Pap smear increases with repetition. With each consecutive yearly Pap smear, the probability of a missed diagnosis becomes less and less likely. Because of the Pap smear, cervical cancer, once ranked as the number one killer of women in the United States, has now been moved to position number 13.[4] Ironically, the success of the Pap smear in reducing premature death due to cervical carcinoma has created unrealistic expectations, which have led to high litigation rates. In a sense, the Pap smear has become a victim of its own success and, as one summary states, "expectations have been raised so high that any result short of perfection is likely to be viewed as malpractice."[5]

Pap smears are unique pathology specimens because, in general, the pathologist of record does not see negative Pap smears. Herein lies the importance of quality assurance screening and overreading of one in ten negative Pap smears. The Clinical Laboratories Improvement Act (CLIA) guidelines address the expectations and screening limitations for cytotechnologists in an effort to standardize guidelines across the United States. The pathologist director of cytology must give careful attention to hiring practices, yearly competency evaluations, quality improvement plans, and adherence to standard operating procedures. CLIA requires that the pathology laboratory re-review all previous Pap smears for a five-year period once a diagnosis of moderate dysplasia or higher is established. This is another step to ensure that adequate controls are in place and diagnostic cells have not been missed in the historic screening processes. This CLIA regulation does not mandate revision of historic reports, and it would certainly be wrong to try to change a report already issued. Many pathologists choose to address this re-review process in the current report noting the case numbers and dates of the reviewed materials. One must be careful when reassessing cases retrospectively in light of new information. The best practice is to ask for re-review of these materials by someone unbiased by the current diagnostic materials. This is true whether the re-reviewer is a partner, an affiliated university pathologist, or an outside consultant.

Fine Needle Aspirates

Fine needle aspiration (FNA) biopsies of peripheral lesions allow rapid assessment and, sometimes, definitive diagnosis of lesions without the additional risks of generalized anesthesia or operating room open-biopsy procedures. FNAs are well-suited for sampling peripheral soft tissue masses, enlarged peripheral lymph nodes, breast masses, and even prostate nodules (with specialized needle adaptors). The procedure is minimally invasive, and the risk of complications revolves around bleeding and infection inherent to any procedure involving a needle puncture. The very strength of the FNA, sampling of superficial lesions with a very thin needle in order to examine the cellular component and make a diagnosis, is also the medicolegal weakness—making diagnoses from very few cells, sometimes too few to be representative of the entire lesion. A lymph node involved by metastatic moderately differentiated squamous cell carcinoma is easily diagnosed with FNA, even when the location of the primary tumor remains unknown. This type of case, with obvious metastatic carcinoma, is most unlikely to become the target of a legal review. However, interpreting the FNA of an enlarged lymph node with a mixed population of cells suggesting a reactive process, even when accompanied by flow cytometry, in a patient who has Hodgkin's lymphoma is a scenario fraught with pitfalls. Another example is the missed diagnosis of atypical hyperplasia or ductal carcinoma-in-situ (DCIS) in a mammographically identified breast lesion that leads clinicians to watch, wait, and rebiopsy in the future. When repeat biopsy occurs months later and the diagnosis of DCIS is established, the question raised relates to the clinical impact of a delay in diagnosis. The pathologist collecting, interpreting, and recommending follow-up based upon FNA sampling is all too aware of these risks. With this said, it is not surprising that FNAs resulting in subsequent legal actions tend to revolve around areas of diagnostic difficulties, such as breast pathology, hematopoietic disorders, and lymphoproliferative processes. The pathologist who communicates with clinical staff prior to FNA biopsy, reviews the medical records, and views radiology studies such as the most recent mammogram provides better care for his patient and mitigates the potential both for misdiagnosis and for misunderstanding of what the pathologist is capable of on the part of the clinical staff.

The pathologist performing FNA always has the option to defer the procedure and recommend further imaging studies or an open biopsy. This is appropriate when the lesion is not easily identified or cannot be adequately localized and stabilized for the aspiration biopsy procedure. If the lesion cannot be secured for sampling, then the resulting cellular materials obtained cannot be deemed representative of the lesion in question. On occasion, the pathologist can defer the FNA when it is deemed that the procedure risks outweigh the benefits, recommending an open approach to biopsy. One of the authors (MAS) was once requested to perform an FNA of a large abdominal lesion in an elderly patient. Chart review indicated no reason to suspect malignancy other than the large lower abdominal mass estimated at 6 x 4 cm in diameter, and no imaging studies had been performed. Consent was obtained and a focused history and physical performed. Significant findings included a long, complex history of atherosclerotic cardiovascular disease and peripheral vascular disease. At physical examination, the pathologist agreed that there was a large abdominal mass but noted that there was also a distinctive pulse. After explaining to the patient that the exam findings suggested that perhaps it would not be best to place a needle in this mass, the pathologist left empty-handed. Regrouping with the clinical care team was initially difficult, as they could not believe that the physical exam of a pathologist should override the findings of the internist. However, after further imaging studies, the team was grateful that we had not performed an FNA on an abdominal aortic aneurysm. As pathologists, we sometimes need gentle reminders such as this to reinforce our role as clinicians, not merely technicians.

Autopsies

That the autopsy does not get the respect it deserves is so often repeated as to be trite. Some clinicians consider that the power of modern-day radiology has replaced the need for autopsies.[6] Studies regularly appear in the medical literature touting that autopsies will uncover a misdiagnosis or important unsuspected diagnosis in as many as 40% of cases autopsied.[7, 8] Unfortunately, even pathologists are in danger of neglecting the autopsy's unequaled power to reveal why a patient has died. In listening to the talk of hospital-based pathologists, it is clear that many, though by no means all, dislike performing autopsies. This disdain for the autopsy by pathologists is unfortunate, for the autopsy is the one procedure that belongs wholly to pathologists. Regrettably, the importance of the autopsy service is one that is overlooked or underrated by many laboratory directors as well. The truth is that the hospital-based autopsy represents the most all-encompassing opportunity to integrate the findings of anatomic pathology, clinical pathology, and clinical care. Pathologists who deny the importance of autopsy in essence have turned their backs on one of the principal procedures that defined our practice as an independent self-sustaining specialty. Autopsies can also be of critical importance to family members, who may not be in a frame of mind to consider this fact when it is needed. This is where the clinical care team has a duty to step in and discuss the need for an autopsy and answer any questions or dispel any myths family members may have concerning the autopsy. Pathologists should be prepared and even welcome the opportunity to interact with clinical teams and family members when questions concerning the autopsy arise.

Why has the autopsy fallen into disrepute in hospitals? The cost of performing an autopsy was traditionally borne by the hospital, and certainly no insurance pays for an autopsy. In fact, insurers have the right to refuse payment for any test completed and entered into the medical record after the patient has died (e.g., tuberculosis and fungal cultures, complex molecular studies, etc.); the "insurance" after all, is a contract between the insurer and the individual, and as soon as the individual dies, the contract dies along with him. The cost of an autopsy is what it is, and there will be no reimbursement for the autopsy any time soon. In these days of careful budgeting of hospital finances, some claim it makes good economic sense to discourage autopsies since every autopsy avoided is a few thousand dollars saved by the hospital. Hospital administrators, however, cannot completely negate the importance of the autopsy as long as accreditation agencies such as the Joint Commission on Accreditation of Healthcare Organizations (JCAHO) include medical record review of autopsy findings as an essential component of each review cycle. Autopsies are reviewed for completeness, clinical relevance, impact on clinical care, and are even considered in the realm of physician credentialing. All of these are a part of the hospital's overall JCAHO score, an assessment sometimes used in hospital advertisements. If, however, accreditation agencies were to drop this component of the review cycle, the autopsy could be in danger of disappearing altogether from some hospital facilities.

There is another reason for the decline in autopsies that is sometimes whispered in the halls of medical centers, namely that autopsies increase the risk that the hospital and the physicians involved in the case will be sued for malpractice. This fear is based on the autopsy's ability to uncover a significant error in diagnosis or patient management in up to 40% of cases, as mentioned above. Of course, the converse of this statement is that the autopsy validates the diagnosis and treatment of the preponderance of patients. It is unlikely that anything written here will change an opinion that is already firmly held by a physician. Nevertheless, the problem cases in both the practice of medicine and in a malpractice suit are not those cases for which the facts are known. The vexing cases are the ones in which no one knows exactly what happened, so both sides in a dispute are free to speculate with no hope that the dispute can ever be resolved. Viewed from this perspective, an autopsy stands a far greater chance of exonerating a hospital and its staff than it does of harming the hospital. Believe it or not, an autopsy that reveals an error can even be helpful, for, damning though it is, it still can mitigate the circumstance by indicating that the hospital and its staff wanted to know what happened and were unwilling to "bury their mistakes," as the saying goes.

In order to assess the truth of the fear that autopsies provide damaging information in malpractice suits, the College of American Pathologists, in a study led by Bove and Iery, reviewed 99 malpractice cases reviewed at the level of appellate court.[9] This study determined that in 40 of the 99 cases an autopsy report contained a finding in discrepancy with the clinical assessment that, if known, had the potential to be treated, possibly prolonging life.

Of the 99 cases that went to trial, the appellate court review affirmed 51 acquittals (that is, the defendant physician was found not guilty of malpractice, and this verdict was affirmed upon legal review of the case). The appellate court affirmed 19 findings of medical negligence by defendant physicians after reviewing the case. The remaining 29 cases were reversed by the appellate court and remanded for second trial. Trials were reversed not for medical reasons but for violations of legal proceedings, such as one side not providing the other side with information during the discovery phase of the trial.

For cases in which an autopsy had been performed, the defendant physician was acquitted in 8 of 13 cases where autopsy confirmed the diagnosis. The defendant physician was acquitted of malpractice in 32 of 36 cases where a discrepancy was revealed by autopsy. In other words, in 89% of cases where autopsy revealed a significant error or oversight in clinical diagnosis or management, the physician was still found not guilty of malpractice by the jury.

Bove et al. list a thumbnail sketch of all of the cases in which the defendant physician was found guilty of malpractice.[9] In two cases, pathologists played a dishonorable role. In one case, the patient underwent an emergency caesarean section, aspirated, and died. The pathologist who performed the autopsy confirmed aspiration but later altered the autopsy report and the death certificate to claim that death was due to an amniotic fluid embolus. Neither the jury, judge, nor the appellate court found amniotic fluid embolism a credible cause of death in light of the scramble to avert a lawsuit. In other words, the pathologist and clinicians who tried to hide the truth did not understand that the procedures of law would decide the case, nor did they understand that the laymen of the court and of the jury had sufficient medical sophistication to question the truthfulness of all the scrambling. The pathologist impugned his honor for nought.

In the second case, the decedent suffered a bowel perforation during a hernia repair and subsequently died, despite a second operation to repair the injury to the bowel. Here the pathologist who performed the autopsy failed to mention anything related to the surgical procedures or complications. Once again, the jury had sufficient understanding to render a verdict despite the pathologist's attempt to cover up the mistake. Here the pathologist attempted to hide the truth by omission, rather than by commission, but again his wrongdoing was obvious in court.

Note that the study by Bove et al. addresses only a subset of those cases that went to trial, specifically the cases that were appealed. The cases that went to trial are in turn a small fraction of all the malpractice suits filed. (Only 7% of malpractice suits filed go to trial.[10]) It is possible that autopsy findings do lead to settlements in some cases, which would effectively be an admission of malpractice. Nevertheless, a side in a malpractice suit is taking a chance not to bolster their claim by the performance of an autopsy. Bove et al. relate the story of a physician sued for malpractice who charged spoilage of evidence by the family for not getting an autopsy and for cremating the remains. The court ruled that permission to refuse an autopsy and to dispose of remains belongs to the family. Rather than make a countercharge against the family, the physician's defense would have been better served by intimating to the jury throughout the trial that the family knew they had no case so they destroyed the evidence.

Obtaining Autopsy Consent

Informed consent is necessary to the practice of clinical medicine. Informed consent calls for physicians to advise their patients of

1.   the nature of the proposed treatment,
2.   the alternatives, and
3.   the significant risks (i.e., those that are common or serious).

Failure to provide a patient with informed consent results in liability for the physician for any complication from the treatment as long as a reasonable patient informed of the foregoing would have refused treatment.

Practically speaking, malpractice suits founded only upon a failure to provide informed consent are rare; informed consent becomes much more interesting and important to attorneys when it is coupled to an adverse complication.

Informed consent is uncommonly encountered in the practice of pathology. A patient who has had a biopsy or from whom a blood specimen has been taken has given implied consent to have a pathologist further test the tissue removed. Permission to perform an autopsy is required, however. Performing an autopsy without permission would constitute a failure to request the next of kin for a kind of informed consent, and a charge of malpractice could be made that was founded wholly in the failure to obtain permission.

(Actually, the permission to perform an autopsy is unique to medical practice. Because the patient is dead, permission to perform an autopsy is not even informed consent in the ordinary legal sense. The nearest kin to the decedent is granting permission for an autopsy based on the right of the next of kin to possession of the body in order to provide decent disposition of the remains. This right extends back to English common law.[11])

The means by which autopsy permission is obtained also differs from obtaining informed consent from a patient undergoing a procedure. Living patients will give consent to the physician who will perform the procedure or at least to someone on the physician's staff. The autopsy, however, will be performed by a pathologist, whom the family has never met. By custom, permission for autopsy is usually obtained from the next of kin by the primary clinical physician of the decedent. This custom puts the pathologist in the position of performing an examination that is more invasive than any other procedure in medicine without having any firsthand knowledge of what the next of kin was told about the autopsy or what the family may expect from the autopsy. On occasion, the family has been misinformed or has unrealistic expectations, as shown by the following case.

A man who was completely bald died due to his metastatic adenocarcinoma of the lung. The team of medical residents who asked for permission to autopsy wanted to know whether the decedent had any metastases to the brain. The decedent's family was reluctant to grant permission to examine the brain because they feared that the decedent would be left with a noticeable incision on the head following removal of the brain. The medical residents assured the family that no mark would be visible on the head from the autopsy, so the family consented to a full autopsy of the head, chest, and abdomen. The pathology resident conducting the autopsy contacted the clinicians who cared for the decedent prior to autopsy to ask whether there was any question the clinicians had that was not covered in the medical chart. Fortunately in this case, the medical resident mentioned the family's concern and the reassurance that the residents gave the family that autopsy would leave no trace of removal of the brain that would be visible at the funeral home. Because removal of the brain from a man who was bald would inevitably leave a visible mark on the scalp, the pathology resident refused to examine the brain, even though the family had given permission to do so. The pathology resident explained to the medical residents that he could not deliver to the family what they had been promised. The medical residents were disappointed that their medical curiosity had to go unsatisfied, but they had the wisdom to see that removing the brain would be perceived by the decedent's kin as a breach of promise.

From the story above, several lessons may be drawn.

1. It is a wise practice to talk with the clinician who got permission from the next of kin for autopsy. Ask the clinician what he hopes to learn from the autopsy. Also, ask the clinician what the next of kin was told could be gained by the autopsy, what the next of kin hopes to learn from the autopsy, and what the next of kin expects regarding the condition of the body following postmortem examination.

2. Depending on the circumstances, it may be appropriate in certain cases to do less of an autopsy than the permit allows. Discuss with the clinician what you are going to do, so that no one will be surprised.

3. Communication is essential to good pathology practice. As the autopsy becomes less and less common, many medical students and young physicians have never seen an autopsy and have no idea what is specifically involved in performing an autopsy. As part of the pathologist's role as an educator, it might be a good idea to make a presentation every year or two to the surgical and medical services, discussing and demonstrating what is involved in performing an autopsy and what sorts of questions an autopsy can answer.

The more involvement a pathologist has in an autopsy, even in the process of obtaining consent to autopsy, the better the job the pathologist will be able to do.

It is never appropriate to do more than has been permitted by the next of kin on the autopsy consent form. If the next of kin restricts the autopsy to the chest only and you proceed through the diaphragm into the abdomen, then you have transgressed the permission you were granted and have violated the property right of the next of kin. If the next of kin ever finds out that this violation occurred, and it could happen if the decedent's family physician, who is an old friend of the decedent's family, casually mentions to the decedent's son that the liver had no metastases, then it is you, the pathologist, who will be sued and you, the pathologist, who will be found guilty of malpractice because you, the pathologist, knew better. You can expect the family physician to get off without penalty, whether he was in collusion with you or not.

The primary care team usually obtains consent for autopsy, but does this extend to physicians-in-training? Within training facilities, the resident is generally provided a graduated level of decision-making independence during his residency program. With each year comes additional experience, knowledge, and responsibilities. After all, residents are physicians who have successfully completed their medical school training, so this level of independence and progression is essential for the apprentice trainee to be able to complete his training and wake up the day after residency enabled to take full responsibility and control of his practice. Generally these degrees of progressive independence are addressed in the Medical Center Bylaws. Medical students, however, are a different story. Students are still diligently striving toward their medical degree. Many medical centers do not allow medical students to obtain informed consent, including consent for autopsy. Pathologists should refer to their Medical Center Bylaws for clarification of how their hospital operates.

Performing a Hospital Autopsy

Confirming the Decedent's Identity

The purpose of this book is not to teach pathologists how to do autopsies but rather to discuss points that pertain to law. With that purpose in mind, the first order of business in examining a body for autopsy is to confirm that the body before you is that of the decedent whose family has granted permission for an autopsy. Compare the name and hospital identification number on the permit with the name and identification number on the hospital identification bracelet on the body. Explicitly state in the autopsy report that the name and identification numbers on the permit and on the body were compared and were identical. Name alone is not enough. Even in a small hospital, two patients may have nearly identical names, just as two pathologists within a small subspecialty may have nearly identical names. Think about what you expect to find on the decedent while performing the external portion of the autopsy examination as well. If the chart had led you to expect many tubes and lines exiting the decedent from every appendage and the body on the table has a single line exiting the left antecubital fossa, then something is amiss. If you have any question, then call the medical team to come and identify the body as the patient for whom they obtained an autopsy permit before you proceed. There is little that can go wrong in the way of malpractice during an autopsy, but performing an autopsy on the wrong body heads that short list.

Toxicological Deaths

The emphasis in pathology is often on the visual, particularly for the anatomic pathologists who do autopsies. Hospital pathologists are accustomed to looking for anatomic causes of death, but some deaths are caused by processes invisible grossly and microscopically. The author (G.G.D.) gets several calls per year from hospital pathologists who have the autopsy slides at their desk to complete a case. In reviewing the case at the desk, the pathologist realizes that this particular case may be a death where toxicological evaluation is needed to determine the cause of death. The pathologist, however, did not retain any specimen for toxicological analysis, so the pathologist calls someone with more experience in toxicological cases to ask for help. Without a specimen to test for whatever substance is suspected of causing death, no degree of expertise can provide the answer; expertise can only agree that such and such a substance *could* have caused death.

The importance of postmortem toxicology testing on hospital cases was also mentioned in the study by Bove et al.,[9] who reported that 9 of the 99 cases were drug-related, usually of a prescribed medication, but sometimes in combination with other drugs, including alcohol and illicit drugs of abuse. It is a vital part of any autopsy examination to save specimens for toxicology testing and, if the clinical picture indicates, for testing for mediators indicative of anaphylaxis.

The specimens routinely saved for toxicological analysis by forensic pathologists vary a little, but not much. Samples collected include blood drawn from the heart or aorta, peripheral blood (iliac veins), vitreous humor, urine, bile, gastric contents, liver, and brain. Many drugs, such as digoxin, redistribute after death, so it is important to have two blood specimens taken from two disparate compartments (central and peripheral) to determine the concentration of the drug. Cocaine continues to undergo hydrolysis postmortem, but this hydrolysis is inhibited by fluoride. Therefore, sodium fluoride is the anticoagulant used in forensic pathology. If cocaine is a consideration in a hospital case, then sodium fluoride is the anticoagulant of choice, and the specimen should be refrigerated after it is collected. Urine is invaluable, if present, for drug screening. Brain is useful because some drugs, such as cocaine, can be protected from degradation in the fatty environment of the brain. Gastric contents are generally useful only in cases of suspected overdose by pills, but forensic pathologists save gastric contents routinely because it is better to have the sample and not need it than to later regret its loss.

Occasionally a urine drug screen will be positive for four or five classes of illicit drugs (e.g., cocaine metabolite, benzodiazepine, amphetamine, barbiturate, and opiate). Perhaps the decedent did take all five of these substances, but remember that an autopsy is a sort of physical examination and that correct diagnoses are made when the history and physical findings are used to corroborate each other. Consider the following case.

In a hospital case that fell under the jurisdiction of the medical examiner the initial hospital urine drug screen was positive for cocaine metabolite, benzodiazepine, amphetamine, barbiturate, and opiate. The clinicians, including consultants, henceforth dutifully recorded that the decedent was a drug abuser who would use whatever he could get. A drug screen is appropriate for any individual beyond the first decade of life who is involved in an automobile accident, but in this particular case the patient was 57 years old, and his social history indicated that he was an engineer who had been employed at the same company for the past 30 years. The history did not sound like the history of someone who would simultaneously ingest five different classes of illicit drugs. Even drug addicts seen in forensic practice seldom have more than three different classes of drugs in their system. Occasionally antibodies in an immunoassay cross-react and give a false positive for many compounds on the enzyme-linked immunoassays commonly used to screen for drugs of abuse, a likely explanation for many positives in a patient or decedent who does not seem to be the drug abusing type.

Any substance found by a screen should be confirmed by an independent method, such as gas chromatography/mass spectrometry, and this admonition goes double for any illicit substance found on a drug screen. If squaring off with the family over whether the decedent had cocaine in his blood, you need to be certain of the truth of your claim that cocaine was present. In the case history just given, GC/MS analysis would show (and in fact did show) that the decedent had none of the compounds detected by the screening assay in his blood.

One must also consider the possibility of an isolated single class false positive drug screen. Many prescription medications, herbal products, and even over-the-counter medications can cause an isolated false positive drug screen. For a laboratory working with a drug rehabilitation program, this can cause havoc if transgressors may be dropped from the program for a positive screen without follow-up confirmation. It is imperative that the clinicians communicate often with the laboratory director whenever doubt regarding a drug screen result is raised. There should be a very low threshold for referring the questioned sample out for confirmatory testing. In turn, there should be a low threshold for testing laboratories to question manufacturers when the laboratories encounter cases in which false positives have been confirmed and no identifiable causes can be established. Recently, such communication with laboratorians across the United States resulted in identifying yet another drug cross-reactivity with opiate screening methods—two of the newer fluoroquinolone antibiotics with a rather complex chemical structure may cause false positive opiate screens.

Another source of a falsely positive drug result is carryover, which can occur in a patient whose serum was run through the gas chromatography/mass spectrometry (GC/MS) analyzer after a true positive, particularly after an unusually high level of true positive. It is prudent to flush the GC/MS lines until clean after any especially large drug peak is obtained.

In one case, the wife of a physician died, and cocaine was detected in her blood. When told of this fact, the physician said that it was impossible that his wife was positive for cocaine and asked that the specimen be tested again. On repeat, the sample was negative. The specimen prior to the specimen from the physician's wife had had an unusually high cocaine peak, and the residual cocaine in the GC/MS line flushed out with the specimen from the physician's wife. The pathologist called the physician to apologize for the error and any distress that the error caused. To the pathologist's surprise, the physician husband's response was that he knew all along that his wife never used cocaine, so he knew all along that the pathologist's result was an error, and thus the initial report had caused him no distress at all.

There is another compelling reason to retain specimens at autopsy for possible toxicology testing that has not yet been mentioned. No article has been published on the topic, but any pathologist who believes that no abuse of illicit drugs occurs in the hospital that he covers is naive. Drug abuse occurs within all levels of society, so whether your hospital serves indigent patients or rich, the possibility of drug abuse, and thus of death caused by an illicit drug, is present. Family and friends can smuggle cocaine in to a hospital patient just as easily as they can smuggle in pizza—more easily, really, because pizza is bulkier and has a distinctive odor. The following case illustrates the point.

The girlfriend of a man in the hospital for his chronic renal failure injected cocaine into his central line. She noticed that he quit breathing, but she did not want her actions to be discovered. After ten minutes, she decided that he probably was not going to start breathing again without help, so she notified the nurses at the station that the decedent was not breathing. Cocaine was in the decedent's blood at autopsy.

The case above was made easy for the hospital pathologist because the girlfriend confessed what she had done. Suppose instead that the girlfriend had quietly slipped out the door, never to return. Drugs of abuse are part of the differential diagnosis for sudden, unexpected death. Both cocaine and the various amphetamine analogues can cause sudden cardiac death, and heroin can cause rapid, profound, and lethal respiratory failure. A completely unexpected hospital death merits the inclusion of drugs of abuse in the differential diagnosis. The screening test is relatively cheap, and a positive result, confirmed by GC/MS, will go a long way toward thwarting any malpractice suit for wrongful death. Again, no hospital is immune from the possibility of an inpatient abusing drugs.

One type of autopsy that is especially frustrating occurs whenever a young patient who was found obtunded is taken to a small community hospital. Then, two or three days later, the comatose patient is transferred to a tertiary care center. The patient remains unresponsive and is taken off life support a day or two after admission to the tertiary care center. The clinicians at the tertiary care center want to know what caused death and obtain consent for autopsy. Once consent is obtained, the autopsy is performed, but it reveals neither anatomical nor toxicological cause for death. No toxicological cause was found because the critical specimen, if it still exists at all, is a blood specimen from the time of admission to the first hospital. The pathologist can solve the case if he calls the laboratory of the first hospital and asks the staff to look for tubes of the patient's blood or urine on a hold shelf, particularly the blood drawn on admission. Some hospital pathologists think that making such a telephone call exceeds their authority and that only the patient's clinical physician can call and request any remaining specimens of the patient from the first hospital. Whether a telephone call exceeds a pathologist's authority would depend on the given situation, but if the clinician and the pathologist wish to determine the cause of death in such a case, then they need to obtain the admission blood. As you might guess, the chance of getting the original admission blood grows slimmer with every passing day. This is another example of where good communication between the pathologist and the clinical physicians can help. The clinical physician is much more likely to recover the admission blood at the time of patient transfer, as long as he knows to request the patient's specimens. Knowing to request will be part of the ongoing teaching responsibility of the pathologists. Lest you think that all this calling and requesting is too much trouble, is it not standard practice, both for surgeons and for pathologists, to request to review microscope slides of a patient's biopsy prior to resection at a referral center?

In the case of an apparent overdose, it is worth mentioning that the family of the decedent may not be nearly as interested in discovering the cause of death as the clinician in a case of this sort, even though the next of kin gave consent for autopsy. The family may already know the cause of death, at least near enough, or else the family may be in denial, in which case they have no desire for anyone to rub their nose in the truth. Again, it is important to confirm any positive drug results found on a screening assay with a separate analysis, such as GC/MS. Do not underestimate the ability of a determined family member to deny the truth if that relative is bent on denial. Even with the GC/MS tracings in your hand, someone in denial will pose excuse after excuse for why the results are in error. You cannot refute excuses in such a circumstance; you can only agree to disagree. If the relative becomes belligerent, which happens, and remains belligerent, which sometimes happens, then the relative may seek an attorney to see what can be done legally to erase the existence of the offensive report. One of us (G.G.D.) has had such experiences, and he has found a useful tack in such instances. When it becomes clear that the decedent's kin refuse to accept a laboratory result (whether positive or negative), the author is quick to send the specimen to an independent toxicology laboratory for independent analysis.

Why shouldn't the author send the specimen out? After all, in the case of the physician's wife recounted above, the cocaine was a false positive. People do make mistakes, and asking an independent lab to assay the specimen shows good faith on the pathologist's part. Just because the independent laboratory returns the same result as the first laboratory did, do not expect that the result will satisfy a relative bent on denial. Sending the specimen out for independent confirmation does help, however, when the relative calls attorneys, the director of the hospital, the board overseeing hospital accreditation, the state board licensing physicians, the governor, the newspapers, and the advocacy hotline touted by a local television news team for searing investigation of outrageous wrongs perpetrated by soulless corporations against helpless citizens. The first question that all these agencies will ask the pathologist is what truth there is to these allegations. If you, the pathologist, are able to reply when first asked that you have already done everything you know to do, including considering the possibility that your lab made an error, but that analysis of the specimen by an independent laboratory showed the same result, then the agencies will be impressed by your thoroughness and professionalism. The news agencies, moreover, will look elsewhere for an exciting story to report because there is nothing exciting about a pathologist quietly doing careful and thorough work.

Forensic pathologists have the liberty to do complete autopsies in every case, but hospital autopsies are subject to restriction by whomever grants permission for the autopsy. Of course, no specimen should be taken for toxicology that is not within the area authorized for autopsy, but even a blood sample from the heart in a chest-only examination will allow the pathologist to answer the question of whether a substance was present or absent in the blood.

Decomposition

In this day of refrigeration, hospital physicians are unaccustomed to postmortem decomposition. Pathologists speak of autolysis, and the pancreatic histology becomes less than ideal quickly as a result of autolysis. But most physicians, pathologists included, have no experience with the putrefactive stage of decomposition. Regular experience in examining and evaluating putrefactive decomposition rests entirely with forensic pathologists. Hospital pathologists, however, should know a tiny bit about the normal process of putrefaction because the process can manifest itself even in a hospital case, as shown below.

A 34-year-old alcoholic female was found unresponsive by her father. Because the two of them lived in a shack without electricity or telephone, the father walked to the nearest house to call for help. When paramedics arrived, they could not see what they were doing in the dim shack, so they transferred the decedent from the couch on which she lay to a gurney. The paramedics were unable to resuscitate the decedent en route to the hospital, and the decedent was pronounced dead in the emergency department of a university hospital. Once attempts at resuscitation ended, the clinical staff noticed that the decedent had raw wounds around her wrists and ankles and a large contusion under her right eye. Speculation arose as to what caused these injuries, and the staff decided that the decedent must have been kept bound hand and foot by her father in order to satisfy her father's perverse sexual desires. The police were called by the hospital staff to arrest the father for murder. The body was transported to the medical examiner's office for evaluation. The medical examiner found that the "injuries" described clinically were all changes due to early putrefactive decomposition and that death had been caused by an untreated pneumonia. The locations of the "injuries" around the wrists and ankles reflected the sites that the paramedics had grabbed in order to transfer the body from the couch to the gurney. The police did not arrest the father.

Autolysis, which is the first stage of decomposition, begins when a person dies. If a person has died, and provided the body is indoors at room temperature, then autolysis will be the only stage of decomposition apparent for about 24 hours. After roughly 24 hours at room temperature, the putrefactive changes of decomposition begin. By this time, bacteria from the gut have begun to grow unchecked within the blood that still lies in the blood vessels. Early putrefactive changes include skin slip or skin sloughing, in which the epidermis becomes detached from the dermis. This was the change that was first manifest in the alcoholic woman described above. Even a slight touch will cause the epidermis to slip aside, exposing a moist, raw dermal surface. The other early sign of putrefactive decomposition is marbling. Marbling is the prominent appearance of blood vessels, mostly veins, that can be seen through the skin. The bacteria growing in the blood can form pigments of green or greenish black as a by-product, and these dark pigments make the veins prominently visible on the surface of the skin, much like veins within polished marble, hence the name. With an additional 24 hours, the green discoloration will spread beyond the veins to involve whole segments of the body, and the face and torso will begin to bloat—that is, to swell with gas formed by the bacteria that are growing throughout the body. By this time, the body will stink of decay, and by this time the case is most unlikely to be in a hospital or brought to a hospital. At that earliest stage of putrefactive decomposition, where the only signs are marbling and skin slip, the odor of decay may be slight, and the odor of decay can easily be masked by the odor of someone who has not bathed in a long time. Hospital personnel, as in the case above, may see this earliest stage of putrefaction and because of their unfamiliarity with the process fail to recognize it for what it is. Remember that skin slip begins to occur when bacteria have seeded the blood within the body's vessels, a process that usually takes 24 hours at room temperature. Patients who are septic when they die, however, bypass that 24 hour window that it takes for bacteria to grow out of the gut and throughout the blood. This is the explanation for the immediate onset of putrefactive decomposition in the alcoholic woman described above. This is why it is possible for hospital pathologists to see early putrefactive decomposition in a hospital autopsy, particularly if there was some delay in the transport of a septic patient from the floor to the morgue refrigerator after death was declared.

(Incidentally, the times given above are the best rule of thumb available, but they are very rough estimates. Processes proceed more quickly at higher ambient temperatures and more slowly at lower temperatures. In a nutshell, the estimation of time of death based on medical findings at autopsy is fraught with conjecture, although divination is probably a more accurate term. Hospital deaths are usually precise in their time, but hedge is the word for estimating time of death based on medical findings on the body if you should be asked to do so.)

Retention of Specimens

Routine

The College of American Pathologists has published minimum guidelines for saving tissue.[12] The guidelines can be boiled down to the following:

Anatomic Pathology
Wet tissue—save for two weeks (surgical specimen), save for three months (autopsy tissues)
Paraffin blocks—save for five years (surgical and autopsy)
Glass slides—save for ten years (surgical and autopsy)
Reports—save for ten years (surgical and autopsy)

Clinical Pathology
Tubes of blood, cerebrospinal fluid, body fluids—save for 24 hours
Specimens from blood bank donors and recipients—save for 7 days posttransfusion (or 10 days postcrossmatch)
Microbiology specimens of permanently stained slides—save for 7 days
Peripheral blood smears/body fluids—save for 7 days
Bone marrow smears—save for 10 years

At Request of an Attorney

At times an attorney may call and ask that a certain specimen be retained, or even that any notes connected with that specimen be retained. A request of this sort is properly followed with a subpoena. News stories regularly arise concerning politicians or companies who are trying to destroy papers that they think an attorney may request. What sort of obligation does a pathologist, or any physician for that matter, have to retain specimens for an attorney? The answer is that the pathologist has no obligation to retain any specimen, or notes, or anything else that is regularly and routinely discarded *until* an attorney makes a request. As soon as an attorney makes a request, however, the law will require that the request be honored or at least considered. (Remember, it is attorneys who write the laws, so of course the law favors their side.) No law requires that a physician retain a specific item until an attorney formally asks the physician to retain that item. In other words, if you discarded the wet tissue from a surgical pathology specimen after three weeks, as is your custom with surgical specimens, and six months later an attorney calls your office demanding that you produce that specimen, then the attorney is out of luck. You may tell the attorney that the specimen was discarded after three weeks as is customary. You can then expect the attorney to huff and puff, but if he wanted the specimen the fault is his for not calling sooner, and he knows it. Sometimes the attorney will go on to make statements that imply some sort of misconduct on your part. Do not let the attorney bluff you into apologizing for your actions when you did nothing wrong. Such apologies can be used later by someone without scruples to imply that you, the pathologist, did in fact do something wrong.

If, on the other hand, you still have the specimen, then as soon as you are asked to retain the specimen you must do so. It may be more than merely the specimen that you will need to retain. When attorneys do request that some item be saved, they typically request that the item be saved along with anything that might possibly pertain to the item. For example, suppose the specimen requested were the tissue from a radical neck dissection, and at the time of grossing in the specimen you jotted down marks on a scrap of paper to help keep count of the nodes recovered (e.g., ʬ l). If that scrap of paper were in the folder with the surgical pathology report at the time an attorney requested that the neck dissection be saved along with anything pertaining to it, then you are honor-bound to retain that scrap of paper for the attorney.

A request for a specimen obligates the pathologist to retain the specimen, but it does not automatically mean that the specimen must be turned over to the attorney who requested it. It sometimes happens that the request to produce a specimen is inappropriate. For example, a relative might, through an attorney, request some specimen without any knowledge of the request by the patient whose specimen is being requested (as may happen in questions concerning paternity). Similar to a request for medical records, a request for a specimen should include the signature of the client whom the attorney represents. Meanwhile, you will need to notify the attorney who represents the group or the medical center, whichever is appropriate, about the request. It is the responsibility of the attorney representing you (or you through the hospital) to determine whether a request is appropriate. The thing that you as a pathologist should not do is to take it upon yourself to decide whether the request for the specimen will be granted. If it comes down to a question of who has the right to possession of the specimen, then the matter will be decided by a judge. If a judge orders that the specimen be released, then you should release it, regardless of your thoughts and feelings on the matter. To ignore a judge's order is to show contempt for the court, and individuals who show contempt for the court earn a fine, time in jail, or both.

In the clinical laboratory, it is perfectly acceptable for the primary care team to contact the laboratory director requesting that urine, blood, cerebrospinal fluid, and sometimes tissues be set aside for potential toxicology testing, even in the face of a negative drug screen. Screens, of course, are not all-encompassing, and if clinical suspicion of toxin or drug effect is raised in a patient who is seriously ill, then the laboratory is obligated to assist in sequestration of this type of sample. A good policy for this rare request is to designate a specific location for holding samples in the refrigerator or freezer and to hold samples for 6 months, if space permits. Labeling the samples as "Hold for Dr. Scott; 6 months if possible" will provide all the information needed to ensure that the industrious technologist cleaning freezers and refrigerators doesn't inadvertently discard a sample you wish to hold, although a word to that industrious technologist would be wise. In addition to the standard types of samples requested for sequestration, there may be the occasional request to hold citrated plasma and EDTA whole blood in a patient with an unexplained coagulopathy. Sometimes, only samples collected in life may provide the additional information needed to answer complex questions after death. Citrated plasma can be used for mixing studies, coagulation factor analysis, and protein assays, while the EDTA whole blood is an excellent sample for extraction of DNA for molecular testing in cases with potential hypercoagulation associated point mutations. Such requests and use of samples have occurred in the practice of one of the authors (MAS).

As you cannot plan for everything, you must be prepared for the unexpected request and work with the needs of the hospital that best meet the needs of patient care. Each event requires careful thought about potential implications for patient care and for potential use in a legal case. Examples of unusual requests encountered by one of the authors (MAS) include: a request to collect, track, and transport a potentially rabid bat killed by a patient (subsequent testing confirmed that the bat was positive for the Rabies virus, and appropriate vaccinations were initiated without any adverse events); a request to store a syringe with 1 mL of clear liquid "found" in a patient's bed by a relative for potential testing (subsequent GC/MS testing was negative); and a request to store a syringe containing clear liquid found in the locker of an employee (subsequent testing confirmed opiate abuse). In each of these cases, the laboratory initiated a chain of custody form, assigned an investigation number working with the facility police, and took photographs documenting the state of the item at the time of receipt in the laboratory. Even when you do not work in the realm of the legal system, brushes such as these require common sense protections such as chain of custody forms and photographic documentation.

A specimen is one thing, but what about a request to give an attorney the original slides and the blocks related to a surgical case, or the tracings related to a case from the clinical laboratory? Your instincts are correct here; never relinquish your original reports, slides, blocks, tracings, etc. The attorney who makes such a request may threaten you when you refuse to turn over the material immediately, but this is a bluff. Hold onto your material firmly until such time as your attorney receives a court order mandating that you turn over the items listed in the court order. Such a directive from a judge to turn over your only defense would be vanishingly rare, and your attorney should be able to make an adequate case for you to keep your original slides and offer the attorney requesting material recuts or the opportunity for his expert to review the original slides so that the slides remain in your possession. In the meantime, assure any requesting attorney that you are keeping the blocks and other materials safe and secure. As before, if you do receive a court order to relinquish items, then you must relinquish them. Do not stand on your honor, or else you and your honor will be spending time in jail. Naturally, if you relinquished certain items at the command of a court order, then you will keep the written order. If the question of why you released the items comes up subsequently, then the court order will serve as ample proof that you relinquished the items at the command of a court.

In the practice of forensic pathology, the author (G.G.D.) is sometimes asked to relinquish items, such as an infant car seat, to an attorney representing a side for a civil suit. The author makes clear that all the attorneys involved in the suit must agree for one party to accept responsibility for the item, after explaining to the attorney requesting custody that by assuming custody the attorney opens himself to the charge that the item has been tampered with or even substituted while in his custody. Usually, the attorney no longer wishes custody, but if all attorneys agree, then the author will transfer the item to the attorney demanding it after recording the signatures to the agreement of all parties in the case file. The clever attorney will not ask for the item in question. Why should he assume responsibility for the custody and care of the item when he can stick you with the responsibility? Why take up the room in his office? Why open his client to a charge that the item was tampered with while in the possession of the client's attorney?

Anatomical Gifts and Unusual Specimens

In centuries gone by, physicians had to resort to disinterring fresh corpses if they wished to study anatomy, and they had to be quick about it. In literature, the practice of stealing a corpse is nicely recorded in *The Adventures of Tom Sawyer*, a book written just over one century ago. Society has since come to accept the practice of physicians studying anatomy by using human remains obtained through the anatomical gift program. An anatomical gift program has even allowed study of postmortem decomposition and putrefaction under varying conditions at the University of Tennessee in Knoxville. The feature that gained society's approval, however, was the donation of the remains inherent in the concept of a "gift."

In 1999, investigation began into the practice of retaining organs removed at autopsies performed at the Alder Hey Children's Hospital in the United Kingdom. The findings of the investigation led to a scandal that ran for weeks in the British press. The printed report of the Inquiry ordered by the British House of Commons is available over the Internet,[13] and a full account of the Inquiry's findings is available there. In brief, the Inquiry found that physicians at Alder Hey were applying pressure on families to consent to autopsies, sometimes by telling the families that a coroner would order an autopsy anyway, so the family had better give the hospital consent. The Inquiry goes on to report that once an autopsy was performed, the organs removed were preserved as part of a growing collection for possible future research, but families were not informed that the organs would be retained. The report from the House of Commons lists other offences, including falsification of records and failure to keep records. The group that conducted the Inquiry considered that "paternalism" on the part of the hospital physicians was at the root of the offences. According to the Inquiry, "Paternalism is defined in the Concise Oxford Dictionary as follows: 'the policy of restricting the freedom and responsibilities of one's dependents in their supposed best interest'." In the United States, paternalism was the approach taken by some medical professionals in the past to explain why consent for a procedure was unnecessary. The necessity of obtaining consent for a medical procedure, and of informing a patient of the true state of the patient's health, seems much clearer today, and the practice of medical paternalism is the exception rather than the rule. Nevertheless, the occurrences at Alder Hey, and the public outcry that those occurrences engendered, need to be considered by pathologists in their own practice, and the wise pathologist would apply the lessons to his practice sooner rather than later.

This section will discuss autopsy and surgical pathology practice in light of the Alder Hey occurrence. First, however, it may help to present a case example on a separate topic—corneal donation—that bears emotional burdens for the relatives of the decedent similar to the burdens in the Alder Hey occurrence. In order to discuss all the ramifications of corneal donation, some background is necessary on the practice of forensic pathology.

Autopsies performed under the jurisdiction of a medical examiner or coroner differ in a fundamental way from hospital autopsies. The law that gives a medical examiner authority over particular sorts of cases also gives the medical examiner or coroner the authority to authorize the autopsy. In other words, medical examiners do not need to get permission of the next of kin to perform an autopsy. In fact, it goes even deeper than that. Medical examiners have the authority to perform an autopsy they think indicated even if, before the autopsy, the medical examiner is contacted by the next of kin expressly forbidding the medical examiner to do the autopsy. The law that empowers the medical examiner or coroner gives such authority and protects the medical examiner or coroner from any legal attack for doing the autopsy. That a forensic pathologist would be given the authority to countermand the wishes of the next of kin is difficult for most people to understand when they first hear of it, until they are reminded that the most common assailant in cases of homicide is a relative. The law that empowers the medical examiner to override the veto of the next of kin exists so that the next of kin, if he happens to be the murderer, cannot dictate how the body is examined. The essence of the matter is the contest between the rights and good of the individual and the rights and good of the society in which the individual lives. Lest anyone misunderstand, forensic pathologists take this authority seriously, and in the face of opposition by the next of kin, they invoke this authority only after careful consideration of the circumstances surrounding death and the wishes of the next of kin.

By extension of the authority to autopsy without permission of the next of kin, a medical examiner has the authority to do whatever procedure he deems necessary to establish the cause and manner of death. As a routine part of a forensic examination, the vitreous humor is aspirated from the globes for chemical and toxicological analysis. A decade or two ago, several jurisdictions around the United States passed laws giving the local medical examiner the authority to donate the corneas from bodies that, by law, fell under the jurisdiction of the medical examiner. This authority was granted by law because of the routine collection of vitreous humor during forensic examinations. Because the medical examiner had the authority to collect vitreous humor in every case he examined, and because the integrity of the globes would be destroyed by collecting vitreous humor, it was reasoned that the corneas could be harvested prior to collection of the vitreous humor, with the consent of the medical examiner and without the consent, or even notification, of the next of kin. Many people across the country had their sight restored as a result of this practice.

There is a logic to the reasoning that led to laws allowing corneal donation at the direction of the medical examiner, but there is also an element of paternalism. If you were to discuss this matter with people, you would find that some individuals see the good of society as more compelling, and others consider that the right of the next of kin to the body takes precedence. Here follows the tales of two jurisdictions, each of which had a law granting the local medical examiner the authority to authorize corneal harvest without any notification or approval of the next of kin.

In one jurisdiction, the eye bank considered that the best course was to discuss the option of corneal donation with the next of kin prior to harvest. Here the eye bank would call the medical examiner's office every day to request a list of the decedents and information on how to contact the next of kin. Eye bank workers would contact the next of kin and discuss the possibility of corneal donation. More often than not, the next of kin refused corneal donation, and that was the end of the matter. Nevertheless, some families consented to corneal harvest, and the eye bank was able to harvest the corneas from about 10% of the medical examiner cases by following this protocol.

In the other jurisdiction, the eye bank considered that the law allowing corneal harvest was sufficient unto itself. No attempt was made to find or notify family. Both the medical examiner and the eye bank worker would review whatever information, such as medical records, the medical examiner received with the body. If there was any record of refusal of organ donation, or even a record of hesitancy regarding the subject, then no corneal harvest was made in that case. Otherwise, provided that the decedent qualified medically as a corneal donor and the medical examiner gave approval, the corneas were harvested. The eye bank in this jurisdiction was able to harvest the corneas of about 75% of the decedents.

Time passed, and the media, both television and newspapers, became aware of the practice of corneal donation by medical examiners without the consent of the next of kin. The local media investigated the practice followed by the eye banks and medical examiners within the area that each covered.

In the first jurisdiction, the media found nothing to decry, so no story was reported.

In the second jurisdiction, the media took the position that the right of the next of kin to the body takes precedence over the good of society. There were stories and interviews, and a few relatives of decedents whose corneas were harvested made passionate statements about the wrong done to them because of the violation of their loved one's body. The stories ran for weeks. In the end, which came within a couple of months, politicians who had supported the law allowing corneal harvest at the discretion of the medical examiner called upon the medical examiner to abandon the practice of granting permission for corneal harvest. The medical examiner complied with the request of the politicians, and henceforth corneas were harvested only if the next of kin granted permission.

The eye bank in the first jurisdiction still follows its original protocol, and it is still able to harvest corneas from about 10% of the decedents. The eye bank in the second jurisdiction now harvests corneas from about 1% of the decedents.

The similarities between the situation involving corneal harvest and the outcry over organ retention at the Alder Hey Hospital are clear. In each case there was intent to do some good on the part of the physicians involved, and there was some precedent or a law to support the position of the physicians. In each case, however, the intent of the physicians to do good ran counter to the perception of what was right by enough members of the public that politicians got involved in order to try to restore sufficient order and decency to alleviate the public outcry.

At the time of the public outcry against the occurrences at Alder Hey Hospital, pediatric pathologists in the United States spoke among themselves about the effects that an investigation like the Inquiry of the House of Commons would cause if conducted in the United States. On the one hand, the proper practice of autopsy pathology sometimes requires fixation of tissue, so that the organ is not returned to the body upon completion of the autopsy. The brain is an obvious organ where fixation yields a more careful look, but congenitally defective hearts also fall into this category. Then there is the matter of saving unusual specimens, obtained either as surgical specimens or at autopsy, for teaching, a practice that has its usefulness. On the other hand, there is the right of the next of kin to possession of the body in order to provide decent disposition of the remains, and there is the right of the patient to his medical record and to his specimen removed surgically.

The matter of patient rights is being reexamined in the United States, and the requirements for the maintenance of patient confidentiality are becoming ever more stringent. Much of the outcry from the occurrence at Alder Hey Hospital arose because the parents of the children autopsied said that they were never told what would be done with the organs of their child after autopsy. Consent forms for surgery and for autopsy in the United States generally make mention that specimens removed may be retained and used for teaching or research, particularly in teaching hospitals. It is easy to infer from the experiences at Alder Hey and with corneal donation that consent to a procedure, whether an operation or autopsy, does not necessarily extend to consent for organ retention and use of the organs for teaching or for research. Despite a signature giving consent, a patient or relative can easily, and perhaps truthfully, claim that the duress of the moment meant that they did not read or understand the fine print. The fine print about consent for organ retention may save a hospital or department from a lawsuit (or it may not), but it will not mitigate media attention or public outcry. Someone who signed a consent form will claim that it is true that the information was in the fine print, but that same someone will go on to say, on television, that he was told by a physician at the hospital that the fine print was just a formality and to hurry up and sign.

Institutional Review Boards oversee matters of ethics regarding research because the penalty for failure to follow ethical guidelines in research is the loss of millions of dollars of federal funding. Teaching is not subject to that same sort of financial penalty. There is no simple answer for coming to terms with how best to practice pathology and balance the demands of a patient's rights with the need to teach and study. Indeed, no single answer will serve for all time, other than to be honest and to treat others as you would wish to be treated yourself. Review of your own group or departmental policy regarding how you handle surgical and autopsy specimens is a matter for regular review, every so often, as part of your quality assurance program. The review may best be done in conjunction with a risk management attorney. One approach is to have paragraphs on consent forms that explicitly address organ retention. The paragraphs on organ retention are discussed with the patient or next of kin by the physician obtaining consent, and the signer must then indicate whether he approves or disapproves of the specimen being used for either teaching or research, or for both. In the case of autopsy, the next of kin can also indicate that he understands that some organs (name the organs explicitly on the consent form) will not be returned to the body unless he indicates otherwise but that returning the organs to the body may delay the body's being ready for release to the funeral home selected by the family. If the next of kin approves of fixing the brain but does not wish for the brain to be either returned to the body or saved for teaching, then discuss how the brain will be disposed of. The purpose of this sort of detailed information is to assure that both the physician and patient have discussed and understand what will happen and to record that discussion for the medical record. The guiding principle is that honesty is the best policy. Unfortunately, in the Alder Hey matter, honesty was not the policy followed by hospital personnel.

Clinical Pathology

Samples for Toxicology Testing (Ethanol and Drugs of Abuse)

Patient Drug Testing

Intoxicating substances found in an individual's blood are of as much professional interest to attorneys as to physicians, albeit for different reasons. This is no news to directors of laboratories. It is common to find some statement on a patient's printed blood ethanol concentration report that indicates that the result is intended for medical use only and that the test was not done for legal use. Such a disclaimer will not keep a test result out of court if an attorney is determined to get the result into court. At the risk of presuming, the message that the disclaimer is meant to send to attorneys is that the specimen has not been handled in a manner that ensures a proper chain of custody as discussed earlier in this chapter. With or without a chain of evidence, if the attorney wants the result in court, then he will get it admitted into court. At that point, of course, the attorney representing the other side (specifically, the now sober patient) will argue against admission of the specimen into court, saying that the specimen is probably from some patient other than his client and therefore has no bearing in the legal case. Should you the pathologist be on the witness stand as director of laboratories, this argument will soon place you in an awkward position. On the one hand, you are being asked to testify that the toxicology result is unequivocally that of the patient being discussed in court. Without a chain of custody, you cannot make a claim of absolute certainty, not with legal weight at any rate. On the other hand, you will be asked whether patient specimens are ever mixed up in your lab. Of course mix-ups occur, so you reply that "Yes, mix-ups do sometimes occur." The next question is the awkward one, and it will be something to the effect of "And mix-ups of this sort are really rather common, isn't that right? They happen all the time, don't they?" Presumably you will have reviewed the case and decided for yourself whether a mix-up is likely or not. If likely, say so. If unlikely, then an appropriate answer would be to say that you cannot absolutely guarantee that no mix-up occurred in this case, but that you reviewed the case and see no reason to suspect a mix-up in this case. An example of such a case experienced by one of the authors (MAS) follows.

A blood alcohol level was ordered on a disoriented patient admitted to an outside hospital for medical evaluation. The specimen was collected at the hospital and then transported to the reference testing laboratory for analysis and reporting. The blood alcohol level was markedly elevated. Many months later, for reasons unknown to the laboratory, this patient was involved in a legal battle in which a history of alcohol use and abuse became relevant to the case. The attorney defending the client contacted the laboratory to establish whether or not this test finding could be discredited in court. No chain of custody had been obtained, however, when questioned, the attorney was informed that the hospital and testing laboratory had a very specific protocol for collection and testing of blood alcohol levels, even when no chain of custody form was required. The standard operating protocol required that the following steps occur before testing was completed: identification of the patient by two parties, both of whom initial the collection tube; collection of the sample without use of an alcohol-based cleansing pad; collection of a dedicated tube for testing, ensuring that the sample is not inadvertently opened as a shared sample for other tests; and transport to the testing facility, which then documents that all protocol steps have been followed and that the tube is received intact for analysis. Although the testing technologist did not remember the case, the name, or anything about the case in question, she knew the procedure and the protocol followed. If the specimen was tested and reported, then this protocol had been followed. The attorney attempting to discredit this test result was never heard from again.

Standard operating procedures and protocols on the outset may seem dull and cumbersome, but they have their place in laboratory testing, particularly as they relate to toxicological test methods. Could a mix-up have occurred in the example presented? It seems exceedingly unlikely, and considering that the laboratory director never heard from the attorney again, it seems he thought it unlikely, too. You might also mention that mix-ups, while they do occur, are uncommon, such as fewer than 1% of cases, which is much different than in fewer than 20% of cases. In the current age of bar-code-driven patient identification methods, the likelihood of misidentification may even approach zero. If this conversation were to take place in a trial, the judge will probably get involved at some point. It will be the judge who will decide whether the evidence of the patient's blood ethanol concentration will be admitted into court.

Let us return for a moment to the disclaimer that a particular laboratory result is intended for medical use only and that the test was not done for legal use. If this statement is meant as a message for attorneys, you might wish to put it more plainly in the terms attorneys are interested in, namely, "No attempt was made to maintain a legal chain of custody for this specimen from the time that it was procured until the production of this report." Some laboratory reports bear a statement explicitly addressing chain of custody in this way, and it makes the legal status of the laboratory result wonderfully clear.

Employee Drug Testing

Collection of samples for clinical toxicology testing in the hospital setting primarily relates to employee urine drug testing. Three types of settings arise for employee drug screening: preemployment testing, random employee testing, and testing for "cause or suspicion." In all three settings, it is best to operate under guidelines established within, and approved by, the hospital facility. Standardized collection protocols should address notifying the employee or prospective employee that a urine drug screen is required and outline the established acceptable timeline for presentation to the laboratory for sample collection. Once the employee presents to the laboratory, he should be counseled regarding how the sample is to be collected and should be given the opportunity to disclose, in writing, any medications he is currently taking, including over-the-counter medications and herbal products as well as prescription drugs. Collection of the sample should be monitored (some circumstances require observed collection), and the samples submitted should be tested for the possibility of common adulterants or misrepresentations. At a minimum, this includes testing for temperature, specific gravity, and pH. Once collected, the sample is usually divided into two containers, taped, and initialed, all in the presence of the employee being tested. The specimens should be kept in a secure, preferably locked location until transport to the testing site. The employee should be informed that the second sample is reserved for retesting and confirmatory testing if required. In some facilities, the follow-up confirmatory testing expense is placed upon the employee rather than the employer. Generally, direct observation of specimen collection is required when the employee is presenting for "testing for cause or suspicion," and these settings can be quite tense. You may consider having hospital security in a nearby location should conflict erupt. In addition, direct observation of sample collection is usually required for those in employee assistance programs, such as the impaired physicians program.

Transfusion Medicine

Medical procedures carry risk, and transfusion of a blood product carries with it the risk of several different types of adverse outcomes. For this reason, transfusion merits a consent form that acknowledges the slight but present risk of infection or hemolytic transfusion reaction or anaphylactic allergic reaction, possibly ending in death. As discussed at the beginning of this chapter, the law makes clear that a physician is in no way legally bound to produce a good outcome; there is no guarantee of success. Of course, nobody wants the bad outcome to be his, and lawsuits are sometimes filed by patients who become infected with Human Immunodeficiency Virus or Hepatitis C Virus through a transfusion. Provided that donor screening and blood product screening for evidence of HIV, HBV, and HCV were performed, there should be no grounds for a successful lawsuit charging malpractice for allowing a patient to receive a unit of tainted blood. Just because there should be no grounds does not mean that the physician is immune to a charge of malpractice, as the following example shows.

During the early HIV era, before testing for HIV was possible, the primary mechanism to screen for potentially infected blood donor products was a careful history for known risk factors. A hospital active in cancer treatment received and gave a unit of blood infected with HIV to a patient. The patient survived chemotherapy only to succumb to HIV infection several years later. The family sued the hospital. In court, the jury was told that this young patient had conquered a life-threatening malignancy, undergoing grueling therapy, only to die of HIV encountered in a tainted blood product. She left behind a loving family with small children. All agreed that the circumstances were tragic, but in defense there was no testing for HIV available at the time of transfusion, and thus there was no good way to avoid the risk of transmitting HIV via blood products. Several physicians from the hospital in question were furious that such a case could reach trial, and on the witness stand they were visibly angry, indignant, and unsympathetic to the plight of this family. Despite the fact that no test at that time could have been used to prevent this occurrence, the jury ruled in favor of the decedent, compensating the next of kin for loss of life.

This case emphasizes the importance of behavior and conduct in court, which can persuade a jury to rule in favor of the prosecution despite any degree of scientific evidence, particularly if the jury perceives that an individual or agency lacks compassion for the patient.

Multiple tests are used today to test for the presence of HIV and HCV; however, even with the use of nucleic acid testing via polymerase chain reaction analysis of donor blood, there still exists a window of potential missed diagnosis between viral infection in the donor and detectable circulating viral load levels. As a rule of thumb, the window for false negative testing using serologic methods is 10–30 days, while the window for false negative testing using molecular methods is 3–10 days. Courts have borne this out in cases of HCV infection from a blood product. Lawsuits charging malpractice due to infection with HIV, however, have led to some cases of juries finding malpractice. As illustrated in the case above, HIV carries greater emotional clout than HCV in the minds of laymen, and greater emotional clout can sometimes carry the day for the infected patient even in the face of law. There is always the possibility of appeal, which is something to discuss with your attorney. In a perfect world, a malpractice verdict of this sort would never occur, but then in a perfect world there would be no sickness to begin with.

The most common cause of a life-threatening adverse reaction to a transfusion has been and remains human clerical error, usually leading to a hemolytic transfusion reaction. With luck, the error is caught early and the reaction is minor, but an ABO mismatch can end in death. If human error causes the poor outcome, then any formal charge of malpractice that comes of the matter is likely to stick, and settlement is the probable course that the attorneys representing you and the hospital will recommend. An example of this type of error involves a case where an O positive patient required transfusion of packed red blood cells. An order for O positive units was made to the local blood donor service, and units were received for transfusion. A standard step in the check-in of blood products included verifying the group and type of the labeled blood products. Upon verification, one of the units was noted to be mislabeled. It was actually an A positive unit of blood labeled as an O positive product. This was caught prior to blood administration, and no harm was done. If, however, the event was a dire emergency and products were released without testing, the outcome could have been a fatal hemolytic transfusion reaction. Because clearly clerical errors can be potentially fatal, blood banking standard operating procedures mandate multiple checkpoints in an effort to identify these errors before harm is done. Fortunately, with these mandated requirements to check, recheck, and re-recheck, this type of error is now exceedingly rare.

Delayed hemolytic transfusion reactions occur when a patient has an antibody titer below the level of clinical detection at the time of typing and antibody screening for transfusion. The patient will improve initially with transfusion, but over the ensuing ten to twenty days the foreign red cell antigen stimulates an anamnestic immune rebound in the recipient, resulting in a boosting of antibodies directed against the transfused cells. The patient will then become anemic and jaundiced from lysis of the foreign red cells mediated by antibodies directed against Rh, Kell, Kidd, and Duffy antigens foreign to the recipient. The risk of delayed hemolytic transfusion reactions can be minimized within a hospital system by keeping (and making use of) transfusion history documentation (cards or electronic files) in the blood bank on patients who have had antibodies documented in the past. There is always the possibility that a patient with a low-level antibody of hemolytic potential will be admitted to your hospital who has never before been seen in your hospital, such as a visitor from out of town injured in an automobile accident. This possibility has led some people to argue for a central blood bank file maintained on a national level. Others fear that a central file offers too great a risk for invasion of privacy. At the time of this writing, the pendulum is swinging toward increased patient right to privacy.

Life-threatening adverse reactions to blood product transfusion may also be caused by transfusion of products contaminated with bacteria. Historically, this risk is greatest with platelet products because they are stored at room temperature, providing better conditions for bacterial growth than products stored in refrigerated temperatures. For this reason, the shelf life of platelet products has been decreased over time, and now all platelet products must be given within 5 days of collection. There are bacteria that can grow in refrigerated blood products, such as *Yersinia* and *Serratia* species, but these are much more limited than those that can grow in room temperature platelet products. Other sources can provide more knowledge than we can about the fine points of bacterial infection of blood products. For this book, we wish to point out that sometimes a simple thing can prevent an adverse outcome from occurring. Visual inspection of packed red blood cells and platelet products prior to release for administration is that simple preventative measure. Visual inspection of a unit of platelets for excessive clumping or of a unit of red cells for hemolysis, purple discoloration, or distention of the bag by gas will reveal to the alert technician that the product may be contaminated with bacteria. In cases where units infected by bacteria are given, inspection with the advantage of hindsight is likely to reveal telltale signs of a tainted unit.

Transmission of an infectious agent via blood product transfusion is not limited to bacterial agents. Protozoan parasites such as *Toxoplasma gondii*, *Leishmania*, and *Trypanosoma cruzi* have been documented.

An adult man undergoing an emergent second heart transplant was noted to have a rocky postoperative course with a striking febrile illness evolving approximately 10 days posttransplantation. Examination of the peripheral blood revealed circulating intracellular and extracellular organisms characteristic of *Toxoplasma gondii*. The patient had been hospitalized for an extended period of time including through the first and second cardiac transplantations, making the possibility of hospital-acquired infection most likely. The search began with evaluation of blood products transfused and with scrutiny of the donor from which the second heart was harvested. Eventually, the exact point of parasite transfer was confirmed. The patient eventually died with overwhelming parasitemia.

Also, transmission of common viral agents such as CMV, which resides in the leukocyte component of blood products, is possible. In fact, the potential for devastating CMV infection occurring in the immunocompromised host is the reason for seeking CMV negative blood products for the immunocompromised CMV negative patient requiring transfusion.

Requests for DNA Confirmation

Paternity Testing

Forensic pathologists are sometimes asked to obtain a sample of a male decedent's blood for use in paternity testing. This request is made a few times per year, but it is made year after year after year. Directors of clinical laboratories say that such a request is far more uncommon in their experience. Perhaps the event of death, and the last chance to make claim to an individual's estate that accompanies death, galvanizes people into action. Even when a request for DNA testing is made, the specimen is usually procured specifically for DNA testing rather than being taken from a leftover tube of blood. Courts will look for some evidence of chain of custody, such as the chain of custody procedure outlined by the American Association of Blood Banks, before they will admit evidence from a test into court. Requests for paternity testing come in many forms, and workers in DNA labs that do paternity testing have interesting stories to tell. For pathologists, the rule of thumb remains the use of common sense. If a request for a sample from a patient for paternity testing is made in a hospital case, then the patient (or the patient's guardians) should know about the request. If the patient is unresponsive, then the next of kin should know of the request.

A clinical laboratory received a request for paternity testing on a patient with a serious closed head injury who was being cared for in the intensive care unit. His injury was the result of an accident at work, and his family stood to gain financial compensation for his injuries or death. The girlfriend of the patient claimed to be pregnant with his child and requested a specimen be obtained from the comatose individual for paternity testing. Given the nature of the request, hospital legal counsel was notified, and appropriate consent was obtained from this patient's next of kin prior to initiation of any specimen collection and testing. Because the patient had undergone multiple transfusions, a blood sample was considered an inadequate choice as it could contain DNA from multiple donors. Instead, the laboratory collected several buccal cavity epithelial scrape samples on the patient for paternity testing to be completed at a later date. The patient died, the baby was born, and paternity was confirmed, allowing appropriate distribution of funds designated for care of his child. (Incidentally, in cases of this sort the parents of the father may either be angry that the woman bore his child or glad that the deceased father has left behind a spark of his life in a child. Expect either response in your initial dealings with the next of kin.)

For establishing and maintaining chain of custody, your laboratory and those requesting the test would best be served by requesting a sample formally with a court order, in the same sort of way that medical records are requested. As indicated in the case example, call upon hospital legal counsel to handle the legal details.

Validation of Specimen Identity

In the busy hospital setting with collection of literally hundreds to thousands of patient blood samples each day, there is the potential for specimen misidentification. Anytime human intervention and judgment are required, the door to potential error is opened. Fortunately, this is an uncommon occurrence in the laboratory. Awareness of any potential problem allows steps to be designed in an effort to intercept and prevent the problem. The results of any laboratory, regardless of the level of sophisticated techniques, are only as good as the sample submitted for testing. This said, it is in our own best interests to identify the problem, look at the process, and identify weaknesses or moments with the potential for error. Having identified potential sources for error, we then need to minimize or, in the best of worlds, eliminate these sources and subsequently monitor for success. For this system to be effective, you must create a system in which not only errors are recognized but also the "close calls." Close calls, which are caught and rectified by a diligent employee, point toward the system weaknesses and a problem that needs to be fixed. The looming question is, "How do we create a system in which both errors and 'close-calls' may be reported without fear of punishment or reprisal?" The Veterans Administration (VA) healthcare system has taken a proactive stance on this issue. If you ask a patient—or better yet, yourself—what level of error is acceptable in the healthcare provided to you as an individual, then the answer is a resounding, clear, unhesitating 0%. However, if you look at healthcare statistics across the United States, the findings are chilling. Schimmel reported from 1964 hospital database reviews that 20% of patients admitted to university-based hospitals were injured during the course of their stay.[14] The findings of this review of hospitals in 1964 are similar to the findings of reviews from the 1980s, 1990s, and today.[15, 16] Multiple tactics have been tried to reduce the number of overall medical errors, however, response has been sparse and results minimal. Today the focus is driven by a model of reporting based on NASA's Aviation Safety Reporting System, which has been so successful in decreasing aviation accidents over the past thirty years. The key is the development of a system that allows evaluation and comparison without the risk of punitive actions.[17, 18]

The obvious question for the pathologist is, "How does the laboratory fit into the overall hospital system error problem?" The VA has performed the most extensive look at laboratory-specific data related to error rates,[19] and the findings are summarized here. Several mechanisms for reporting of failures in laboratory quality exist in the VA system. These include inspection processes by both internal and external groups, participation in internal and external proficiency surveys, the VA Patient Incident Control Reporting System (blood transfusion problems, sample or patient misidentification, etc.), the Office of VA Medical Inspectors oversight (review of surgical pathology reporting and misdiagnoses), and the VA Office of General Counsel (tort claim review system). All of these reports contain an element of laboratory reporting that is extracted and presented to the VA Central Office (VACO) level Pathology and Laboratory Medicine Service managers. All reports of corrective action are returned to VACO for incorporation of follow-up steps, declaration of planned monitors, and ongoing activities for the reported errors. Based on these databases and the reporting systems in place, VACO estimated a possible 5% error rate within laboratories; however, these reports were not linked to potential patient injury or adverse effects. In an effort to determine actual laboratory error rates in the VA laboratories that affected patient care, VACO reviewed 5 years of Patient Incident Control Reports from 1986 to 1990. During this period, there were a total of 1,127,000,000 tests performed and a total of 102 laboratory errors/incidents reported through this reporting mechanism. All reports and follow-up actions were reviewed for each incident. These errors were then divided into those attributed to clinical staff operating outside the laboratory (physicians, nurses, etc.) (46% of total errors), those attributed directly to the laboratory (43% of total errors), and those in which the errors were either not substantiated or were related to an outside blood donor service (11% of total errors). Analysis of the errors directly related to the laboratory was further divided as noted in Table 3-1.

Table 3-1: Summary of laboratory errors in VA patient incident reporting system (5 year period from 1986–1990).[19]

Laboratory activity, process, or section	Percentage of total laboratory errors
Blood bank clerical error or misidentification	43%
Blood bank typing, crossmatch, or antibody identification error	23%
Surgical pathology misdiagnosis	16%
Clinical laboratory errors in chemistry, hematology, microbiology, etc.	11%
Phlebotomy or computer errors	7%

Given the raw data, the actual error rate for the VA laboratory system over this 5 year period of reporting would be calculated as 44 errors of laboratory origin with adverse patient impact per 1,127,000,000 tests performed during this period. The shorcoming with any study of this nature is that not all errors are actually reported. This error rate was then adjusted for probable unreported errors using the Government Accounting Office (GAO) adjustment factor based on medical record chart reviews. The GAO investigation indicated that overall only 13% of errors found in medical record reviews are reported. Using this correction factor, the "missing 87%" of laboratory errors were added into the calculation. This resulted in a rate of 314 laboratory errors for 1,127,000,000 tests for 5 years (0.0003%). Even if you increased the potential unreported cases another thousandfold, the laboratory error rate associated with negative patient impact would be less than 1%.

Despite this low incidence of laboratory errors resulting in negative patient impact noted in the VA nationwide review, the fact remains that we all desire that the incidence of error be zero. Mechanisms used in the laboratory workplace to mitigate these potential errors focus on identifying and minimizing potential system weaknesses and recognition of errors before reporting occurs, thus negating the possibility of negative patient impact. This is where the clinical impact of laboratory performance improvement plans, quality assurance, and quality control is critical. Laboratories may use the delta check concept for identification of potential misidentified blood samples. In this system, the patient blood sample is run through an automated instrument with dual-interface host query capability. When the instrument in chemistry or hematology encounters a significantly different value (set by the medical director for the laboratories according to the patient population for that laboratory), a delta check alert is generated by the automated system, the host laboratory information system (LIS), or both. One of the key indicators for detection of mislabeled samples is the Mean Cell Volume (MCV) component of the red blood cell indices. Regardless of the white blood cell count, platelets, hemoglobin, or hematocrit, the MCV is relatively constant throughout a given patient's hospital stay. Small changes take extended periods of time to develop. For these reasons, a delta check alert for an MCV can be used to trigger sample identification verification as a first step. The principles of quality control, quality assurance, and performance improvement plans will be described in more detail in Chapter 7. At this juncture, suffice it to say that performance improvement programs (sometimes called Total Quality Improvement plans) must be a living, breathing, growing part of laboratory operations. The better you perform, the higher you raise the bar. It is a constant process of review, change, evaluation, re-review, and reestablishing goals, always striving for the lofty but impossible goal of perfection. Of course, if your goal does not exceed your reach, then what's a heaven for?

Citation of References in Reports

Some pathologists like to cite references for further reading as part of their report on a case. The practice is especially common in departments with a residency training program. Autopsy reports, for example, often have a list of references at the end. Some pathologists also cite references in surgical pathology or clinical pathology reports when the case is an unusual entity outside of daily experience for both the pathologist and clinician. Other pathologists cite references so that, should questions arise in the future, the "standard of care at the time" will be clear. Discussions of the practice of citing references with an attorney who works in a private firm that represents physicians in malpractice suits and with attorneys in hospital risk management yielded similar responses. Both the risk management attorneys and the private practice attorney think it appropriate to cite references if doing so to point others in the direction of additional information; no one expects that a few reference citations represent an exhaustive review of the literature. Nevertheless, the hospital risk management attorneys went on to say that they were concerned by the statement that a reference will serve to justify the actions of the pathologist by showing what the standard of care was at the time the diagnosis was made. Years hence it may be just as easy to show that another standard was also appropriate or that the standard used was just plain wrong. Should you think that the inclusion of an article may make life unnecessarily difficult later on, you should not attach articles to your report. You will never remember all the articles that you have attached to reports over the years, and in any case it is wrong to alter the medical record. Rather than regret an action later, it is better not to commit it.

The two types of attorneys differed in their opinions concerning the inclusion of a photocopy of an article with a report or in a hospital chart. The attorney in private practice said that any such article would make no difference in the process or outcome of a trial concerning malpractice. The attorneys in risk management, however, were opposed to including a photocopy of the article cited with a pathology report, just as they are opposed to a clinician putting an article into a patient's chart. The chart concerns the patient and should contain reports directly related to the patient's care. The articles are in the library and may be looked up there. The distinction in the risk management attorneys' minds is that making an article a part of the chart gives the article an appearance of importance not given by a simple citation. As a group, forensic pathologists are opposed to putting any article in a report or in a case file because it gives the impression that you consider the article authoritative, and, as we will discuss in Chapter 5, no text is authoritative. An *individual* makes a diagnosis, even if he has some input from his colleagues during the process. An article or two hardly represent all the training and experience that went into making the diagnosis. Do not sell yourself short.

Transmitting Information to Clinicians and Clinical Staff

Reporting Critical Values

Some laboratory results, such as a serum glucose of 36 mg/dL, represent a medical emergency and merit immediate notification of someone caring for the patient with the critical (or crisis) value. It is insufficient to call and leave a message with a secretary or on an answering machine, because a critical value demands immediate clinical assessment and treatment if treatment proves to be clinically indicated. Someone in the laboratory must call and transmit the critical value to a member of the team providing care to the patient. Depending on the particular test and its value, it may be appropriate to notify the patient's nurse, or the value may require notification of the attending physician in charge of the patient's care. None of this is news to a director of clinical laboratories, and the computers that generate lab results are programmed to draw attention to a lab result that falls outside whatever critical range the director of laboratories has set.

Should a lawsuit that revolves around a critical value arise, then the same rule that governs other aspects of patient care applies to the act of calling a critical lab value to a member of the patient's clinical team—if the call was not written down, then it never happened. Some clinical laboratories keep a log of critical value calls on a clipboard or in a three-ring notebook. The log looks something like Figure 3-2, albeit the entries are handwritten.

Patient No.	Critical value	Called to	Called by	Date	Time
1845588-9	Glc 36	Anne Johnson (patient's nurse)	Bob Givens	09/16/02	8:24 AM
1845621-7	WBC 97k, 87% lymphs	Dr. Ellen Hess (patient's physician)	Sara Lucas	09/16/02	1324H

Figure 3-2. A sample log sheet recording calls of critical values. Electronic charting can replace such logs, but a log sheet remains a succinct source for this information within the laboratory (see the text).

A log sheet serves the purpose of recording that a call was made by a laboratory worker to a member of the clinical team, but there is an advantage to the pathology laboratory in having notification recorded as part of each individual patient record in each case. The advantage is that the medical record is the document that any attorney (whether for or against you) will review to determine what care was rendered when and by whom. A critical call log sheet is ten thousand times better than no record at all. Nevertheless, to produce the log sheet independently as proof of calling, after the attorneys have been unable to find record of any call in the chart, has the potential to weaken the evidence that exonerates the pathology laboratory. It is true that all the laboratory employees will be able to testify that the log sheet is always there, that all calls are entered onto the sheet as they are made (there should be other calls from around the same time on either side of the call in question), and that the log sheet has been the mechanism for recording calls of critical values for years before the case in question arose. Even so, the log sheet can be made to look self-serving, if an attorney should choose to paint the log sheet as being contrived after the fact when he is arguing the case before a jury. The attorney representing the laboratory will be able to present evidence to the jury that the log sheet is not contrived, of course, but sometimes planting a seed of doubt is sufficient for the purposes of the plaintiff's attorney.

The previous paragraph is leading to the argument that a log sheet is fine to keep track of things in the laboratory but that an entry into the patient's formal medical chart is better still as a way of recording that the call took place. There is no reason that a pathologist cannot make an entry onto a patient's chart. Traditionally, pathologists do not write notes in the patient's chart, which is inconveniently far from the pathology laboratory. Traditions in and of themselves are unworthy of veneration, and inconvenience must be weighed against benefits. Fortunately, there is now a convenient way to record laboratory notification of clinical staff of a critical value in the patient's chart through electronic charting. Electronic charting makes it easy to append a note to the laboratory report that Dr. X or Nurse Y was notified of this critical value by Lab Technician Z at such a time on such a day. Thus a record of notification becomes part of the medical record. Having the note in the patient's medical record ensures that any thought of the plaintiff's attorney (or of the clinical physician's defense attorney) that the lab is to blame for not notifying someone of a critical value dies aborning. It is much easier to keep a thought from developing into a legal strategy than it is to undo a legal strategy that has already been set into motion.

In the era of electronic documentation, even hospitals without a sophisticated electronic medical record often have portions of the hospital database available electronically. The two most likely areas to be computerized are the laboratory and pharmacy services. Make use of the Laboratory Information System (LIS) to help link documentation of the critical value call and the results. Most LIS systems allow free text entries via "comments" that can be linked to the test results. In older LIS systems where this is not possible, you can use "canned comments" to document the contact electronically. This may be as simple as "critical value called; see call log." This option provides an electronic documentation trail, even when electronic charting is not possible, that points back to the laboratory call logs. Paper medical records contain a section for laboratory data usually filled with the LIS summary or cumulative reports. Comments associated with these data points may also serve as chart documentation of the clinical contact.

Finally, even with the advantage given by making notification of the patient's clinical team in the chart, it may still be of some use to the pathology laboratory to keep a call log for critical values or to keep a copy of lab reports with the note of notification in a binder. There are times when you may wish to check quickly whether a call was made, and it can take several days to get a chart out of deep storage in medical records, particularly if the patient's primary care physician requested the chart first or medical records has sealed the chart at some attorney's request.

What to Do When You Discover that an Error Has Occurred

The business of pathologists is providing information to clinicians so that clinicians can decide how to proceed in treating a patient. The information may be easily interpreted, such as a neutrophil count of 50.0×10^3 µL in a febrile patient, or it may be a difficult case best reviewed by the clinician and pathologist together, such as a dysplastic nevus with uncertain malignant potential. The one thing that is expected in all cases, however, is that the information provided by a pathologist to a clinician will be correct. Pathologists strive for the asymptote of perfection, but everyone makes mistakes. In Chapter 4, we will discuss what to do when you are notified that you have been named as a defendant in a malpractice suit. At this point, the discussion concerns what to do if you discover that you have made an error.

Because no one is perfect, all pathologists make mistakes now and then. Some mistakes have no meaningful effect on the patient. An example of a trivial mistake would be the failure to notice transposition of two digits in a report on a placenta, so that the pathology report states that the mass was 920 grams rather than the correct mass of 290 grams. Although embarrassing, the mistake is obvious, is an understandable human oversight, and does little harm. In some cases, however, the mistake on the part of the pathologist does cause the course of a patient's care to go terribly awry. A missed focus of dysplasia on a Pap smear, a frozen section diagnosis of malignancy that is seen to be incorrect on permanent sections, or a specimen mix-up leading to the wrong patient being warned that her unborn child is likely to have a neural tube defect are examples of errors that can lead to terrible consequences for the patient. The one thing that you must *never* do when you discover such a terrible error is to try to alter the medical record in some way. We will discuss legal reasons not to alter the medical record (including slides) in Chapter 4, but it is wrong to lie, and you will learn of the many deaths a coward can die if you lie about your work.

If you as a pathologist discover that you have made an error of such great magnitude, then you need to immediately make it your business to start getting the truth out. Because you are a pathologist, you need to call the patient's clinician and discuss the matter with him privately in a calm and professional manner. Certainly it is no one's business but the parties involved, so privacy is appropriate. Nor should there be interruptions during the conversation; everyone should turn off their pagers and cellular phones. A mistake of this magnitude calls for a face-to-face discussion—the stakes are too high to discuss the matter over the telephone. Each physician needs to see the other physician during this conversation. Expect the clinician to ask how such a mistake could have happened. Bring the pertinent laboratory report or microscope slides with you. If no microscope is handy, then be able to get to a microscope if necessary.

Having discussed the matter with the clinician, it will be the clinician who calls the patient to come in for a discussion of the matter (or else the patient's parents or guardian if the patient is a child or otherwise unable to care for himself). Given that the pathologist is the physician who made the mistake, it is appropriate for the pathologist to meet with the clinician and affected patient. For one thing, the pathologist is the one who is best able to explain to the patient what happened. For another, the pathologist will know exactly what is discussed with the patient and how the patient responded if the pathologist is part of the conversation. If the pathologist leaves the conversation to the clinician to handle, then the pathologist must trust that the clinician will present the matter to the patient accurately and that the clinician will throw no more stones of blame at the pathologist than the pathologist deserves.

The conversation of the physicians with the patient merits a face-to-face discussion without any threat of interruption, just as the conversation between the pathologist and the clinician did. It is likely that the pathologist has never met the patient, but the clinician is there to introduce the pathologist to the patient. Some words of explanation by the clinician may help establish the pathologist's role in the patient's care, as in the following example (fictional names are used for convenience):

Clinician: Hello, Mr. Thomas, and welcome. Thank you for coming today as I requested.

Patient (tensely): You're welcome.

Clinician: This is Dr. Alan James, one of the pathologists here at the hospital.

Pathologist (offering hand to shake): It is a pleasure to meet you, Mr. Thomas.

Patient (shaking hand with little enthusiasm): Hello.

Clinician: Mr. Thomas, are you familiar with pathologists and what they do in a hospital?

Patient: Not really.

Clinician: Pathologists are medical doctors who are involved in patient care, but at a distance from patients. It is pathologists who run the medical laboratories where patient specimens are sent. When you have a tube of blood drawn in my office, for example, my staff sends that tube on to the hospital laboratory, which is a pathology laboratory, where pathologists run the tests necessary to determine what your white blood cell count is, whether you have enough iron in your blood, and things of that sort. Because pathologists run the laboratories and have no personal patients of their own, most patients never see pathologists. Does that make reasonably clear how pathologists fit into the scheme of things here at the hospital?

Patient: I suppose so, but why did you call me to come to your office?

Clinician: You recall last month, when you had that persistent cough after returning from your mission trip to South America?

Patient: Oh yes, I was worried that I had cancer.

Clinician: Remember that your chest X-ray had a new nodule on it that wasn't present a year ago and we took a tissue sample using the "tiny needle" approach through your rib cage?

Patient: Yes, I remember. I worried a lot and was finally told that it was "not diagnostic." I'm not looking forward to my surgery scheduled for next week.

Clinician: Dr. James, our laboratory director, called me last week to tell me that your case was reviewed again and actually the changes are diagnostic. We need to do some follow-up studies, and we are going to cancel the open lung biopsy we had discussed.

Patient (a bit antsy, speaks softly as he fidgets with a paperclip): I understand.

Clinician: I have asked Dr. James here to explain all of this to you and answer any questions that you may have.

Patient (obviously very nervous over this new information): Okay.

Pathologist: Mr. Thomas, the first thing I want you to know is that the biopsy is negative for cancer. Please put your mind at ease regarding that.

Patient: Thank you, that's good news. This whole recall thing had me really worried.

Pathologist: I am very sorry for the distress that this has caused you. I thought that it was very important to talk to you in person, explain the findings, and also follow up with a couple of questions to help us determine the best steps to take next. One of the things we do routinely in the laboratory is have other pathologists randomly review biopsy cases signed out by other pathologists. We use this as a kind of "control" system to find any errors and alert us to any problems. Your biopsy was reviewed as a part of this process and it turns out you *do* have diagnostic changes in the biopsy tissue. What the first pathologist thought was "fibers or contaminating debris" was actually parts of a parasite organism. We immediately recognized that a mistake was made and called your doctor to explain this to him. We also sent the biopsy to a specialist to help determine exactly what kind of parasite this is...

The conversation continues with the physicians explaining the significance of the parasite and the need for stool sample testing, which will probably be negative. If the repeat chest X -ray shows that the nodule is getting smaller and the stool testing is negative, then no further treatment needs to be done. The patient, pathologist, and the primary care physician review the chest X-ray and the pathology slides together.

In this scenario, had the pathologist fretted over the case and waited until the outside consultant called back with the definitive answer, this patient would have undergone an unnecessary open lung biopsy. Quick confession and communication averted any untoward patient impact.

In the case above, the patient got news better than he feared, so his joy will go a long way toward dispelling any desire on the patient's part to sue for malpractice. When the news is worse than the patient expects, the scenario may not end so happily. Regardless of what the outcome is for the patient, once a mistake is discovered, you must discuss it with the patient. However upset, or ashamed, or frightened you as the pathologist who made a mistake are, maintain a calm, professional demeanor throughout your conversation with the patient. Honesty is more important than anything else you can do, but like unto honesty is having the human decency to feel empathy for the patient. Especially at this moment of confession, the patient's thoughts and feelings, concerns, and grief outweigh your concerns for your own professional welfare. Your time is the patient's in this situation, so do not hurry the conversation along. If you have the habit of glancing nervously at your watch, then leave your watch behind in your office. Giving of yourself to the patient at this moment is of paramount importance. It will be best if you can empathize and give of yourself simply because it is the right thing to do. If you cannot empathize, then you are worsening your position in any coming lawsuit. It might surprise you what can be accomplished by the quality of mercy, both on the part of you and on the part of the patient. Here is another example.

A pathologist presented some autopsy cases as an invited guest at a medical grand rounds at a hospital where the pathologist did not work. As part of the presentation, the pathologist showed some photographs of a body, including the face of the decedent, to make a medical point. Afterward, one of the hospital staff members, who happened to know the pathologist, called the pathologist to let him know that a relative of the decedent worked at the hospital and had been in the audience. This relative was extremely upset that the photographs had been shown. The pathologist asked the staff member to tell the relative that the pathologist was coming back to the hospital immediately to discuss the matter with the relative. Once there, the pathologist actually did little talking. Mostly, the pathologist listened to the relative grieve and recall how much the relative had loved the one who had died and how hard it was to see the photographs of the decedent presented publicly for all to see. The pathologist said that he was asked to give a talk on a certain topic and that the particular case shown best illustrated the medical point that needed to be made. The pathologist went on to say that had the pathologist realized that a relative of that decedent would be in the audience, the case would not have been shown. After twenty minutes, everything was said that needed to be said. Two days later, the pathologist made it a point to return to the hospital to see the relative again and ask how things were going. The relative replied, "The night that you showed those photographs I had dinner with the whole family, and I told them what you did." The pathologist asked, in the calmest voice manageable, what happened when the relative told the whole family. "They all wanted to sue you," the relative said, "but I told them that they couldn't do that, because you were a nice person." The relative and pathologist spoke a few minutes more, and the pathologist again apologized for upsetting the relative. Neither has seen the other since.

In the situation just described, the pathologist made one big mistake, namely showing autopsy photographs with identifying features. The pathologist also did some things correctly. First, the pathologist showed the images of the relative's decedent to make a specific point and, having made it, moved on. More important, however, was that the pathologist dropped everything to present himself before the relative to discuss the matter, and the pathologist made sure to listen attentively and patiently to whatever the relative had to say. People respond to a show of honest vulnerability. Again, it might surprise you what can be accomplished by the quality of mercy.

After meeting with the clinician and again after meeting with the clinician and patient, the pathologist should record a thorough note of the discussions. The note should record the date and time (including duration) of the discussion, the names of the parties present, and the points discussed. It is difficult to make a note recording the conversations too detailed, but it would be disastrous, of course, to take notes or make a tape recording during the conversations. Your memory and the record you write down immediately afterward are appropriate. You can be sure that your memory will be sharp immediately after a conversation of this sort.

Some say that, even if a physician has made a mistake, he should still bill for his services because the failure to bill will look like an admission of guilt. Others say not to bill. Those who advocate not billing, however, tend to be clinical physicians who have established a relationship with their patients. Given that you decide to bill, the patient may balk at paying, and it might be the better part of valor not to collect. Nevertheless, you did provide a service, and you are entitled to bill for your service. Remember that a physician owes a patient his best effort, but the physician does not guarantee a good outcome. Therefore, it is appropriate to bill even for a bad outcome.

Statute of Limitations

Decent honesty is the first reason that a patient should be notified when a mistake of consequence has been made concerning his health care. Even if you do not find honesty a compelling reason, there is still another reason that you should be forthright in admitting a mistake to a patient, and that is the statute of limitations. In law, there is a point in time after which a person's right to sue expires, and that point is determined by the statute of limitations. The statute of limitations defines the amount of time during which an individual has the right to sue for recompense of damages. Once that time has passed, the person can no longer sue.

The critical questions, of course, are when does the clock start ticking, and how long does it tick. The statute of limitations will define the answers to each of these questions. Each state has its own state law, and each state has its own statute of limitations that defines the starting point and the duration for malpractice (among other offences) in that state.

The question of when the clock starts can be difficult to answer because even with carefully worded laws the time of the infraction, if you will, may be unclear. Three different attempts at defining the starting point for the clock follow.

The oldest rule of law, which is still law in some states, is that the clock starts at the time of alleged malpractice. It is an easy matter to determine when the malpractice occurred if the contention revolves around a misread frozen section. It is harder to determine the starting point for a patient with hemophilia who claims he contracted viral hepatitis from a blood product he received.

The plight of the hemophiliac is addressed by a statute that states that the clock starts when the patient receives the "last related treatment" for the condition. In other words, the clock starts the last time the patient was treated for the condition. In the case of the hemophiliac, the hemophilia will not be cured, but one might argue in court that the last related treatment was for the particular episode in which the infected blood product was given. Note that with this statute of limitations any medical treatment based on a pathologic diagnosis would make the pathologist culpable based on the date of last related treatment. If the pathologist diagnosed a malignancy, then the clock starts when the oncologist discharges the patient from care after his chemotherapy and follow-up are completed. If the pathologist diagnosed an infection that required treatment with an aminoglycoside and the patient developed renal failure as a complication of antibiotic therapy, then the last related treatment might never come, if the courts decided that the renal failure was a consequence of the treatment for the infection, because the patient would require either regular dialysis or immunotherapy for a transplanted kidney.

The third statute has the clock begin at the time the patient discovers the alleged malpractice. This is sometimes called the "Discovery Rule." Here the clock does not start until the patient discovers the alleged malpractice. If the patient learns that a clamp was left in his body at surgery 15 years after his previous operation, then the clock begins 15 years after the mishap. In states where it is law, it is the Discovery Rule that makes revealing a mishap to a patient as soon as it is discovered the wise course of action from a legal point of view. A patient may forgive a mistake that is admitted immediately. A mistake that is hidden will, when discovered, create ill will and double the desire to sue.

Pathology Leadership of The Laboratory

The laboratory medical director is a leader, and as such you set the tone for management in your laboratory. In today's climate of regulatory recommendations and mandates, combined with ever-increasing workload and hospital economic restrictions, it is a daunting task to develop a laboratory with a positive team spirit approach toward their ultimate mission—quality patient care. Many management styles can be effective, but they must match your personality. No management style fits all. Strong positive laboratory leadership is best demonstrated by pathologists who understand the operational functions of the laboratory. This doesn't mean that you can step in and operate the equipment, but you go the extra mile to understand and appreciate the challenges of those who do this for you.

The laboratory director is the primary interface between the laboratory and overall hospital operations. This, mind you, must not be viewed as an adversarial role. The laboratory director and hospital administrators are working toward the same goal, but invariably your primary focus will differ and that is not a problem. The goal is for you to be the representative for the laboratory, seeking each opportunity to highlight how your goals are similar. Administrators will focus on money, and you will focus on care. In reality, both must be considered at each crossroad encountered in the strategic planning process. You are not necessarily a politician, but as laboratory director you have to get out there and meet the people. For too long, faceless pathologists have allowed the hospital staff and administration to think of the laboratory as a "black box," and this is why so many hospital administrators have chosen to contract this service to outside consultants.

Take every opportunity to involve the laboratory in multidisciplinary leadership roles. Take every opportunity to add value to your services by going beyond the call of duty. Take every opportunity to get your laboratory technologists, histotechnologists, and cytotechnologists involved in multidisciplinary workgroups. Think creatively, including listening to creative personnel within your lab. Challenge your employees to understand the system and seek to improve the system.

Finally, strong laboratory directors involve themselves with regulatory bodies, accreditation agencies, proficiency programs, and inspection agencies. You are the link for the laboratory both internally within the hospital and externally within the community. Lead by example, and let that example reflect a proactive, positive attitude. Take every opportunity to reward good behavior and good work and take pride in showcasing the expertise of your employees and your supervisors.

Disciplinary Actions

Every laboratory medical director, service chief, and laboratory supervisor spends much too much time dealing with personnel problems. In general, we as pathologists are not socially driven personalities, and we did not spend years in training to settle disputes. (Attorneys do that.) Time spent exploring a difficult case is usually pleasant for a pathologist, but the same amount of time spent in arbitrating a dispute or disciplining an employee is interminable. Despite our disdain for the task of disciplinary actions, this is part of our responsibility as the laboratory director or section chief. A few practices are helpful in all personnel interactions:

1. Be a good listener. Avoid the urge to complete the thoughts of an employee who seeks your ear. Sometimes the only request is to listen and understand the problem presented. Pay special attention to the very first thing the employee says because people tend to lead their case with what they consider the problem to be.
2. Be fair and equitable in all of your interactions. Consistency is key. Communicate your expectations and make the ground rules clear from the very beginning. Every laboratory director has management skills and styles uniquely his own. Make your style known to everyone in the laboratory. Establish a chain of responsibility and authority, and honor it. Don't let employees short-circuit the system, and, in the same way, you should not short-circuit the system either.
3. Never take action or promise decisive action based on one side of a complaint. All parties involved deserve to be heard. (That is why both sides in a trial get to present their side of the story.) You have plenty of time to formulate your decisions. You may be surprised by the degree of misperception and miscommunication involved in a stressful situation. Sometimes an unbiased, emotionally neutral party can bring two

sides together to understand the problem and sometimes even develop solutions to avert similar problems in the future.

4. Never assume that anyone understands the problem. After listening and voicing what the problems seem to be, get the employees to reiterate them using their own words. You will uncover areas that need clarification in most cases.

5. Document your interactions. These are not intended as legal document trails but rather memory-joggers for future reference. However, if definitive disciplinary actions are being taken, these should be documented, dated, and signed as part of the official personnel files.

6. Rely on your resources. Many pathologists are unaware that they have tremendous internal resources and expertise available to them. These include personnel/human resources specialists, the office of general counsel, risk managers, and the employee assistance programs. Consult the experts to gain their insight, but always remember that the final decision is yours. There is no weaker reason than "so-and-so told me to do it," and it is especially weak in court. Any disciplinary action taken should be in concurrence with your wishes. After all, you will be the one on the witness stand—not your consultants.

7. Communicate, communicate, and communicate. As soon as you stop talking and working through problems, the game is over. You don't have to like each other in order to talk to each other. You don't have to like each other in order to work together in a professional, respectful manner. Sometimes job expectations are difficult—that's why we call it work.

Dismissal

Termination of an employee is a serious action. Be certain that with each step in the disciplinary system of your hospital system, you have made well-thought-out decisions. Think and rethink each action to be sure it is the best decision. The goal should never be to terminate an employee, rather, the goal should be to work with the employee so that he may become a productive part of the laboratory team. Alas, sometimes, this is just not possible. Work with your human resources specialists and take advantage of their vast expertise, but remember, the final decision has your name on it. It must be appropriate and justified for reasons that you can elucidate. Many a civil battle has been lost and personnel reinstated because the laboratory leader's justification amounted to "Hospital Personnel told me to fire them." With every dismissal, expect grievances, Equal Employment Opportunity complaints, or civil actions, or all of the above. Do not worry, just be prepared to respond to the inquiries from any such source with honesty, professionalism, and a mindset of mutual respect. The idealistic purpose for any of these processes is to seek out and reverse any potential injustice levied toward an employee; this is an admirable goal. Work with these representatives. There is no reason to fear them as long as you have made the right choices and can back those decisions with appropriate documentation.

Confronting a Colleague

Sometimes dismissal, or at least the threat of dismissal, is necessary for a physician colleague with whom you practice. Psychiatric illness, substance abuse, sexual harassment or molestation, and criminal fraud are examples of situations that demand confrontation. With the hope that this will be a rare occurrence in your practice, this topic will be discussed further in the next chapter.

Consultations and Liability

Consultation should follow the basic tenets of sound clinical interaction with a patient. As a physician, a consultant should do no harm. As a human being, a consultant should treat others the way that the consultant would want to be treated. Finally, communication that is both timely and clear is essential. Pathologists serve as consultants for clinical physicians and are accustomed to the practice of consultation.

The legal view of consultation is that of a joint venture. Joint venture states that two or more persons may join their properties and services to carry out a single enterprise for profit. Two physicians can be sued for malpractice if their combined care led to a medical misadventure. Moreover, two physicians can be successfully sued for malpractice if the joint effect of their actions led to a medical misadventure, even if the individual's actions, taken in isolation, would not lead to the adverse outcome. This legal responsibility exists because the proper care of a patient does not occur in a vacuum but within the context of what other physicians are doing.

The following example illustrates how a pathologist can be guilty of malpractice through a joint venture. A routine cervical smear reveals some dysplastic cells. The pathologist sends the report to the gynecologist without personally notifying the gynecologist. The gynecologist's office files the report in the patient's file, and the gynecologist does not read the report until the patient returns for her next visit, at which time an invasive squamous cell carcinoma is discovered. Both the pathologist and the gynecologist bear some blame, and both may well point the finger of blame at the other. Law says that both physicians bear some responsibility because they undertook a joint venture in the care of the patient. Setting law aside, it is still clear enough to an impartial observer that both are partly to blame. (It is likely that both physicians in this example would be urged to settle the case out of court in favor of the plaintiff patient rather than to stand trial.)

Informal (Curbside) Consults

In the past, courts have almost always held that a physician–patient relationship does not arise from an informal request by a colleague for advice on a case, even if the name of the physician consulted is recorded in the chart, although a few courts have ruled otherwise within the past five years.[20, 21] Generally, courts have ruled that in the absence of a formal referral or consultation, which would form a contractual agreement, no physician–patient relationship exists. Physicians may take heart that there still exists some understanding of the practice of medicine by legal professionals, for one judge's written opinion has held that "The mere discussion between professional people of hypothetical situations cannot be viewed as a basis for liability. To hold otherwise would tend to adversely affect the quality of the services they offer to members of the public. Physicians, lawyers, dentists, engineers, and other professionals, by comparing problem-solving approaches with other members of their disciplines, have the opportunity to learn from one another. Possessing this freedom, they are better positioned to bring theory into practice for the benefit of those whom they serve."[22]

Nevertheless, courts have made it clear that each case must be evaluated on its own merits and that no physician can expect to hide behind a curtain without fear of scrutiny.[22] Courts in Arizona and New York have ruled that an informal consult does place upon the physician consulted at least the possibility of bearing some responsibility for the patient's adverse outcome. In each state, the court itself declined to rule whether the physician consulted informally had established a physician–patient relationship, leaving this decision to the jury in each case.[21] In other words, the courts in Arizona and New York declined to excuse the physician consulted from the malpractice suit, as has been done by courts in the past, and instead gave the jury the responsibility of deciding the part that the physician informally consulted played in the care of the patient.

Given the possible shift in approach by courts, a physician consulted informally in the hall should make certain that the one asking questions knows that the review of a case in the hall is no substitute for a formal review of the case and that without a formal review your comments as an informal consultant are of a general nature rather than a specific diagnosis tailored to the specific situation being discussed. Actually, the physician who would cite a colleague's response in a passing hallway conversation may be taking on additional liability rather than protecting himself because such a citation makes clear that the physician failed to get a formal consultation and tried to provide medical care by shooting from the hip. Pathologists are less vulnerable to this mistake, but the principle is still applicable to a pathologist dispensing a diagnosis.

In a separate legal case, the court ruled that a physician asked to offer an opinion based on a hypothetical question during a lecture had not established a physician–patient relationship and could not be sued for malpractice by the patient whose physician asked the question. Simply answering a question posed by a colleague does not impose a physician–patient relationship upon the person asked, but always there remains the duty to act as a reasonably prudent person would act under similar circumstances. There should be no flippant answers, and a physician serving as a supervisor should take his supervisory responsibilities seriously.

Regarding call and oversight of resident physicians in training, some courts have held the on-call physician responsible for adverse outcomes by a resident physician, while other courts in other cases have taken the position that the on-call physician is merely on-call and that he has no control over the actions of the residents until such time as he actively engages in care for the patient. In other words, some courts have held that an attending physician is responsible for the mistakes of residents, while other courts have held that residents have sufficient training and experience to be responsible for their own decisions. This sort of matter is decided case-by-case.

By Clinical Staff of You Concerning an Opinion of Your Partner

Sometimes a member of the clinical staff will seek out a pathologist whom he knows or trusts especially well to ask that pathologist to give him the diagnosis on a case signed out by one of the pathologist's partners. If the particular pathologist is the group expert on liver biopsies but was out of town when the biopsy was performed last week, then such a request is sensible. If the pathologist is routinely asked to cover for a member of the group whose diagnostic skills are less than the clinical staff expect, then you have what may be a sensible request, but you also have a problem. The reasons for being asked to double-check on your partner are myriad, and the politics of the situation are delicate and unique. You know best the relationship that your partner has with you, with the rest of the group, and with the clinical staff. In your dealings, consider the others involved (the patient, the clinical physician, and your partner) and do what is right and best for all parties. If the requests occur because of a recurring problem, such as an incompetent partner, then the pathologists need to assume their mantles as leaders and address the problem.

By a Partner on a Difficult Case

Consulting your partner on a difficult case often occurs as an informal curbside consultation. Anyone in practice has realized that unless someone's name is on the case, then that someone lacks the complete commitment necessary for a difficult diagnosis. Therefore, some offices send formal consult sheets with the slides in question, asking whether the members of the group agree or disagree and requiring each pathologist's signature. By signing the sheet, you give additional reason, beyond simply being a partner in the group, for your name to be added as a defendant should a malpractice suit arise from the case. Do not sign without considering the case as if it were your own.

Obtained by You from an Outside Expert in a Difficult Case

If you need to send a difficult case for outside consultation, then choose your consultant with care. Careful choosing is expected of you as part of your duty to the patient. Some primary care physicians have been found liable for failure to follow the advice of a clinical consult that they requested. For any physician, including a pathologist, it is permissible to choose not to follow a consultant's advice, but you had better have a carefully reasoned explanation recorded in the patient's chart for why you have chosen not to take the consultant's advice.

Obtained of You by an Outside Pathologist in a Difficult Case

Chapter 5 includes a discussion of generating a report when reviewing a case as an expert witness. An expert witness serves as a consultant to an attorney rather than to a physician. The items discussed in Chapter 5 are appropriate for consultative reports to physicians as well, however. A consultative report should record the reason for the consultation (i.e., what question are you as consultant being asked to answer), the material available to the consultant for review, the consultant's findings, any additional materials needed by the consultant for better evaluation, and the consultant's diagnoses and recommendations. Furthermore, the consultant should also document that his diagnoses and recommendations were communicated (when and how) to the physician who requested the consult. Any factor that hindered the consultant's diagnosis, such as failure of the consulting physician to provide additional blocks after material was requested, should be recorded.

References

1. Pike v. Honsinger, 155 N.Y. 201 (1898).
2. Mackauf SH. Neurologic malpractice: the perspective of a patient's lawyer. Neurol Clinics 1999;17:345–53.
3. The Holy Bible. New International Version. Grand Rapids, MI: Zondervan Publishing House, 1989. Luke; 10:25–37.
4. Gatter K. Pap test perils. CAP Today. 2003;17(2):64–9.
5. Steigman CK, Vernick JP. The Pap smear: a victim of its own success? Med Lab Observer 2002;34(8):8–14.
6. McPhee SJ. Maximizing the benefits of autopsy for clinicians and families. Arch Pathol Lab Med 1996;120:743–8.
7. Baker PB, Saladino AJ. Q-Probe 92-06: Autopsy Contributions in Quality Assurance: Data Analysis and Critique. Northfield, IL: College of American Pathologists, 1994.
8. Nichols L, Aronica P, Babe C. Are autopsies obsolete? Am J Clin Pathol 1998;110:210–8.

9. Bove KE, Iery C, Autopsy Committee of CAP. The role of the autopsy in medical malpractice cases, I: a review of 99 appeals court decisions. Arch Pathol Lab Med 2002;126:1023–31.

10. Taragin MI, Willett LR, Wilczek AP, et al. The influence of standards of care and severity of injury on the resolution of medical malpractice claims. Ann Intern Med 1992;117:780–4.

11. Holder AR. Medical Malpractice Law. New York: Wiley Biomedical Health, 1975.

12. College of American Pathologists. Minimum guidelines for the retention of laboratory records and materials [online] [cited 2003 Jan 8]; Available from http://www.cap.org/html/LIP/autoprec.html .

13. Redfern M, Keeling J, Powell E. Report of the Royal Liverpool Children's Inquiry [online] [cited 2002 Nov 25]; Available from http://www.rlcinquiry.org.uk .

14. Schimmel EM. The hazards of hospitalization, 1964. Qual Saf Health Care 2003;12(1):58–63.

15. Lemonick MD. Doctors' deadly mistakes. Time. 1999 Dec 13;154(24):74–6.

16. Richardson WC, Berwick DM, Bisgard JC, Bristow LR, Buck CR, et al. The Institute of Medicine report on medical errors: misunderstanding can do harm. Quality of health care in America committee. Med Gen Med. 2000;Sep 19;E42.

17. Morrissey J. Encyclopedia of errors. Growing database of medication errors allows hospitals to compare their track records with facilities nationwide in a nonpunitive setting. Mod Healthcare 2003 Mar 24; 33(12):40,42.

18. DeRosier J, Stalhandske E, Bagian JP, Budell T. Using health care failure mode and effect analysis: the VA National Center for Patient Safety's prospective risk analysis system. J Comm J Qual Improv 2002; 28(5):248–67.

19. Travers EM. Legal risk management in the clinical laboratory. In: Travers EM. Clinical Laboratory Management. Philadelphia: Lippincott, Williams & Wilkins, 1997.

20. Kinderman K. Professional liability: informal consults give rise to the physician–patient relationship? J Med Pract Manage 2002;17(6):305–7.

21. Hendel T. Informal consultations: do new risks exist for this age-old tradition?. J Med Pract Manage 2002;17(6):308–11.

22. Fox BC, Weinstein RA. "Curbside" consultation and informal communication in medical practice: a medicolegal perspective. Clin Infect Dis 1996;2:616–22.

4
Impact of Law on Practice of Pathology—Malpractice

Gregory G. Davis and Margie A. Scott

What Is Malpractice?

Handling laboratory specimens with potential forensic importance is an every-day occurrence for a pathologist, but being called into court is not. If you are honest, you should never be called into court on criminal charges. If you are lucky, you will never be called into court as a defendant in a civil case asserting malpractice, but the truth is that many physicians become involved in a mal-practice suit during the course of their career. Some specialties are renowned for their propensity for being sued—obstetrics and neurosurgery come to mind. Pathology is not as prone to lawsuits, but anatomical pathologists still remain aware of the sword suspended overhead at the frozen section microscope. In the clinical lab, the laboratory director will inevitably be called into the preliminary hearing stages in court cases because his name is a recurring theme on every patient's medical record. Attorneys cast as broad a net as possible in naming defendants, and often the laboratory director's name is amongst the catch. The charge of malpractice may dissipate in the initial discovery phase, but not al-ways. If there is a laboratory test of interest to the case, then the laboratory di-rector can expect to be called to testify on the witness stand as a material witness even if not a defendant in the case.

What is malpractice, and how is it defined legally? There is no single an-swer, which troubles attorneys not at all. (Recall that it was a Supreme Court Justice, Potter Stewart, who, when trying to define "hard-core" pornography, said, "I shall not today attempt further to define the kinds of material I under-stand to be embraced...[b]ut I know it when I see it."[1]) A similar approach is taken to the definition of malpractice by the legal profession. Everyone has a reasonably accurate concept of what is meant by "malpractice" that serves them from day to day. Then, in a specific malpractice case, the judge presiding over that case will instruct the jury on what constitutes malpractice for that case. The judge's definition will perhaps incorporate a portion of the opinion from the case of Pike v. Honsinger quoted at the beginning of Chapter 3. Other common themes in defining malpractice for a jury are "that which a reasonably prudent physician would do," or "that which the average physician would do," or "that which is generally accepted in medical practice," or "that which is in accordance with the accepted standards of practice," As discussed in Chapter 2, a remarkable strength of the American legal system is that judges are not on the take, so you can expect that the definition a judge will use for a given case of malpractice will be similar, if not identical, to the definition he gave a different jury in a case alleging malpractice heard in his court the month before. In other words, if you are a defendant in a malpractice suit, you need not fear that the judge has already decided that you are guilty prior to trial. The judge will not give the jury some definition of malpractice carefully worded so that the jury has no choice but to find you guilty—that is not how law is practiced in the United States.

The Four Pillars of Malpractice

A judge will instruct the jury in each case about what malpractice is, but the process of the trial will establish whether each defendant rises above or falls below the judge's definition. Because each malpractice case is unique (just as every medical case is unique), a unique standard will be established in each case based on the testimony of the expert witnesses. This unique standard established during the trial will be the standard by which the jury will measure each defendant physician. In order to convince a jury that malpractice has occurred, the patient's (plaintiff's) attorney must build his case with a foundation of four pillars: duty, dereliction, damage, and cause. If any one of these four pillars is absent, then the attorney representing the plaintiff cannot make a sound case for malpractice.

Duty concerns the obligation of the defendant physician to treat the patient. If the plaintiff is the established patient of a clinician, then the clinician has a duty to treat the patient. Duty extends to a pathologist whenever that pathologist accepts a clinical or surgical specimen. At the beginning of Chapter 3, we discussed the duty that can exist between a pathologist and a patient if a pathologist begins treating a person found injured or ill; that duty exists until the helpful pathologist turns the care of the patient over to another physician.

Dereliction is established if the patient's attorney can show that the defendant physician was derelict or negligent in performing his duty toward the patient. It is over dereliction that arguments will be offered about whether the defendant physician did or did not meet the standard of care. The judge will have instructed the jury about the physician's obligation to meet the standard of care, but witnesses will testify to the jury what the "standard of care" is. The standard of care reported to the jury may differ substantially from witness to witness. The jury of laymen has the authority and responsibility to decide what "standard of care" applies to the case being considered, based on what the expert witnesses have said is standard. Having decided the standard of care for this specific case, the jury will then decide whether each defendant provided or failed to provide that standard of care.

Damage must have occurred for malpractice to take place. Worsening of the patient's condition is not enough. Physicians are only human, and some conditions may worsen despite exemplary medical care. That a patient with metastatic renal cell carcinoma dies of his neoplasm is not damage. Damage occurs when a patient with a renal cell carcinoma has the wrong kidney resected.

Cause must be shown; that is, the damage done to the patient must be shown to be the direct result of the defendant physician's action or inaction. This concept is gotten at in court by the "but for" or "substantial factor" test. Expert witnesses will be asked whether the defendant physician's actions were a "substantial factor" in causing the damage. Or cause may be shown by another question: Would the damage to the patient have occurred "but for" the physician's actions? If the answer is "no," then the physician's action (or inaction) caused the damage. If the malpractice charge concerns resection of the wrong kidney, then a pathological diagnosis of renal cell carcinoma on a biopsy was not a substantial factor in resection of the wrong kidney, and the pathologist should not be found guilty of malpractice. If, on the other hand, the diagnosis of renal cell carcinoma itself were in error, then but for that wrong diagnosis the patient would not have undergone a nephrectomy, and the pathologist may well be found guilty of malpractice. The pathologist might also be found guilty of malpractice if the biopsy is submitted as a right kidney biopsy, and the pathologist fails to notice that his final diagnosis states: "Kidney, left, ultrasound guided percutaneous biopsy: Renal cell carcinoma."

As stated above, if any one of these four pillars of malpractice is absent, then the attorney representing the plaintiff cannot make a sound case for malpractice. The attorneys in a malpractice case are playing a sort of game, with identical tactics for each side but with opposite goals. The attorneys representing the patient must establish all four pillars. The attorneys representing each defendant will try to establish that one of the four pillars does not exist. If the attorneys representing a defendant can show that two or three pillars do not exist, then so much the better, but the absence of one pillar is enough.

Duty is usually clearly established and not contested by either side. Law is a big field, however, and just as wise physicians have learned that almost anything is possible in medicine, so too lawsuits may be begun without proper investigation into their merit. If you are wrongly named on a lawsuit, you will still need to have an attorney handle the legal matter of having your name dropped from the suit. You cannot simply ignore the suit; once a lawsuit has begun, the points of contention must be satisfied. Still, if attorneys knew about zebras and horses, then they would think of failure to establish duty as a zebra.

Causation and damage can sometimes be difficult to prove in a medical malpractice case. In a violent event, such as an automobile wreck, it is easy for all to see that an individual in the wreck was able to walk prior to the wreck but was left paralyzed due to a spinal cord injury caused by the wreck. In medical cases, however, the patient is already sick to some degree, and it can be a difficult matter to tease apart what portion of the sickness is due to natural disease and what portion was compounded by poor care on the part of the physician. Remember that the law requires physicians to provide good care, not a good outcome. In order to sue successfully for malpractice, the four pillars must be established. The pillar of "damage" requires that the care provided by the physician caused some outcome solely due to the physician's treatment and distinct from the effects of the disease itself. As an example, it sometimes happens that a patient must visit his physician several times before the correct diagnosis becomes clear. If the correct diagnosis proved to be a glioblastoma, then it would be difficult to prove that malpractice occurred if the suit charged that a physician's delay of two months in diagnosing the condition caused death. If the two month delay were in diagnosing bacterial meningitis, however, then a delay of two months in treating with antibiotics could well have led to death and be the subject of a successful malpractice suit against the physician. Notice, though, that even in the case of meningitis, an argument could be made by the physician's attorney that meningitis is a life-threatening condition and that delay did not alter the outcome. (A two month delay in diagnosing bacterial meningitis is unbelievable, but it is assumed here to make a point. In malpractice cases concerning a delayed diagnosis of bacterial meningitis, the delay is on the order of hours, not months.)

Establishing damage and cause are hurdles that the attorney representing the plaintiff patient must clear. When damage and cause are difficult to establish, an attorney who makes a living suing physicians and hospitals for malpractice will be less likely to accept a case. When, on the other hand, damage and cause are reasonably easy to establish, dereliction is left as the only pillar that must be established for a jury in order for a plaintiff patient and his attorney to sue successfully for malpractice. Dereliction is the point around which malpractice trials often revolve. Medicine is a complicated field. Two capable, conscientious physicians can differ honestly in their opinion of how a certain situation should be managed. These opinions may be hotly debated, an occurrence often seen in medical or surgical grand rounds. Legally, the interpretation or management of a given medical situation is at the heart of standard of care, and it could not be otherwise. Grey areas are always at the heart of debate, both legally and medically. (In the science of medicine, the fiercest debates always surround a topic that is unproved; after all, no one now debates whether blood circulates through the body.) Where there are two differing opinions, there exists the condition that court was designed to settle, and there lawsuits may be won or lost.

The Business of Malpractice Law

Patients as Plaintiffs

Reasons Patients Sue

Why do patients sue for malpractice? Patients sue if they received an incorrect diagnosis, such as a false positive for malignancy that led to resection or a false negative that has turned into metastatic disease. Like it or not, receiving an incorrect diagnosis that leads to devastating consequences ("damages" in the attorneys' parlance) makes sense, even to physicians, but there are other reasons that patients sue. Patients or their families sometimes sue simply because they need money. Of course, that is not what is said, but the old saw that when a person says " 'It's not about the money...', then it really *is* about the money" applies in medical malpractice suits. It may not even be that the patient is trying to profit. Some sue because the size of their debt after a hospital stay is so great that suing becomes a viable option for releasing them from that debt.[2] Occasionally relatives may seek to sue because to accept responsibility for their own actions is intolerable to them. For example, a wife who had noticed that her husband had less stamina than before may, when she loses him to lung cancer, blame herself for not insisting that he see a physician sooner. Rather than live with this blame, she may seek to transfer the blame to another party, the physician who did not save her husband's life. It is the job of attorneys to hear such complaints and turn the complaints that are invalid away.[3] Finally, the patient (or his family if he died) may sue because of dissatisfaction with the medical care received or with the result of that medical care.

A mistaken diagnosis, a patient's desire for money, and a relative's guilt require no further discussion, but patient dissatisfaction does. Patients will accept an adverse outcome because they themselves can find it difficult to distinguish between what part of the outcome is due to the disease and what part to the physician's negligent treatment. Much clearer in a patient's mind, however, is whether the patient was treated with courtesy, dignity, and respect. Patients who are treated rudely or lied to know that this much in their treatment by the physician was wrong, and the seed has been planted that perhaps more injury was done to the patient by the physician than merely a social injustice.[3]

No one enjoys being dissatisfied, frustrated, embarrassed, or demeaned. Whenever one person treats another person shabbily, the human tendency is for the injured party to want redress for that shabby treatment. Although some individuals choose to turn the other cheek when treated poorly, others want vengeance. Vengeance is hard to get, however, when the offending person has authority over the person injured, especially when the two parties rarely see each other. Workers have ways of exacting vengeance on a cruel or thoughtless boss, but there is little that a patient can do to punish a physician other than to sue for malpractice.

Vengeance as a root of malpractice claims is a theme in a book by James Schutte.[4] Dr. Schutte's book is directed toward clinical physicians, but in the book he discusses reasons that patients sue and ways that physicians can reduce their risk of being sued.

Patients moved by vengeance to sue their physician do not do such a thing hastily. The patient's anger toward the physician develops over a long time. Because it takes a long time for such anger to develop, it follows that it is not one big mistake that angers the patients but rather repeated insults that grate upon the patient until a mistake occurs that breaks the camel's back. A patient's anger may not even begin with the physician but with the physician's staff—his clerical and nursing staff. Patients come to see physicians because they are sick, and to be greeted by staff who are rude, indifferent, overly busy, or annoyed at the patient's presence is an affront. To be treated rudely by the staff every time soon grows tiresome, as does waiting long past the scheduled appointment every time. Patients are sufficiently intelligent to ask themselves who but the physician hired and keeps the staff. Should the physician's rudeness rival that of the staff, then that is one mystery solved for the patient and a second strike against the physician. Some patients switch physicians at this point, but there are still people who hold the attainment of a medical degree in high regard and thus make allowances for a rude physician, assuming that rudeness is the price of good care. Despite a patient's respect for a medical degree, however, there will be an inevitable loss of rapport between the physician and patient. Up to this point malpractice cannot be proved because the legal pillar of damage is still missing. The frustrated patient needs only for damage to occur to complete the foundation for a lawsuit. Damage may take the form of breach of patient confidentiality by the physician or his staff who are overheard talking on the elevator by the patient's cousin. Damage may be an untoward outcome, further compounded by a lack of concern by the physician at that outcome. Once damage occurs, you can expect a patient in this situation to be smart enough to see that the means for retribution is now in his grasp. You may think this vignette overdone, but Schutte's book relates story after story that plays out these themes. That the story repeats itself is no surprise to attorneys and should be no surprise to you. In general, just as a relatively few sick patients account for a large percentage of a hospital's inpatients over time, so a few physicians repeatedly treating patients like kine rather than kin are sued over and over again, accounting for a disproportionate number of malpractice suits. It is not necessarily the money that patients who have been mistreated want. Suing is the only means to vengeance that is available to a patient. Some patients have had such a bad experience that they hope by their lawsuit to put the physician out of business so that no other patient will ever again suffer such indignities under the physician's care, as the following example suggests.

An elderly woman reported to her doctor's office for her physical examination. The receptionist noted that this lady had excessive mud on her shoes. This was perceived as unacceptable, as she was getting dirt and mud on the floors of this plush office. When this was brought to the attention of the physician, he immediately chastised the patient publicly for tracking mud all over the office floor. He had her shoes removed and bagged. She left the office barefooted, carrying her shoes in a plastic bag and trying to balance her purse, her paperwork (bills from the office), and her shoes, while navigating her walker to the door. The elderly woman was ashamed and quite visibly upset when her daughter arrived home from work. After hearing about the encounter, the daughter was justifiably angered and sought advice. She was advised to write the state medical licensure board to file an official complaint. The state board followed up with an official investigation followed by a letter to the physician.

Fortunately for this physician, this patient did not fall on the well-polished linoleum flooring or in the gravel parking lot while returning to her transportation. Had she fallen and broken her hip, the liability of this physician for his denigrating actions and resulting injury could have devastated his career. Pathologists typically do not see patients, but the example above could just as easily have taken place in a clinical laboratory where patients have blood drawn. Physicians who do not treat patients with dignity and respect are provoking a lawsuit.

Areas where the pathologist can encounter an angry patient are limited but represent a real liability. These include the inpatient and outpatient phlebotomy area, the therapeutic apheresis service (in many hospitals managed by the clinical laboratory), the stem cell collection laboratory, and the fine needle aspiration biopsy service. The patient who has a poor encounter with blood collection generally will not contact the faceless laboratory director but instead will go to a higher level by calling or writing letters of complaint to the hospital director, the chief of staff, the media, or even to congressional representatives. Such letters can brim with the patient's anger. (Nor is it to be dismissed as the raving of a madman, for a single disgruntled patient writing a letter to the editor of the local paper can cause an entire community to question the quality of the services your laboratory renders, damaging the reputation of your laboratory.)

When a patient does complain about your laboratory services to your hospital and you as laboratory director are made aware of the complaint, the best action is to contact the patient directly and apologize (regardless of your perception of whether the injury was real or perceived). This approach almost always calms the troubled waters. The apology, and the willingness to listen will enable you to get to the heart of the concern, which may not be in the letters. Do not call the patient in anger to fight fire with fire. A complaint of this type is simply a patient begging for a person-to-person interaction with a medical system he does not understand. As soon as the laboratory director or the technologist laboratory manager has a face and personality, the problem (real or perceived) can usually be resolved. In directly contacting unhappy customers, the laboratory director occasionally uncovers an internal issue that needs to be addressed. Consider the following:

The hospital administrator's office notified the laboratory director of a complaint from a woman who was quite upset that "the laboratory had intentionally ruined her child's blood sample." The woman and her daughter now had to return to have a new sample collected, after a first procedure that was very traumatic and during which the laboratory worker who had collected it was rude. The laboratory director called the mother to apologize (once you apologize, a patient will start to listen) and to discover exactly what had gone amiss, explaining to the mother that as director of the laboratory the pathologist was in a position to do something to correct the problem with the hope that this would never recur. The mother then explained in detail. The laboratory worker traumatized her child during the blood collection. After mother and child returned home, they received a call from the girl's doctor, who said, "The lab screwed up and clotted your child's blood sample. You need to return to the hospital to have her stuck again." The laboratory director promised to find and counsel whomever it was that collected the sample. The director also explained that "the lab doesn't clot blood—but sometimes when there is difficulty collecting the blood, it may clot by itself before the preservatives have a chance to stop clotting." The mother was appeased, but still very unhappy about a repeat visit. She was told to ask for the laboratory director when she returned and that the lab would have one of its most experienced phlebotomists collect her daughter's blood.

The laboratory director's investigation revealed that the pediatrician had an inexperienced person collect the blood in his office and then, when things went awry, blamed the laboratory. A phone call to this clinician was in order; he was chagrined when the cards were laid on the table regarding his blame-shifting behaviors. A follow-up report to the hospital director outlining the fact-finding discoveries and follow-up actions (copied to the pediatrician of record) absolved the laboratory of these charges. The patient's mother, however, was not informed of the pediatrician's misrepresentations—this would have returned one unprofessional act for another in a spirit of vengeance and would have planted a seed of distrust in this mother's mind that could have been detrimental for patient care.

The pathologist that performs procedures on patients such as fine needle aspiration biopsies, bone marrow biopsies, and therapeutic apheresis procedures must also consider the potential impact of a disgruntled patient. As one of many providers that the patient sees, the pathologist may always be added to a patient's malpractice suit. The pathologist who discerns an unhappy patient is wise to inform the physician leader of the health care team for that patient. Regardless of whether a pathologist sees patients, it behooves the pathologist to be certain that he and his staff are polite, professional, and discreet. You never know when you and your staff will suddenly be talking with an angry patient or relative.

Contributing Factors

An incorrect diagnosis, guilt, dissatisfaction with medical care leading to vengeance, or the need for money may all lead to a malpractice suit being filed, but a suit is more likely if the case contains an element that heightens the emotional involvement of the patient or the patient's family. Any case that brings an unpleasant surprise or that involves a child or a pregnancy is attended with heightened emotions by the patient and his relatives.

Obstetrics and neurosurgery are at the heart of this truth about emotional involvement. When parents' hopes for a newborn baby are dashed by an untoward outcome of labor and delivery, or when parents' hopes for their college-aged child are crushed by a head injury in an automobile accident, then that same human desire for vengeance is more likely to take hold. In each of these scenarios, both an unpleasant surprise and a child are involved, so the obstetrician and neurosurgeon are caught on two horns. In a way, it is immaterial to the parents whether the physician in such trying circumstances did everything right or not. It is, however, material to the attorney who represents the parents. Provided the attorney can find some aspect of the physician's care that can be believably presented to a jury as a mistake (i.e., dereliction) the foundation for a malpractice suit exists. The heightened emotion of the parents will influence the members of the jury, for anyone's heart should go out to someone who has suffered such a grievous loss. Heightened emotions lead to larger monetary awards for malpractice.

Hospitalization is another factor that can lead to a malpractice suit because of heightened emotions. It is obvious that patients who are hospitalized are sicker than patients who are being seen intermittently in a clinic. The emotions of a patient and his family are tightly strung in a hospital. A patient going for a yearly physical examination is not accompanied by his extended family. A patient undergoing an operation, on the other hand, may well have his extended family in the surgery waiting room. The relatives in the waiting room are there to show their love, and they are eager to hear that the operation was a success. That eagerness to hear is the key to how a physician can best handle a situation fraught with heightened emotion. Patients and their families want to know what is going on. Lack of communication between a physician and his patient (or his patient's family) leads directly to dissatisfaction. In their study of characteristics of potential plaintiffs, Huycke and Huycke reported that the patients seeking to sue invariably considered themselves ill-informed,[2] and this dissatisfaction is increased in a tense situation.

Lack of communication includes lack of effective communication, that is, misunderstandings. A simple misunderstanding can be corrected easily enough. If, however, the patient expected one outcome and got another, then the patient has received an unpleasant surprise, and unpleasant surprises lead to heightened emotion. A particularly awkward misunderstanding can lead to a legal accusation of breach of contract on the part of the physician by the patient. No physician should make claims or promises that he cannot keep. There is an old joke about this in which a patient asks his surgeon whether he, the patient, will be able to play the piano after surgery. When the surgeon says, in a reassuring tone, "Yes, of course you will be able to play the piano," then the patient replies, "That's funny. I've never been able to play the piano before." A tired joke notwithstanding, a verbal commitment, by a physician or even by his staff, can and will be held in court to be a contract. Despite the amazing abilities of modern medicine, the ability to grant life, or even health, is beyond physicians. A physician should tell a patient, "I will do everything in my power to restore your abilities," not "I will restore your abilities." If you as a physician guarantee a good result, then you have given up some protection that law affords you. This protection is summed up in the last sentence of the judicial opinion quoted at the beginning of Chapter 3 from the case of Pike v. Honsinger, the final sentence about no guarantee of a good result—"[The physician's] implied engagement with his patient does not guarantee a good result, but he promises by implication to use the skill and learning of the average physician, to exercise reasonable care and to exert his best judgment in the effort to bring about a good result." No wise physician will promise more than this. Pathologists, who are renowned for hedging, should be able to avoid this pitfall with ease, but even a pathologist can make this mistake, as in the following example.

A pathologist received a call from a child's mother asking how much longer it would take to complete the report. The pathologist had received all his special stains and was planning to complete the case that day, so he told the mother that the case would be completed by the next morning. After the conversation with the mother, the clinician came by and discussed the case further with the pathologist. The clinician relayed additional patient history and concerns making additional studies necessary, and those studies had to be sent to a consulting laboratory. This delayed the completion of the report for another week. The child's mother was frustrated when she called the pathologist the next day to confirm that the report had been completed. Not only had the pathologist failed to keep his promise, but he failed to call and notify the mother of the new development and the need for additional tests. The mother was frustrated, and the pathologist got a telephone call later that day from an attorney whom the mother had contacted.

It would be incorrect to say that the pathologist was ever able to satisfy the mother, but after many additional conversations with the mother and with the attorney, the pathologist was able to avoid being sued. The rapport between the pathologist and the mother was irreparably harmed by the pathologist's breaking his promise to her, and then that harm was compounded by his failure to keep the mother informed when the situation changed. It would have been better not to have made the promise. Some would say it would have been best of all never to have spoken with the mother in the first place, but once the pathologist was involved he was required to see the thing through to the end.

Which Patients Sue

Many more patients are given reason to sue for malpractice than actually sue. So which patients choose to sue for malpractice? There is no simple answer for what prompts one patient to sue and another patient to accept the hand dealt. Huycke and Huycke interviewed 500 potential plaintiffs when the potential plaintiff called a law office to discuss their case for malpractice with an attorney and found that only one-quarter of the callers had sued someone before.[2] Obstetrics, family practice, orthopaedic surgery, emergency medicine, and general surgery as specialties accounted for half of all calls. Pathology was not recorded as a specific complaint. The patient, who would have dealings with his primary care physician rather than with a pathologist, will register his complaint against the primary care physician, whom he knows. The pathologist might become a defendant later, after the plaintiff's attorney has researched the case.

Whatever the reason that a patient decides to explore the possibility of suing for malpractice, the first step in testing the water is for the patient to talk about the possibility with an attorney. Consulting an attorney to see whether it is a good idea to sue for malpractice is like consulting a surgeon to see whether a troubling condition could be cured by an operation. Surgeons like to operate, otherwise they would not have gone into surgery. If there is any reasonable suggestion that a patient's condition might merit an operation, then what do you suppose the surgeon is likely to advise? Likewise, an attorney consulted about suing for malpractice can be expected to recommend suing if he finds that the case has sufficient merit to hold up in court. Why not sue, as long as the case seems likely to promise some amount of monetary award? After all, the patient does not owe the attorney any money until the award is received. Literally, if nothing is ventured, then nothing is gained, and the patient has nothing to lose.

(Actually, the patient does have something to lose. Many a lawsuit grows out of frustration borne in turn out of a sense of wrongful damage, extending even to wrongful death. The damage may truly be wrongful, caused by inept care that any conscientious physician would decry as foul. The loss caused by the damage calls for grieving on the part of the injured party, his family, or both. Grieving begins, but speaking as an observer who is not an attorney, the initiation of the malpractice suit stops the process of grieving at the stage of anger until the matter is resolved legally. Few mechanisms are as effective at delaying gratification as court. It will be long years before the malpractice suit works its way to completion, and for all that time the process of grieving is stunted. The process of grieving suffers further if the case is won by the patient and then that decision is appealed, so that the patient's elation must be forced back into anger. Should the patient lose the case, then grieving must expand to encompass this second injustice that the patient perceives has been worked upon him, and the grieving must begin anew with denial. The following account is anecdotal, but the lesson is no less important. The author (G.G.D.) knows of two cases of death that occurred under circumstances likely to lead to some sort of payment in answer to a charge of malpractice. One family chose to proceed with a lawsuit. The other family decided that no amount of money would bring back the one they had lost. Ten years later, both families still mourn their loss. The family who chose not to sue has accepted their loss and, though always mindful of their loss, have gotten on with their lives. The family who sued is still in court following appeal. For the family seeking damages, each round in the lawsuit knocks the scab off the wound of their loss. The purpose of this long parenthetical comment is to present the viewpoint of the plaintiff who is suing for malpractice. It is hard to be sued for malpractice, particularly if you as the physician did nothing wrong. It may help you to maintain an appropriate demeanor in court, however, if you realize what battles lie ahead for the plaintiff. Even if the plaintiff wins the suit, he still must come to terms with his loss. No amount of money will bring him to terms with his loss. Whenever you become frustrated, it may help to remember how difficult the road is that the family must walk and how distant their goal of peace of mind. If you are capable of that sort of empathy, then you are more likely to be a help than to prove a stumbling block to everyone involved, including yourself.)

Practice of Medical Malpractice Law

In business there are two basic models that describe how you can earn money. You may produce your product in high volume and then sell it at a low profit margin. If you are a pathologist, then chances are you think that the high volume/low profit margin model describes your professional situation accurately. The converse model is that of producing in low volume but selling at a high profit margin. Low volume/high profit describes the practice of malpractice law for attorneys representing plaintiffs, that is, for patients who wish to sue. A malpractice attorney may take only a half dozen cases per year, compared to dozens of cases per day for a pathologist.

Contingency

Because a malpractice attorney deals in low volume, he will study the few cases that he does take both inside and out to better his chance of winning his case in court. Plaintiffs' attorneys typically work on contingency, that is, in lieu of payment up-front, the attorney agrees to accept a percentage of whatever settlement or award the plaintiff receives. The legal arena considers working on contingency a way to assure proper legal representation for all citizens. Just as few individuals can afford to buy a house without borrowing the money and paying it back with interest, so few individuals have sufficient cash reserves to hire a malpractice attorney to work for them by the hour. Because most patients who would seek to sue a physician for malpractice cannot afford to do so, the legal system set up contingency payment as a way of offering legal representation for all while assuring payment of the attorneys representing such clients. A typical contingency is 33%, although the figure is negotiated and agreed upon by client and attorney in each case. It is obvious that 33% of $50,000 is less than 33% of $5,000,000, so the contingency system serves as incentive pay for the plaintiff's attorney to do good work. It is also obvious that 33% of nothing is nothing, so an experienced malpractice attorney is unlikely to accept a case brought to his attention unless he thinks that the case has merit, that is, that the patient has a good chance of winning (and of winning enough to make the work worthwhile).

Finding Cases

There are several ways that attorneys specializing in malpractice prosecution find their clients. Law offices may cast a fishing line into the water by running advertisements urging individuals who think that they may either have suffered medical malpractice or received a dangerous medication to call for consultation. Calls to the line are bites that are reeled in and considered. If the patient's claim of malpractice is insufficient to hold up in court, or if the claim concerns a matter so trifling that the potential award is too small to bother with, then that fish is thrown back. A few calls, however, show great promise, and patients with a good fish story are accepted as clients. According to Huycke and Huycke, malpractice attorney firms that advertised their services on television received three times the calls in a day as firms that did not advertise on television.[2]

There are law firms that keep one file of complaints they get from patients and patients' families, a second file of complaints that they get from staff members of this or that health care facility, and a third file of the public accreditation reviews of health care facilities. Workers in the law firm review the three files, and when the firm finds a patient complaint in a facility with disgruntled workers and poor inspection reports, then the law firm knows that it has a sure thing that will yield a large cash award.

The most common way that law firms get clients, however, is by referral, just as clinicians get most patients by referral. Often the referral is made by a mutual acquaintance of the patient and the attorney, and in this case the referral is not necessarily to an attorney who practices malpractice law.

Choosing Cases

Attorneys who represent patients in a malpractice suit must choose their cases wisely. Because a busy malpractice attorney may handle only a half dozen cases in a year, he would want to win each case. Or, to put it the other way, he cannot afford to lose cases. Few businessmen, be they physicians or attorneys, can afford to commit two months of their time and thousands of their own dollars for no return on their investment. It is heartening to know that attorneys check into a case to see whether the case has merit before they accept it. Not every patient who wishes to sue gets to sue, as seen in the following example.

A 46-year-old male with a history of prescription medication abuse died, and autopsy revealed that death was due to an accidental overdose of several pain medications and anxiolytics. At the time of the autopsy, the pathologist was told that the decedent had a signet ring carcinoma of the stomach resected five years prior to death. No tumor was evident at autopsy. The pathologist thought the most likely reason that the man had lived five years after his gastric resection was that the original diagnosis was in error, but review of the slides from the gastric resection by the autopsy pathologist made clear that the decedent had had a signet ring carcinoma of the stomach. The wife of the decedent called the pathologist to discuss his death at the time of death, and she seemed to accept that death was due to an overdose. A year later, the pathologist was called by an attorney whom the wife had approached about suing the surgeon who resected the gastric carcinoma. The attorney said that the wife told him that her husband would have lived longer if he had received proper medical care at the time of his gastric resection. The pathologist stopped the attorney at that point by saying that it was nothing short of a miracle that the dead man had lived as long as he did after gastrectomy and that he had certainly been cured of his cancer by the operation. Autopsy showed that the man had died of a drug overdose, that the decedent had no tumor when he died, and that cancer had nothing to do with the death. The attorney said, "You know, every physician I talk to says the same thing, that it is a miracle that the man lived as long as he did. Either every one of you physicians is part of a vast conspiracy or else you are all telling me the truth. Either way, I am telling the widow that I will not accept this case."

Most likely the surgeon never knew that a lawsuit against him was stopped before it began by an attorney determining that the suit had no merit. It is not just the unlikelihood of winning a financial award that prevents attorneys from accepting a potential malpractice suit that has no merit; attorneys have a professional reputation among other attorneys to think of, and they do not wish to tarnish it by taking cases that they know are frivolous. Most attorneys have the same opinion of "ambulance chasers" that physicians do, perhaps even more so, because "ambulance chasers" reflect on attorneys professionally.

Some who seek an attorney are misguided at best and crazy at worst. Successful attorneys take into account the impression that their potential client will make on a jury. Even if a patient has a valid complaint of malpractice, an attorney may turn him away if the patient's appearance or demeanor is so far removed from what is acceptable in society as to impeach the patient's credibility before a jury. This is, if you wish, another form of prejudice against the down and out, and of course the attorney would never state such a reason for declining to accept a case. Nevertheless, the successful attorney takes cases that he is likely to win.

Formal Notification of a Malpractice Suit

It may be that you have heard that a formal notification of a malpractice suit against you is to be delivered to you. You would probably hear of such a thing through your hospital or group's attorney, who may have heard rumblings or rumors to the effect in his own professional circles. Notice of a malpractice suit against you is supposed to be delivered to you personally. Do not make the mistake of trying to avoid delivery if you have received a warning in advance that notice is coming. For one thing, you can run but you cannot hide. More importantly, it is to your advantage to get the notice (or "summons," as it is also called) to your attorney as quickly as possible so that your defense can begin.

The notice of a malpractice suit against you will list several things—the court where the trial will take place, the names of the plaintiffs and the defendants, the alleged offence (breach of duty), and the amount sought to recompense for damages claimed. All this, of course, will mean more to your attorney than to you. Still, there are a few points that may be of interest to you, even beyond the boggling fact that you are being sued. You would expect that the name of the plaintiff (or names, if there is more than one plaintiff) would be of a patient who has had some sort of specimen pass through the pathology laboratory. We will discuss the relationship that you as a defendant have with your codefendants shortly. The specificity with which the breach of duty is worded gives an indication of the experience that the plaintiff's attorney has with malpractice law. If the breach of duty is some vaguely worded complaint, then the plaintiff's attorney probably does not have much experience with malpractice law. Experienced malpractice attorneys, on the other hand, know something of medicine and know much more of malpractice law, so the breach of duty written by an experienced attorney will be a specific complaint. It may even be frighteningly specific.

The final item on the notice is the amount requested to recompense for damages claimed. Remember that there is a gaming aspect to the practice of law, and often the game being played is poker. The amount listed may be low, with the hope that you will settle rather than be bothered by the case. The amount listed may be high, so that a settlement for a smaller amount may seem like a bargain. Should the trial go to a jury, then the jury may well never even know the amount that is being requested. The number given for the amount on the notice really is used more for its bargaining power prior to trial.

Reaction to a Notice

Up to this point, we have been speaking in general, but now we will assume that you yourself have just learned that you have been named as a defendant in a malpractice suit. Being sued for malpractice brings upon you a crisis of conscience. "Did I make the right decision?" "Wouldn't any other responsible pathologist have done the same?" "What did I miss?" "How can they do this to me?" All these thoughts pass through your mind, instantly and nearly simultaneously. As a pathologist in a pathology laboratory, you are a boss and usually in control. Notice of a malpractice suit thrusts you into a situation over which you have no control, and you can expect to be upset and confused. You are likely to pass through Kubler-Ross's stages of grief—the author (G.G.D.) did. You are certain to experience denial ("This can't be happening to me") and anger (How can they do this to me?"). If you are to get any sleep in the nights ahead (and there will be many nights ahead), then you must move beyond bargaining (there is no bargaining, of course) into acceptance—not acceptance of the validity of the accusation but acceptance that you are in this situation.

The soul-searching that accompanies an accusation of malpractice inevitably leads to some form of prayer, if no more than a call of "Why?" from the darkness of your situation into the unknown. Physicians should be familiar with the role that prayer and the acknowledgment of a higher power to which humans are subject plays in rehabilitation programs such as Alcoholics Anonymous. While in the midst of a malpractice suit in which you are a defendant, you too will understand that you can enter into a situation that you are powerless to control. If you seek solace in literature, the biblical book of Job eloquently expresses many of the frustrations that one feels when sued for malpractice. You may believe in prayer, or you may not. If you feel called to reflect, to meditate, to pray, then do so in whatever detail you wish. The one to whom you call never betrays a confidence, and you may be surprised at what eventually happens.

Regrettably, there is no inalienable right not to be sued. Rather, not being sued is like enjoying good health. There are some things you can do to make good health more likely, but you can do everything right and still get a malignancy that will kill you. A malpractice suit is neither as quick nor as lethal as pancreatic carcinoma, but there are things you can do to reduce your risk, as we will discuss.

It is unlikely that yours is the only name listed on the notice of a malpractice suit. Once a lawsuit is filed, the attorney representing the plaintiff has initiated a sort of statute of limitations that will prevent the addition of any other name to the list of defendants after a certain span of time has gone by. Therefore, the attorney filing the lawsuit will list every person and corporation that he thinks may even remotely be part of the health care process over which the patient is suing. It is easy to drop a person from the list of defendants at any point in the process; after a certain time, it becomes impossible to add a person to the list. Usually all physicians involved in the patient's care (including consultants and residents) are named along with the entities to which those physicians belong (a university, an incorporated group, or a health maintenance organization). The hospital involved will probably be named as well, because the hospital allowed the physician defendants to practice medicine there.

There are several other reasons that an attorney names anyone and everyone he can think of who might be involved in the care of his client.[5] As a defendant, a physician will be forced to provide what he knows about the case for free rather than be called as an expert witness and paid as an expert witness. No good attorney wants to exclude any physician who cared for a patient from being sued, lest the other physicians claim the whole thing was the fault of the man not charged (and now safely beyond the statute of limitations). The more deep pockets an attorney can charge with malpractice, the more likely someone's pocket will be held accountable. In addition, a house divided against itself cannot stand, so by pitting physicians against each other, the plaintiff's attorney makes success more likely.

Response to a Notice

You will probably first learn that you are the target of a malpractice suit when you receive a notice as discussed above. If you receive a notice informing you that you are a defendant in a malpractice suit then you should do five things:

1. Keep your mouth shut.
2. Call your hospital's risk management department, if they cover your malpractice insurance, or call your malpractice insurance carrier and tell them that you have just received a notice.
3. Keep your mouth shut.
4. Work with the attorney representing the hospital or the insurance company. Whatever your thoughts about the legal system, if you are a defendant in a malpractice suit, then you must remember that the attorney representing you is your advocate. You need to work with him. He may represent the legal profession in your mind, but he is your advocate and he is trying to help you.
5. Keep your mouth shut.

The Importance of Keeping Your Mouth Shut

It is important to keep your mouth shut because in that volatile time just after you receive a notice you may say something that you would later regret. The temptation is to tell anyone who will listen about your misfortune, but any statements you make can be used in court if they are discovered by the plaintiff's attorney. It is better not to provide the opposing side with additional fodder. The importance of maintaining an appropriate silence cannot be overemphasized. The following paragraphs discuss parties to whom you may be tempted to talk and reasons not to talk to those parties. Some parties, such as the partners in your group, do have a legitimate reason to know that you have been sued. (Your group will probably know about the lawsuit already because, as a corporation, it has likely been named as a separate defendant in the same malpractice suit.) Even your group, as we will see, need not know every last detail. When you do have a legitimate reason to talk to someone about the case, then talk with discretion. The worst talking you can do is the reactionary blabbing you are tempted to do upon receiving a notice. Don't blab.

Parties to Whom You Should Not Speak after Being Named as a Defendant, and Why

The Patient (Plaintiff)

The primary care physician is more likely to be tempted to call the patient and ask, "What's the big idea, suing me?" than would be a pathologist. As pathologists, our tendency to remain one professional removed from a patient serves us well in this regard. In any case, the time for talking to the patient, who is now a plaintiff in a malpractice suit against you, has passed. By choosing to become a plaintiff, the patient has chosen to do his talking to you, the defendant, through an attorney, and you should henceforth respond in kind.

Family and Friends of the Patient

It may be that you know relatives or friends of the plaintiff patient. Those friends and relations may ask you questions about the case. Even if there were no lawsuit, the patient's case is confidential, and it would be wrong for the physician to divulge any information about the patient's case. All the more reason, then, not to disclose any information if friends or relations of the plaintiff patient should ask you questions about the case. They can hear about it from the patient, if the patient chooses to tell. For your part, it is a violation of patient confidentiality (and of good sense) to discuss the matter. Politely decline to answer, never failing to speak courteously. A curt, "Look, it's really none of your business" is the wrong answer. An appropriate response will be professional and sincere, such as "I beg your pardon, but I must never betray any patient's trust that I will hold confidential the facts concerning his case. To answer your question would be to betray that trust, and I will not do such a thing." One hopes that a gentle rebuttal will be sufficient, but some people do not take a hint. Stand firm. Do not fall for being pressed to answer so that they can "hear your side of the story."

Staff

You probably would prefer that the malpractice suit against you be kept quiet, but if a half dozen physicians and two groups in the hospital are named as defendants, then you can expect that the lawsuit will not remain a secret for long. After all, some laboratory staff members saw the man who announced himself as representing Thomas, Olsen and Jennings bring you a notice. A secretary in another office served with a notice overheard the conversation of her boss with risk management. Word gets around. The lawsuit may even have been listed in the local newspaper as a matter of public record. Well-meaning staff may come to you and ask about the case. Other staff, who have long looked for an opportunity to settle a score with you, may also come and ask about the case. Always be polite, but none of your staff has reason to be privy to the details of the case. If word is out, there is no need to deny that you have been sued; just do not divulge any details. One response would be, "Yes, I have been sued. It happens to the best and brightest in my profession, and now it has happened to me. Thank you for your concern." If pressed for details, you can reply that your attorney has told you not to talk about the details of the case. In this one way, you may paint the attorney representing you as the bad guy.

Your clinical colleagues who have been sued are in a more precarious spot still. In addition to their staff, they must contend with other patients of theirs coming in for an evaluation and asking about the malpractice suit. Most pathologists are blissfully free of that awkward moment and of the fear of losing patients. If you are a pathologist who does see patients, then the reply given in the previous paragraph, coupled with a reminder about the importance of patient confidentiality, which you know the patient would want for himself as well as others, should serve if you are asked about the lawsuit.

Colleagues

Your colleagues may offer you their sympathy and encouragement, but you do not owe them any details concerning the case in return. A colleague who offers his encouragement has given you all that he has to give. You have nothing to gain and much to lose by divulging details to your colleagues.

Attorney of the Patient

Once a patient consults an attorney, then battle has been joined, even if you have not been served notice that you are a defendant in a malpractice suit. Once you are named as a defendant, the legal profession considers it unethical for that plaintiff's attorney to talk with you. Therefore, some devious attorneys sidestep this unethical behavior by calling the prospective defendant physician before notice is sent and asking to review the case with the physician in order to clarify a misunderstanding and avoid a lawsuit. You might think that the case is so straightforward and the correctness of your position so strong that presenting your information to an attorney would deter the attorney from suing you, but such thinking is muddled. The plaintiff's attorney has already reviewed the case with a physician (or two) who will not be named as defendants in the case before he asks to meet with a physician whom he may sue, as we saw in the example concerning a signet ring gastric carcinoma above. The plaintiff's attorney hopes that, in the process of discussing the case, the physician will admit something, or make some inaccurate statement, or otherwise expose some weakness that the plaintiff's attorney can exploit. If you think that insufficient reason to decline to meet with the plaintiff's attorney under these conditions, consider that malpractice insurance policies often prohibit such meetings and renounce coverage of any physician who has an unauthorized meeting with a plaintiff's attorney. Whether the money comes from your pocket or from your insurance carrier's is of no concern to the plaintiff's attorney, but it should concern you. A third reason not to meet with the plaintiff's attorney on your own is that an attorney who tries to meet with a potential defendant before serving notice is obeying the letter of the law concerning not speaking with a defendant, but he dishonors the law's intent. Do you suppose that a plaintiff's attorney would skirt the law's intent for your benefit, or for his? Refer such a request to your risk management department or to your malpractice insurance carrier and let them represent you. That is the appropriate and professional response, and it is also the wise response. The game being played is one of nuance and bluffing, so it is preferable to start your role in the game correctly and thus establish that you are not an easy mark.

A variation on this theme of meeting with you to stave off a lawsuit is for an attorney to ask you, the pathologist (or any other consultant, for that matter), for a written report because the attorney is suing a clinician. After you provide such a report, you may find that the lawsuit has expanded to include you as a defendant. Your written report had already been written when the attorney called you; it is your surgical pathology report, cytology report, clinical lab report, etc. To reiterate, a second report serves only to give an attorney an additional opportunity to look for extra information that he can exploit to incriminate either you or a colleague. Either way, you are better served not to provide an additional report.

After you are named as a defendant in a malpractice suit, it is definitely unethical for the plaintiff's attorney to speak with you, but that does not mean that it has never happened. It is a good idea to have any calls concerning the case come through your secretary, not through your private phone. If you do not recognize the name of the person who has asked to speak with you, contact the attorney representing you and ask him whether you should speak with this individual.

News Reporters

If your story does get into the media, you may be tempted to try to tell your side of the story, especially if reporters call asking for you to tell. Of course, here is another situation where you become guilty of violating patient confidentiality if you tell details to the media. There are other problems with talking with reporters about a case as well. For one thing, you will not be the editor of the version that will appear on television or in the newspaper. The job of the media is to sell advertising, not to defend your reputation. The newspaper and television editors will edit your story in whatever way best suits that purpose of selling advertising. If dragging your reputation through the mud will boost the ratings, then the mud is what you can expect. Although it might be denied, the people who run the media are human, and they have opinions and biases as does any other human. The media are able to decide *a priori* how they want a story to be pitched. (Indeed, no story can be told effectively if the teller does not have a clear vision of where the story is headed.) It is possible for a decision to be made about how the media wants a story to be presented and then conduct an interview. Regardless of what you may say, the media have the ability to determine how the story will sound when it runs; that is, the media can put their spin on the story. Quotes can be taken out of context. Or it may be that your story will be run on one day portraying you as a sympathetic character. Then, on the following day, the media may be shocked to report that as a physician you violated a patient's trust in maintaining confidentiality. What could be more efficient for the media than to get two days worth of news out of one interview with you? It will not be just one interview, however. When you grant one reporter an interview, then all the other reporters covering the same story for the other newspapers and stations will demand equal time. Part of your attorney's responsibility is handling the media, so refer requests for interviews with the media to your attorney's office. Better yet, have your secretary refer such requests to your attorney's office.

If you do end up talking with a reporter on the telephone who is badgering you to give an interview, remain polite and firm in your refusal. Let the reporter end the conversation. After all, proper etiquette requires that the person who makes a telephone call be the one to end the call. Remain polite in your refusal and adhere to etiquette. Then the media can claim neither that you would not return their calls, that you would not talk with them, nor even that you hung up on them. They simply will not mention calling you at all.

Codefendants

Beware of thinking of your codefendants as your brothers in arms. One or more of your codefendants may be your enemy rather than your ally. Although you may think that as codefendants you are all in the soup together, other codefendants may see things differently, get together, and change the game to hot potato with a plan to leave you holding the potato. If a codefendant asks to discuss the case with you, you should answer that you still do not understand all the legal issues involved and that the two of you should make an appointment when each of you and the attorneys representing each of you can all sit down together. If your codefendant cannot see that such an arrangement is in the best interest of everyone, then he either desperately needs the legal advice that you have just given him or else it is not your best interest that he has in mind.

Codefendants' Attorneys

What went for codefendants in the preceding paragraph goes for the attorneys of your codefendants as well. Malpractice lawsuits with a half dozen defendants are complicated affairs, and all defendants and all their attorneys need to sit down and talk together. To talk in groups of twos and threes is to do things piecemeal.

Potential Codefendants

A warning that you will soon be served notice of a malpractice suit naming you as a defendant leaves you in a void, not knowing who other defendants might be. All the reasons listed above for not talking with a codefendant about the case apply to potential codefendants. Likely codefendants are any physician who evaluated and provided care to the plaintiff patient during the episode in question. This includes the patient's attending physician, consultants, cross-cover physicians, and any physician who is a partner of those listed already. Depending on the matter in question, nurses or other health care professionals may also be listed as defendants. The easiest and best course to follow is not to talk with any health professional about the particulars of any case for which you are named as a defendant in a malpractice suit.

Family and Friends

All the parties mentioned above are individuals with whom you as a physician have a professional relationship. What about family and friends? Loving, caring, supporting family and friends are priceless in any circumstance, and doubly so when you stand accused of malpractice. Before you bare your griefs to your family and friends, however, it is necessary to define what is meant by *friend*.

In the United States, which is the land of the free and the home of the brave, we use the word friend to describe almost anyone with whom we have a cordial social relationship. We are fortunate to be able to do so because the freedom of speech guaranteed to us by our constitution leaves us little to fear from speaking freely in front of others in a cordial social gathering. In other countries, things are different and have been for centuries. The Russians have a different concept of what constitutes a friend from that of Americans. In Russian, the word translated as *friend* is reserved for those few individuals for whom the speaker would die if asked or who would die for the speaker if asked. If the relationship is not so close that each party would give his life for the other, then a Russian describes the relationship between the two individuals as an acquaintanceship rather than as a friendship. The importance of distinguishing between a *friend* and an *acquaintance* is obvious in a country where for centuries speaking your mind into the wrong ear could lead the speaker to a prison term, if not worse.

The stakes in a malpractice suit are financial rather than time in prison, but a physician being sued for malpractice would do well to learn a lesson from the Russians about what constitutes a friend. Before telling anyone any detail about a malpractice suit in which you are a defendant, consider whether the hearer is a friend who would take up a burden for you just as you would take up a burden of his. If your friend to whom you are considering sharing details of your malpractice suit is not one of the few individuals whom you would trust with your life (because it is your professional life that is at stake here), then do not talk about the matter with him. Even if he is, do not divulge the details of the case, lest this come out in court as discussed below in the section "The Virtues of Keeping Your Mouth Shut."

Closer than friends should be family, and your spouse closest of all, but it is a sad truth that not every marriage enjoys the intimacy that is implied in the Russian concept of *friendship*. Just as a malpractice suit is a trial for you, it should and will be a trial for your spouse, who is, after all, your better half. "Whatever does not kill you makes you strong," they say. The personal trial of enduring the legal wrangling to the eventual end of a malpractice suit will be a trial even upon your marriage. It is to be hoped that each partner in your marriage will persevere and prevail, whatever the outcome of the trial, and that your marriage will thereby prevail as well. In the face of a trial such as a malpractice suit, the following statement may sound callous, nevertheless, it is necessary. If you have been named as a defendant in a malpractice suit, consider carefully and honestly whether you and your spouse are friends in the Russian sense. If you and your spouse are not friends in that way, then you would do well not to share overmuch detail with your spouse—no more detail, say, than what you share with your partners in your group. No one is in a better position to do you harm by betraying you than is a vengeful spouse.

On a slightly lighter, although still serious, note, there is another reason to consider curtailing the amount of detail that you share with family or *friends* about the malpractice suit in which you have been named as a defendant. The easiest secret to keep is the one that you never tell. If you have learned in the past that certain friends, dear though they are, let slip some things about you that you had preferred remain private, then you should tell those friends no details of your malpractice suit. If your spouse has divulged confidences before, then think twice before burdening your spouse with details about your malpractice suit. Family and friends who love you truly can still support and encourage you without knowing every last detail of the case. Whatever detail you reveal has the potential to be passed on and to grow and change in the telling as the tale becomes rumor.

The Virtues of Keeping Your Mouth Shut

As soon as you realize that a patient for whom you have provided care is contemplating a malpractice suit, you risk weakening or even destroying your defense by talking about the case. Convincing curious co-workers or friends of your innocence is inconsequential. The people that you want to convince of your innocence are a jury of twelve individuals whom you have never even met who will not be convened for another several years. In medicine there are certain conditions that are best treated with tincture of time. Once you are served notice that you are a defendant in a malpractice suit, then it is you who needs to realize that this lawsuit requires, among other things, that you yourself take a dose of tincture of time, and that can prove a bitter pill to swallow. Bitter though it may be, you risk nothing by maintaining a judicious silence until your case is heard in court.

What could happen if you spoke with any of the parties above about the charge of malpractice that has been brought against you? Certainly if someone is out to stab you in the back they can do so no matter what, and any sensible physician should be aware of those who might benefit from his downfall. And is it not the responsibility of a physician, particularly a pathologist, to teach others, particularly the house staff and students who need to learn? It is, and you can best teach by providing an example of correct conduct. As for what could happen if you spoke to parties about the malpractice charge against you, you might be asked the following questions at deposition (the physician's replies are left to your imagination)[5]:

> **Attorney**: Doctor, have you discussed this case with anyone other than your attorney?
>
> **Attorney**: What was the gist of the conversation you had with your colleague/resident/medical students/secretary?
>
> **Attorney**: What specific part of the case did you discuss?
>
> **Attorney**: Did you tell this person why you were being sued? What did he reply? Did you mention aspects of the case that you wish had been handled differently?
>
> **Attorney**: How can I contact this person with whom you spoke?

A simple and truthful "No" in response to the first question ends this particular path of questioning. You can see how easy it would be for someone in whom you confided but who bears a grudge or does not have your best interest at heart to wreak terrible damage against you. And what of the well-meaning resident who, after all, has only a fraction of your understanding and experience? How will that resident represent you in court? Better not to give anyone an opportunity.

Parties to Whom You Should Speak after Being Named as a Defendant, and Why

Something about being sued makes you want to talk to someone about it, so you may be glad to hear that there are a few individuals with whom you can talk freely about your case. This select list is headed by the attorney who will represent you. From the risk management department you should also learn what procedure the hospital has for notifying your hospital administration. Not only can you talk with these people, but you should talk with these people.

The Attorney Representing You as a Defendant

As soon as you receive notice that you have been named as a defendant in a malpractice suit, call your hospital's risk management department, if the hospital covers your malpractice insurance. If your malpractice insurance is covered by a policy with an insurance agency, then call your malpractice insurance carrier and tell them that you have just received a notice. Regardless of whether you call risk management or your insurance company, the conversation you then have will be the same. You will be asked a few questions such as when you received the notice, when the notice says a trial is scheduled, who sent the notice, and so forth. The person asking you these questions will likely be an administrative assistant in risk management or else, if you have called your malpractice insurance carrier, a claims representative. After the few basic questions, you may be assigned an attorney, or you may be told that you will hear from an attorney in a few days. Do not panic if you do not hear back from the attorney within five minutes. Your attorney may be very conscientious and still not call you immediately. (The wheels of justice grind slowly, and although the lawsuit is very important to you, you are probably a good year or two away from any sort of resolution.) If, however, you do not hear from the attorney in a few days then you need to call and ask when you should meet with him. We will discuss how to recognize and respond to a recalcitrant attorney later in this chapter.

Work with the Attorney Assigned to Represent You

No one knows your part in the medical care of the patient suing you for malpractice better than you do. No one is more motivated than you are to see that you are exonerated. Therefore, there is no one in a better position to try to help your attorney to prepare a defense for you than you yourself. When you are sued, the depression that follows can lead you to be angry with the whole legal system, and that anger can extend to the attorney who is defending you. "After all," you may think, "he is an attorney, and attorneys created all the rotten laws that got me into this mess." If you are tempted to think such a thing, then stop thinking it. Cooperating with your attorney is vital to your defense. Your attorney is there to defend you; his is the lone voice of reason that may be able to stop the insanity that has befallen you. Being rude to, sullen with, or suspicious of your attorney plays into the plaintiff's hand. You might just as well have cursed an attending physician you did not like when you were a medical student. In either case, your actions will cause the object of your wrath no real harm, but your actions are likely to destroy your hopes of practicing medicine.

Recall that in order to make a successful case of malpractice, a plaintiff's attorney must establish the four pillars of malpractice (duty, dereliction, damage, and cause). The attorney defending you, therefore, will make himself familiar with the case and develop a plan for showing that at least one of the four pillars does not exist. As discussed above, the most likely pillar of contention will be the pillar of dereliction. During the course of care of the patient who is suing, there may have been several different standard and appropriate courses of treatment that the patient's physicians could have chosen to follow. Choosing one course and then having a bad outcome does not mean that malpractice has been committed, although you can be sued for any action. The legal system decides whether a suit against you has merit (i.e., is reasonable). In the gastric carcinoma example above, the legal system dismissed a suit at the point where an attorney refused to take a case because he deemed that the case had no merit. If an attorney takes a case without merit, then the suit may still be dismissed without further consideration if the suit is deemed frivolous by a judge, as shown below.

A woman with a history of psychiatric illness became disgruntled with the care that she had received from her physician, so she told the physician that she was going to sue him. The woman sought an attorney to take her case, but since she had no reason other than not liking the medical recommendations that the physician made, no attorney would take the case. Despite her psychiatric disorder, the woman was intelligent. She was also determined. She studied and got high marks on the LSAT, applied for and was admitted to law school, and, upon graduating from law school, filed a suit on her behalf suing the physician for malpractice. The physician, when he was notified of the suit, thought that the notice was a joke and did not respond. When the day and hour came for him to appear in court, he received a call from the judge to appear in court immediately. The physician explained that his patient of seven years ago could not sue him, to which the judge replied that in the intervening years the patient had become an attorney who could do such a thing and that the physician had to show up in court to answer the charge against him. The judge did intimate to the physician that the judge would handle the situation, however. When the physician presented himself in court, the judge dismissed the case as having no merit. (What became of the patient is unknown.)

In another case, a patient was diagnosed as having tuberculosis. The patient was treated with a course of antitubercular antibiotics. After the course of isoniazid was completed, it was decided that the diagnosis of tuberculosis was in error, so the patient sued for malpractice. No grounds for malpractice was found, however, because the patient could demonstrate no damage that had occurred as a result of the misdiagnosis. (The court did not consider the necessity of abstaining from alcohol for four months to be damage.)

Despite the preceding anecdotes, the pillar of malpractice most likely to be attacked in your defense remains dereliction. Bad outcomes occur daily in medicine, but a bad outcome does not prove dereliction. You need to sit down with your attorney and tell him what happened, both the good and the bad. Your attorney cannot mount an effective defense for you unless he knows all the pertinent details. The importance of knowing points in your favor should be clear enough—it is with those points that you hope to establish your innocence. If there are points concerning your case that do not seem to be favorable to you, or points that are frankly against you, then you need to own up to them at your initial meeting with your attorney. Trying to hide the information is unrealistic because the plaintiff's attorney can be expected to know the information independently. Failure to level with your attorney about any points that may tell against you hamstrings your attorney in preparing your defense by leaving your position open to a broadside attack from which you cannot recover, as shown below.

A pathologist was named in a malpractice suit charging wrongful death in a case of a man who died of a metastatic melanoma seven months after a skin biopsy was read by the pathologist as negative for tumor. The patient who died had moved to the pathologist's city one year before he died, and the pathologist was told by the patient's clinician that the patient had had a skin biopsy five years prior that showed melanoma. The pathologist never reviewed the pathology slides of the melanoma diagnosed at the outside hospital, but he decided not to mention that he had heard about the existence of the outside slides to the attorney representing him in the malpractice suit. At trial, the plaintiff's attorney, representing the patient's widow, asked the pathologist on the witness stand whether it was common practice for pathologists to review microscope slides on patients with a malignancy and to compare those slides to new material received on the patient. The plaintiff's attorney soon had the pathologist admitting that review of outside slides was good practice and that he had not done so in this case. (Alternatively, the plaintiff's attorney soon got the pathologist angrily defending his actions as something that should only be questioned by people who are trained in pathology, and not by any attorney who reads a few medical articles.)

By failing to tell the attorney representing him about the microscope slides from five years prior, the pathologist robbed himself of his attorney's counsel in how to handle the situation when it would be discussed in court. The pathologist's attorney would have asked the pathologist why the slides were not looked at in this case just as the plaintiff's attorney did, but the pathologist's defense attorney would have done so in the privacy of his personal office rather than in the public forum of court. There may have been a good reason why the pathologist did not review the slides, or there may not. In either case, the pathologist damaged his own defense by assuming that the practice of reviewing previous material was so esoteric that his failure to do so would never come to light, then rubbed salt in the wound by being unprepared to answer the question when it did come. Had he known about the prior slides, the pathologist's defense attorney would have planned with the pathologist how to handle the question when it came, and the defense attorney would have had ready his own list of questions for the pathologist designed to show why the pathologist was not to blame in this case for failing to review the earlier slides if, in fact, the pathologist was not to blame. (If the pathologist was to blame then claiming otherwise would be perjury, and no conscientious attorney would counsel perjury.) By telling your attorney the good and the bad, you give your attorney a realistic view of the landscape on which he will battle for your sake in court. The attorney must have a realistic view of the landscape in order to plan effective attacks and defenses on your behalf.

An advantage that lies with the plaintiff and his attorney is that it is easy for a jury of laymen to put themselves into the shoes of the plaintiff patient. This can be especially true if the jury's attention should be diverted from the case, say, to the plaintiff patient, who is now handicapped as a result of his malady and is sitting in plain view of the jury throughout the trial. The jury's heart may go out to the plaintiff, especially if the plaintiff is young or was the wage earner for a young family. However much the jury may wish to provide some financial assistance to the handicapped plaintiff, it is wrong for the jury to do so unless malpractice has been committed. Nevertheless, the perceived unjustness of the plaintiff's condition is an advantage held by the plaintiff's attorney. The attorney defending you from a charge of malpractice must overcome this advantage held by the plaintiff's attorney with logic, reason, an understanding of the medical problems involved, and an understanding of the limitations of medicine. If you wish, you may think of the job that lies before you and your defense attorney as teaching the jury how to see the case medically as you saw it at the time you provided your services as a pathologist in the treatment of the patient. Teaching the jury to understand the medical problems involved and the limitations of medicine regarding those problems so that the jury can draw a conclusion based on reason rather than emotion is an attainable goal.

Signs that You Need a New Attorney

It may strike you as impersonal that the attorney who will defend you against something as personal as a malpractice suit is a complete stranger, assigned to you at the whim of the risk management department or by the carrier of your malpractice insurance. It is impersonal, but that does not mean that the attorney will not work hard on your behalf. The hospital or the insurance company stands to lose money if your defense is bungled, and neither entity will continue to employ an incompetent attorney. Remember that part of what makes your defense attorney effective on your behalf is that he does not take the case against you personally, and thus his emotions do not cloud his experience and reason during the proceedings.

On the other hand, situations do arise that call for you to seek and hire an attorney who will represent you and only you. The $64,000 question (literally) is when do you need to begin to retain an attorney for yourself out of your own pocket. Fish, Ehrhardt, and Fish, in the second chapter of their book *Malpractice: Managing Your Defense*,[6] list circumstances that call for a physician to seek his own attorney. Those circumstances are:

1. The claim of the malpractice suit exceeds your coverage.
2. The insurer disclaims liability in your case.
3. The insurer suggests a quick, cheap settlement.
4. You cannot get along with the attorney assigned to you.
5. You doubt the competence of the attorney assigned to you.
6. You suspect the attorney assigned to you is not on your side.

Malpractice Claim Exceeds Your Coverage

If the attorney representing you has been assigned to you by the risk management department of your hospital, then that attorney is either an employee of the hospital or has been retained by the hospital. The same sort of relationship holds true for an attorney assigned to you by your malpractice carrier. In ordinary circumstances, this should not be a problem; the attorney will work on your behalf since you are an employee of the hospital or a policy-holder of the insurance company. If, however, the malpractice suit against you seeks ten million dollars in damages and you only have coverage up to three million dollars, then you need an attorney who will represent you for that extra seven million dollars. In other words, the attorney hired by your insurance carrier will provide you only three million dollars worth of service, leaving you seven million dollars short.

Insurer Disclaims Liability in Your Case

There are circumstances in which your insurer may renounce responsibility for covering you, as has been mentioned. Those circumstances are the sort of thing covered by some clause within the fine print of your insurance policy, and they include things such as dishonesty on your part. If your insurance carrier does disclaim liability for covering you, then you still need an attorney to represent you in your case. Provided that the insurer has defaulted on you, you will have to use your own money to hire an attorney to represent you. You will have to hire an attorney to contest being defaulted upon, too, but if the attorney you hire says that the insurer has good reason to have defaulted, such as dishonesty on your part, then there is no use chasing after wind.

Insurer Suggests a Quick, Cheap Settlement

In some cases, insurers like to make quick settlements for a smaller amount of money than it will cost to defend the case in court. Settlement can occur without your even knowing it unless your insurance policy has in it a specific portion that states that you, the insured, have the right to consent to any settlement before it occurs. If you have no explicit "right to consent" guaranteed by your policy, then the insurer does not have to notify you before settling. Settling quickly is the best approach in some circumstances, but settling is not without ramifications for you. State licensing boards commonly asked whether any judgment or settlement has been rendered against you when you renew your medical license. Nowadays, that information is made freely available to any interested person over the Internet, whether posted by your state licensing board or in the National Practitioner Data Bank. If you think that your case merits a fight and the attorney appointed to you by the insurer urges you to settle and settle now, then the money you spend on getting a second legal opinion may be money well spent.

You Cannot Get Along with the Attorney Assigned to You

If you and the attorney assigned to you just do not get along, then you should request a different attorney from the insurer. Expect to explain why you need a different attorney. Be ready to relate some concrete anecdotes that make the problem clear. It may be the attorney who is the problem, you may be the problem, or it may be that the two of you have personalities that are combustible. Regardless of who is the cause of not getting along, your attorney is your advocate in this lawsuit, and it is essential that the two of you be able to work to-gether for the good of both of you and for your personal good.

The insurer may ask for proof beyond your say-so that a problem exists. If that is the case, then what is needed is for you to document the difficulties that exist, including your efforts to redress the problem with your attorney. Legal documentation is just like medical documentation: if it isn't written down, then it didn't happen. If the insurer is unwilling to assign you a different attorney even with documentation, then you would do well to at least meet with a second attorney with whom you choose to review the case. If you cannot get along with this second attorney then ask yourself whether you are the problem, because, if you are, you need to correct your behavior and apologize to whomever deserves your apology.

You Doubt the Competence of the Attorney Assigned to You

Obviously, if the attorney assigned to you is incompetent, then you need to re-place him with a capable attorney. Since you do not practice law, how can you tell whether your attorney is competent? You start by assessing your attorney in the same sort of commonsense way that patients assess a physician. If the attor-ney tells you that yours is a standard case and that the two of you do not need to meet to discuss it, then you need to call the insurance company or risk manage-ment and tell them that you need another attorney. Every medical case is unique, and every legal case is unique. All legal cases require preparation on the part of the attorney. (The legal case certainly is unique in your experience, and you need preparation, too.) If the attorney is inexcusably inconsiderate of you as a human being, then you should request a different attorney. Examples of incon-siderate behavior are that the attorney is uncooperative or that he seems reluctant to meet with you and is always putting off your meeting. It is unprofessional to always run late without bothering to call to notify you of the delay, and it is doubly so for the attorney to imply that you are the one at fault when he does show up. No patient appreciates that sort of behavior from his physician, and inconsiderate behavior says something about the professional character of the one who is inconsiderate. Patients should not have to put up with an unprofes-sional, incompetent physician, and you should not be stuck with an unprofes-sional, incompetent attorney defending you for malpractice. Discuss the problem with the attorney, and document the discussion by recording notes of what was said. Writing a letter to the attorney in which you list the problems and asking for a response is a different way to document your problem for the benefit of you and your insurer. Again, when you ask your insurer to assign you a different attorney, give concrete reasons for why you need to switch. If the attorney is that unprofessional, then the matter is too important for you to refrain from speaking out.

You Suspect the Attorney Assigned to You Is Not on Your Side

If your attorney's actions indicate to you that there is someone or something other than your defense that is uppermost in his mind, then you need to consider hiring an attorney to represent you. Fish, Ehrhardt, and Fish give a good example of this in their book:

> In a certain case, all the defendant physicians had the same malpractice insurance carrier, and so all were assigned the same attorney to handle their defense. It became clear to the physicians that the attorney had looked up their policies to determine who had the lowest policy limit. The attorney then set about contriving a defense that would place all the blame and liability onto the physician with the lowest policy limit.[6]

Deciding where liability should lie based on policy limits was a sound decision for the accounting department at the insurance company, but it is unethical. The legal profession recognizes that such a practice is unethical, and such an action should be reported in writing to the insurer and to the state bar association. The physician who was being framed needed a new attorney. If you recognize that you are being unfairly represented by your attorney, then you need a new attorney, too.

If you do need to hire an attorney to represent you, then remember that you do not need a personal friend who practices law to represent you. You do not need the attorney who overlooks contracts for your group to represent you. What you need is a seasoned professional in medical malpractice law with a proven record of success in representing his clients. Seasoned professionals in medical malpractice law with proven records of success do not come cheap, but you get what you pay for. If you are going to nickel and dime your defense in a malpractice suit, then you are penny wise and pound foolish. Seasoned malpractice defense attorneys do not grow on trees, and you probably do not know such an attorney personally. Your local or state medical society has a list of attorneys that they recommend. (The societies may also be able to tell you about the attorney that you have through risk management or the insurance company.)

Regardless of who is paying for your attorney, review the case with him. Explain the good and bad to the attorney as forthrightly as you can. The mistake that you are most in danger of making is not telling the attorney enough. Remember that your defense attorney is the one person to whom you can bare all your thoughts about the case for which you are being sued. In discussing the case with your attorney, try to apply the concept of signs and symptoms to the plaintiff patient. Any frustrations or anger that you have toward the patient are a subjective symptom and will do you no good in your defense. Any objective signs, however, are something to share with the attorney. For example, if you remember that the patient's clinical physician mentioned to you that the patient was always trying to finagle prescriptions for pain medications, then tell that to the attorney. Some people do sue in hope of getting a little money, and any sign of that sort may prove useful to your attorney in your defense.

Discuss whether your defense needs an expert medical witness. You probably do. Recall that the standard of care by which the jury will judge you will be determined by the testimony of expert witnesses, so the importance of expert witnesses cannot be overemphasized. The plaintiff patient will have an expert witness who will testify that you failed, and failed badly, to meet even the minimum standard for acceptable practice. You will probably need some sort of expert witness who will explain to the jury how your actions were perfectly in keeping with a caring standard of acceptable practice. The plaintiff's expert witness has as an advantage the emotional sympathy of the jury for a bad outcome, or at least a claim of a bad outcome. Once the outcome is known, even physicians regularly remind themselves not to use the retrospectoscope to look backward and second-guess decisions. How much more, then, does the jury need to be told of the fallacy of judging the appropriateness of a medical decision after the consequences of that decision are known! A good expert witness for the defense will know how to correct the jury's tendency to use 20-20 hindsight.

Assuming that your defense will require the testimony of an expert medical witness, then you as a physician are able to assess the expert's medical qualifications in a way that the attorney is not. The expert you are considering should be:

1. qualified,
2. willing to devote the time necessary to prepare for the trial,
3. current on the literature in his field, and
4. impressive.

Any expert witness in pathology that you hire should be qualified to practice pathology. Get a copy of his curriculum vitae and check it out. An expert testifying on your behalf should be licensed to practice medicine. He should be board certified in his specialty and subspecialty. He should have a license to practice medicine in some state, although it need not necessarily be within the state where the alleged malpractice took place. He should belong to appropriate professional organizations as a member. As an expert, you would expect that he would have published some articles in peer-reviewed journals. Does he have any publications, and do any concern the area that is being contested in court?

"He should belong to appropriate professional organizations as a member" means that he should belong to professional organizations that you as a pathologist recognize as professional organizations. A century ago, some medical schools in this country trained physicians, and other medical schools existed that exchanged diplomas for money and a take-home exam. Abraham Flexner separated the wheat from the chaff then. Today, some professional organizations exist that promote the practice and science of pathology, whether the organization's emphasis is on research, teaching, service, or policy. Other professional organizations exist that exchange a certificate of "expertness" in exchange for completing a take-home exam and paying the fee to join the organization. As a

pathologist, you can distinguish between the legitimate organizations and charlatans. Your defense attorney should be able to distinguish, too, provided he is
experienced.

Publications serve as a useful measure of whether a potential expert witness
has remained current in his field by contributing to it. Publications, however, are
not the most important point. The worth of a particular expert witness to your
defense is not measured by the mass of his CV. The point on which you are being accused of malpractice probably relates to the daily practice of pathology.
You need an expert witness to testify on your behalf who regularly practices the
aspect of pathology on which you are being sued, whether anatomical or clinical
(or both). A career researcher with an impressive list of grants is probably not
what you need in court.

Any expert witness who testifies on your behalf should be able and willing
to devote the time necessary for him to prepare for your trial. A Nobel laureate
who is too busy to review the case will be a detriment to your defense. Plowing
through the patient's chart and other documents is yeoman's work, and if you
fear that the expert you are considering seems too noble for such a task, then
keep looking.

Any expert witness should be current on the literature in his field. If he is
not, then he ceased to be an expert shortly after he ceased learning.

An expert witness should be impressive. Impressive is in the eyes of the be-
holder, but there are some traits that you want your expert witness to have. The
expert should be confident in himself, inspire confidence in others, and yet be
appropriately humble (i.e., not overbearing). This may sound like too much to
ask, but the impression that the expert testifying on your behalf makes on the
jury is vital to his testimony being accepted by the jury. If the expert you are
considering is slovenly, condescending, or else absent-minded or comically naive in many ways, then the jury will think less of his testimony. One attribute to
beware of is the academician who can only see both sides of any coin. For example, the appropriate response in court to the question "Do women typically
carry their developing infant *in utero*?" is "Yes." If the expert you are considering is compelled by his nature to answer the preceding question by saying "Actually, there have been reports of women carrying an infant to term outside the
uterine cavity," then you need to keep looking. Such an answer bespeaks an avid
reader but one unable to see the forest for the trees. Of course it is appropriate to
acknowledge both sides of an area that is still being debated in pathology. If,
however, the expert you are considering cannot weigh the evidence presented to
him in a question and give a reasonable answer, then he will do your defense
more harm than good.

The qualifications to look for in an expert witness just discussed are sound
guidelines, but the decision belongs to you and your attorney. You yourself
should be convinced that the expert witness whom you and your attorney choose
to testify on your behalf is an expert in his field. If his qualifications and professional manner are impressive to you, then they should be all the more impressive
to the jury.

Having chosen an expert witness to testify on your behalf, make certain that your expert will be paid reasonable fees for his time. Have the attorney check that the insurance carrier will pay the fee requested by the expert before the expert takes the case. A sullen, belligerent expert testifying on your behalf will be a stone around your neck.

Possible Outcomes

Once a lawsuit has begun, it must come to some sort of legally acceptable end. Lawsuits cannot simply fade away. A suit may be dismissed, settled, or tried in court.

Malpractice Suit Dismissed

We have already discussed some examples of malpractice suits that were dismissed in the section on working with the attorney assigned to you. Whenever the plaintiff's attorney does such a poor job of researching or presenting his case that he fails to convince the judge that all four pillars of malpractice are at least reasonably present, the judge may choose to dismiss the case. (Reasonableness is in the eye of the individual judge presiding over the case.)

Malpractice Suit Settled

In Chapter 2 we discussed that the purpose of the legal system is to settle a dispute between two parties upon which they cannot agree. If the parties remain in disagreement, then a jury renders a decision by which both parties must abide. Once a lawsuit has been initiated, it can be stopped at any such time that all parties are able to reach an agreement because as soon as all parties are in agreement, there is no longer any disagreement for a court to resolve. The term that attorneys use to describe the agreement of all parties is a settlement. As the name suggests, a settlement is a sort of compromise with concessions on all sides, thus settling the accounts and the matter in dispute. A settlement in a malpractice case would typically consist of a physician conceding that his actions, even if inadvertent, caused harm to the patient. In order to recompense the patient for this harm suffered, the physician (represented by his insurer) agrees to pay a given sum of money. The patient accepts the physician's offer, thereby conceding, implicitly, that the sum of money he is accepting is just recompense for the harm he suffered. Agreements are signed, money exchanges hands, and everyone goes home. The physician's insurer agrees that it will pay the patient the sum settled upon, and in return the patient agrees that he will never again sue for malpractice concerning this matter.

Why settle? Attorneys dislike risk, and a trial represents a risk to the attorney. No matter how carefully an attorney chooses the members of a jury, the jury is composed of a dozen individuals, each with his own mind. However hard attorneys try, they can only persuade a jury, never control it. If the parties in a lawsuit are able to settle on a mutually agreeable resolution to the dispute, then the attorneys for all sides consider that they have more control over the situation. This is why some attorneys may settle for a relatively small sum of money in a case where the facts suggest that no malpractice was committed; the attorney who would urge such a settlement has in his mind the knowledge that a jury may be persuaded to rule against the physician and the hospital and award a financial penalty of millions of dollars. If the plaintiff will accept $50,000, and if the estimated cost of going through a trial is $50,000, then the attorney may counsel the physician defendant to take the best economic course.

The best economic course for the attorney, however, may not be the best course for you. If you settle, you have admitted culpability. There is a time to settle and a time to fight. As said earlier, it is in your best interest to assess the situation honestly. If you are a defendant in a malpractice suit, and you know that your carelessness or negligence or lack of proper attention led to the harm the patient suffered, then you have committed malpractice. Any jury convened to hear your case will likely see that you have committed malpractice, too. In that situation, if your attorney suggests that you admit culpability and try to settle, then the attorney is giving you good advice, namely, to go hat in hand, admit your mistake, and offer to make it as good as you can. A likely penalty for being dishonest in your self-assessment, if you truly did commit malpractice, is to be stunned by the size of the financial penalty assessed against you by the jury in a trial.

If, on the other hand, your honest assessment is that you did nothing wrong, then it is probably not in your best interest to settle. Admitting legal culpability in this day is akin to wearing a scarlet letter. State licensing bureaus typically ask whether you have had any judgments rendered against you since you last renewed your license. Those physicians who have had judgments rendered against them, and that includes a settlement, will be listed on a Web site available to the public. Additional licenses or hospital appointments become harder to get. Any new job may come at the cost of a larger malpractice insurance premium.

Settlement involves negotiation. The attorney representing you will handle the negotiations, but he is representing you, so it should be your decision whether to accept or reject an offer toward a settlement brought to you by your attorney from the plaintiff patient's attorney. As in any negotiations, bluffing is part of the art of the deal. The negotiations can be unsettling, especially if you do not have the stomach for such a game. Attorneys love to test your mettle. Testing you is part of what bluffing and negotiating are all about. Schutte tells the story of two physicians who were sued for malpractice.[4] For reasons that Schutte relates, the suit had little merit. Nevertheless, one physician could not stand the pressure of waiting for the suit to be resolved; when a low sum was offered by the plaintiff's attorney for settlement, the physician took it. The other physician, and his attorney, let it be known that there was no settlement to be had from them, so the plaintiff and his attorney eventually dropped the second physician from the malpractice suit. Notice that it is possible for a malpractice suit to be settled entirely in favor of the defendant. Notice, too, that an offer to settle for a bargain price may be a sign that the plaintiff's attorney recognizes the weakness of the case but that he still holds hope that by pestering you he can gain the plaintiff (and himself) something rather than nothing. Do not give in too soon.

Some malpractice defense firms take the philosophical approach that settling, and thus controlling the damages paid, is the best tack. Other malpractice defense firms fight like a lion when sued. Attorneys and firms have professional reputations just as surely as do physicians. Which type of legal firm do you suppose is the recipient of more lawsuits? What is the philosophical approach and reputation of the group of attorneys who would represent you if you were sued for malpractice? You might wish to do what you can to be represented by a firm that has a philosophical approach in line with your own. If you are opposed to a prolonged hassle, then a group that tends to settle would represent your interests more accurately. If you are a fighter, then the aggressive group may be better. Each case is unique, however, so settling or fighting will largely be determined by a given case, regardless of your own temperament.

How do attorneys convert damages into dollars? Damages that have altered the life of a patient will have altered the patient's ability to work, led to ongoing medical expenses, and caused pain and suffering. Loss of work and ongoing medical expenses have adversely affected the patient's economic fortunes and are relatively simple to compute. Prior to this event, the patient had a $45,000 per year income, but he is now bedridden, requiring $30,000 per year in medical expenses. Assuming that the patient lives his threescore and ten and retired at age 65 years, this 30-year-old patient has incurred $2,775,000 in lost income and extra expenses by age 65. Pain and suffering are more intangible and will be played up by the plaintiff's attorney and minimized as much as can be by the physician's defense attorney. Notice that, after the plaintiff's attorney takes his cut and the charges incurred on behalf of the plaintiff's case are paid, the plaintiff patient will wind up with far less than the 2.8 million dollars he is out.

In a case of malpractice leading to wrongful death, the calculations are simpler because there is no ongoing pain and suffering for the decedent on this earth. Most states do not allow for financial reimbursement of the decedent's survivors for their grief or anguish. Some have argued that the inability to add extra financial punishment in cases of wrongful death amounts to discrimination against the poor, the old, the very young, the disabled, and homemakers. Be that as it may, in the United States the dead are what they earned in life when it comes to assessing damages.

Having discussed how a monetary value is placed on damages, how do attorneys go on to broker a settlement? Because a civil suit represents a disagreement between two parties, it can be resolved satisfactorily in the eyes of the law if both parties agree on the differences that separate them, usually by some payment. Following is an example of how the attorneys representing each side can reach a financial settlement, which is really what is at issue. The attorneys estimate the likelihood that the plaintiff patient will win the case. We will suppose that attorneys for both sides agree, based on their past experience, that the plaintiff patient has a 60% chance of winning the case. This factor of 0.60 is then multiplied by the full value of the case, again determined by the attorneys' experience in similar such cases. If the financial settlement that the plaintiff patient can expect, based on past experience, is one million dollars, then the insurance company is likely to offer $600,000, and the plaintiff, who will be counseled by his attorney, is likely to accept such an offer. Notice that the percentage chosen for example is near 50%, but it does favor the plaintiff patient. If the likelihood of a side winning were 10% or 90%, then the negotiations between the two sides will be altered accordingly, and the side with a 90% chance of winning is holding most of the trumps.

Suit Tried in Court

If no compromise can be achieved between the parties on either side of a malpractice suit, then the suit will end up in a trial, where a judgment binding on both parties will be determined. Of course, a judgment may be appealed, thus starting the process all over, but at some point a judgment will be made from which there is no further appeal. Chapter 5 covers the mechanics of a trial.

Note that different defendants in a single malpractice suit may have different outcomes. Some defendants will probably be dropped from the suit. Other defendants, such as the hospital, may choose to settle. (After all, settling may be the financially safest course, and a hospital's accreditation is not sullied by settling in the way that a physician's license may be.) Still other defendants may go on to have their week in court, where they may win or lose.

The legal system realizes that juries can make mistakes, such as demanding an egregiously unfair sum be paid for pain and suffering, so the law has several checks and balances built into it. Both sides in the dispute must agree to the members of the jury in the first place. A trial judge is required by law to dismiss any case that he deems has insufficient evidence of malpractice prior to commencement of a trial (such a happenstance is rare but not unheard of). Once in place, the jury is instructed in what malpractice means in this case, and the jurors swear to follow the legal concepts of malpractice as given to them by the judge. Of course, an overwhelming majority of the jurors must vote to convict the defendant physician of malpractice or else the defendant is acquitted. Even if the jury convicts a physician of malpractice, the judge can set their verdict aside if it is clear to the judge that the jury is incorrect (so in this sense, a physician on trial does have a "peer," in regard to professional standing, who will consider his case). Finally, the case can be appealed by either side. Financial damages awarded to the plaintiff patient are covered by similar safeguards, and both the judge and the appellate courts are sworn to reduce any excessive verdict to a fair and reasonable verdict.[3]

Only 7% of malpractice suits are tried in court before a jury. The other 93% are either settled, dropped, or dismissed by a judge prior to trial. Of the 7% that go to trial, roughly half are settled during the course of the trial. Thus, only 3%

of all malpractice suits filed go to a jury for deliberation, and roughly 80% of jury verdicts are in favor of the defendant physician (find for the physician, in legal parlance).[7]

When the Physician Is Found Guilty of Malpractice

Whenever a physician settles a case by accepting some sort of charge made against him by the plaintiff patient, he is guilty of malpractice. When a judge or jury rules that the physician is guilty of malpractice, the physician is guilty of malpractice. It may be that the physician's attorney considers that the physician has some grounds for appeal if the guilty verdict was handed down in court; that will depend on each individual case. If the physician agreed to settle, then there can be no appeal, because the physician's agreement is a voluntary admission of malpractice. Depending on the laws of the states in which the physician holds licenses to practice medicine, he may have to notify the licensing board of the judgment against him. Hospital regulations may require him to notify the hospital as well. The malpractice road is a lonely road to walk, but it does not mean that the physician's medical career is over.

What of the plaintiff patient who wins a verdict of malpractice against a physician? He receives the money awarded to him either in settlement or in court. And what becomes of the money awarded to a plaintiff patient who wins a suit charging malpractice? Assuming that the plaintiff patient hired an attorney based on contingency (which is almost always the case), the money gets divided. Lobe gives an illustration of how the money is divided in his book *Medical Malpractice: A Physician's Guide*.[8] For the sake of ease, we will assume that the patient was awarded $100,000. A common contingency fee is 33%, so the attorney will receive a third of the money. Expert witness fees and deposition costs on behalf of the plaintiff will be deducted from the plaintiff's award; let us say that is an additional $10,000. Finally, there is the money that the patient owes the hospital for care rendered. If the patient was self-insured, then the hospital will take whatever is necessary from the plaintiff's award to settle the account. If, on the other hand, an insurance company paid the patient's medical bill, then the insurance company will claim whatever it paid to the hospital from the plaintiff patient's award. Assuming a cost of $8,000 per day for a five day hospital stay, the plaintiff will actually take home $17,000, or less than 20% of the amount awarded to him. Looked at another way, the plaintiff patient in this example will take home about half of what the attorney who represented him does.

When the Physician Is Found Not Guilty of Malpractice

A physician who has been found not guilty of malpractice by a judge or jury cannot be tried again for that same offense, according to the laws of the land. The same immunity would hold true if the plaintiff patient dropped all charges against the defending physician in a settlement; that is, if the plaintiff patient essentially admitted that he had no case against the physician.

Difficulty of Countersuits

An early response to being sued is the thought that you will sue back in order to inflict the same sort of heartache and damage on the plaintiff that the plaintiff has inflicted upon you. Having formed this thought, promptly forget it. In order to win a countersuit, you must convince an impartial jury that the preponderance of the evidence indicates that the plaintiff who sued you did so maliciously, knowing that you were not at fault. This is essentially never the case, and thus a countersuit is virtually impossible to win.

Reducing the Chance of a Malpractice Suit

"How can I win once I have been sued for malpractice?" is a fine question, but a better question is "How can I minimize my chance of being sued in the first place?" The best way to minimize your chance of being sued is to be a careful, caring physician.

That you can best protect yourself from being sued by doing good work and by being thoughtful of others sounds trite, but practicing medicine as a careful, caring physician is hard work. Two things determine the mettle of a physician. One is how you conduct yourself in a crisis. Panic does no good, of course. In a crisis, a physician must first check his own pulse and then calmly and carefully act. Crises are fertile soil for malpractice suits, particularly if something goes wrong. Nevertheless, a patient and his family are less likely to seek retribution against the physician who handles the crisis with a level head and who then keeps the patient and the patient's family informed as soon as it is reasonable to do so.

In some ways, handling a crisis is the easier test of a physician's mettle. Crises tend to bring out the best in people. The other test of a physician's character is how he practices during the daily grind. A physician who always maintains a sense of his responsibility to his patients, even when he bows under the burden of that responsibility, is less likely to be sued for malpractice than a weary, bored physician who seeks relief by cutting corners or indulging himself in improper outlets for his stress. Patients respond favorably to a physician with a sense of fairness and duty. Having a patient's good will is of paramount importance in preventing a malpractice suit from being brought against you.

The preceding paragraphs are true for all physicians, pathologists included. Pathologists who do not see patients cannot expect to develop a cordial professional relationship of mutual trust with patients, and therefore that particular means of guarding against a malpractice suit is lost to most pathologists. Pathologists can, however, maintain their sense of obligation to provide good patient care. Do not forget that the relationship between the pathologist and the clinician will be reflected in the dealings of the clinician with his patient. Schutte's book emphasizes that a common attribute of physicians who have been practicing for years without being sued for malpractice is that those physicians communicate with their patients. Communication will overcome much patient dissatisfaction because it indicates to a patient that the physician cares about the patient as a person. For pathologists, the implication is plain. The effectiveness and speed with which a pathologist communicates with a clinician directly determines the effectiveness and speed with which the clinician is able to communicate with his patient. Whether you are in private practice or academics, you should make it your business to get all your laboratory reports out promptly, preceded by a verbal communication with the clinician when the situation warrants that extra service. By providing exemplary service both in quality and in timeliness, you give your clinician no reason to blame you or to make excuses for you, and you lessen the chance that the patient will be frustrated with the care he is receiving. A satisfied patient is a patient unlikely to sue. And, as we have been discussing, the attorney who represents a patient who does sue will look for the weakest link to attack. The pathologist who always runs behind, who keeps sloppy records, or who never has it all together presents a particularly easy target for a plaintiff's attorney. It is in this hypothetical case, moreover, that all the admonitions to beware of betraying confidences concerning a lawsuit against you are most needed. A lackluster pathologist may find that his clinical colleagues have no reason to desire to leap to his defense, especially if by doing nothing the clinicians can at least enjoy a little payback and at best see the pathologist turned out of his position.

Effective, caring communication with others is essential to good medical practice as well as an essential means of thwarting malpractice suits. Another form of communication is also important in protecting you from malpractice suits, and that is communication to yourself (and to others) in the future in the form of carefully kept medical records. Despite all the training in medical school and the experience in the use of medical records as a physician, physicians all too rarely take sufficient time to carefully document what happened in every case. "But I am so busy," you may say. Of course you are, but keeping detailed medical records will save you time in the future. You can think of the medical records that you generate as an investment in your professional future because that is exactly what they are. The records are what you use to treat a patient, and they are the first thing you consult when that patient returns for evaluation, whether it is in six weeks, six months, or six years. The author (G.G.D..) considers himself busy, too, but he has noticed something when reviewing the records he has kept on his own cases—he never reads a record and says to himself, "You know, I put way too much information down on paper about this." What the author says over and over is, "Why did I not write down more about this or that aspect of the case. I remember that it came up at the time, but I failed to realize its importance." Obviously no one can see the future with clarity, but we as physicians still are in the prognostication business, although we prognosticate based on epidemiological statistics rather than by using augury. No one can record every detail and every nuance of every encounter, nor should they, because that would show no discernment. Discernment begins when you consciously begin to practice making shrewd guesses concerning what aspects of the case (or specimen) have a reasonable chance of being important in the future. One approach that has helped the author is to remember that he is mortal and that he could die on his way home from work in a traffic accident every day. (This possibility is an easy thing to keep in mind when your practice is forensic pathology.) The author writes notes and reports not to jog his memory but to provide a record of what happened so that, if the author should die on the way home that evening, someone with the author's training could figure out what the author was presented with, how he evaluated the case, and how he reached his conclusions. The author would like to be missed, of course, but he does not wish to take any essential knowledge of his cases to the grave with him.

Perceptive, detailed notes will be a benefit to any physician who develops the discipline to keep them. The foremost purpose of good notes is improving the quality of medical care provided to each patient. The legal benefit is that those notes will be what are used by both sides in a malpractice suit against you to determine your part and culpability in the matter that is the subject of the suit. If your notes are sloppy, haphazard, illegible, or nonexistent, then it will be unclear what you did or thought. It may be clear to you, but it will be unclear to the jury, particularly if you write your notes for yourself only. This is why writing your notes with the thought that you will one day not be there to interpret them is a useful approach. Believe it or not, the notes that you yourself have written will serve as a sort of independent witness in your malpractice suit. Whether your notes incriminate you or exonerate you is determined by you and the care with which you record your notes.

Pathologists typically do not leave handwritten notes on a patient's chart. In this age of the complete electronic medical record, handwritten notes may not even be left by the clinical physicians. As a pathologist you do have interactions that touch upon patient care that deserve notation, at least in your own office, and preferably on the patient's chart as well, as discussed in Chapter 3. Consultations over a microscope with clinicians, calls to clinicians to tell them the result of a biopsy or laboratory test, or conversations with a consultant in a case all deserve to be recorded on paper. The recording need not be onerous. The recording should include the date and time of the interaction being recorded, the name of the participants in the conversation, and a brief description of what transpired. For example, let us consider the case of Patient Mills, an adult male status post marrow transplant for lymphoma. Mr. Mills has developed a fever and is beginning to develop some haziness in his chest radiograph. The infectious disease team swings by the cytology laboratory to check on the results of a bronchoalveolar lavage on Mr. Mills just as the slides are coming out. You know the attending oncologist and the consulting infectious disease specialist, and you know that the oncologist would not mind if the infectious disease specialist heard the results first. You sit down at the multiheaded microscope with the team and look at the slides. Branching yeast forms consistent with *Aspergillus* are on the slide. You show the organisms to the infectious disease team, mentioning that, while suggestive, the forms are not diagnostic for *Aspergillus*—only microbiology cultures can prove that the organisms are *Aspergillus*. The ID team leaves, and the consultant, of course, will begin empiric treatment immediately. You call the oncologist to tell him of the finding. Then is the time to jot down your notes of what transpired. The note can be handwritten on a sheet of plain paper from a spiral notebook dedicated to such notations, on your daily calendar (which you would have to save), or you can dictate it, but in any case the note must bear the unique case number and the physician contacted. Adequate notes could look something like this:

17 October 2003, 1425 H
Reviewed BAL slides on Patient Mills (998123-5) with ID team, led by Dr. X, who is consulting on this case. Showed team presence of fungal forms consistent with *Aspergillus*, final identification deferred to cultures.

17 October 2003, 1435 H
Called Dr. Y, attending oncologist. Transmitted finding of fungal forms consistent with *Aspergillus* on BAL, final identification deferred to cultures.

Should something else come up the next day, the sequence of communications can be extended. You should initial each entry at its end. The format of the date and time are, of course, up to the individual, but the date and time should be on each note.

One way to approach keeping such records is to write the communications on the back of the copy of the formal report that you keep in the pathology office, which has the benefits of ensuring that the case number is on the sheet and conserving paper and the need for filing space within your office. Should Mr. Mills die, and should his family sue for malpractice, the attorney defending the pathologist would easily be able to show that the information concerning the fungal infection got from the pathologist to the clinicians as quickly as possible, especially with a note appended to the report placed in the patient's chart. The plaintiff's attorney would be hard-pressed to show that the pathologist somehow failed in performing his duty for the patient. The notes make clear that the proper things were done to evaluate the specimen pathologically and that the pathologist made certain that the clinical physicians got this vital information immediately. Winning a malpractice suit against you is nice, but stopping one from ever starting is preferable. Think of keeping notes like the sort shown above as the ounce of legal prevention that will one day prove to be worth a pound of cure.

In addition to being careful and caring, Schutte mentions one other characteristic shared by physicians who had not been sued after years of practice—they all maintain direct control of the patient billings for their practice.[4] In the United States, money commands attention. Money often causes disagreements in marriages, and it can cause disagreements in physician–patient relationships. If disagreements over money can lead to a divorce, then disagreements over money can lead to a malpractice suit. Schutte's point is that physicians who know their patients know when a patient is in financial straits. By showing mercy when an honest patient is in a hard place, the physician communicates to the patient that the physician–patient relationship is more important to him than money alone. Showing mercy does not mean always writing off a debt. Mercy can mean accepting payments over time until the bill is settled, or half paid, or whatever the physician and patient work out.

Clinicians such as general practitioners are in a field of medicine that depends upon sustained patient-physician relationships, and this extends to interactions concerning billing and payment. Pathologists, who do not typically develop any physician–patient relationships, are not necessarily able to handle their billing in the same way. Academic departments may have their billing contracted out by the university hospital and have little control over how things are done. Nevertheless, the fact remains that a common feature of physicians who were not sued in the studies quoted by Schutte is that those physicians maintained control of their billing practices. Think of it in this way: if the bill comes to a patient from an automated system, followed by form demands for payment or else, and if the patient gets a telephone system runaround when he tries to question an item on the bill, then the patient's frustration is easily converted into a desire to sue and punish "the system." Patients who genuinely like their physicians as individuals will think twice before suing old Dr. Pritchard, who helped them out when things were tight. There is no reason to think twice before suing a soulless system.

Indefensible Positions

We have been discussing things that can be done to minimize the chance that a malpractice suit is filed against you as a pathologist. Some are within your power to control, such as keeping good records. Some, such as billing, may be harder to control. There are situations, however, that cannot be controlled at all once they have been allowed to occur. Whenever you or your attorney find that you are in an indefensible position, it will be the attorney who will spell it out to you and advise you to seek a settlement. When you are in an indefensible position, you are going to lose the malpractice suit against you. The attorney will advise settling as a means of controlling just how much loss you incur. Indefensible positions are described below.

Lack of Any Record in the First Place

The importance of documenting what was found or what was done has been discussed above. Believe it—in court, if you did not write it down, then it never happened. Consider a frozen section being called into question in a malpractice case. You can say all day long that you always pull the old material from previous biopsies and resections to compare to frozen material on a patient. You may even be telling the truth. It matters not at all, however, what you say unless you dictated "The frozen material was compared to the appearance of the patient's primary lung carcinoma, surgical pathology specimen No. 98-12345." If you recorded what happened at the time it happened, then it is believable evidence. If you say you did it and there is no evidence to back up your assertion, then at best you look incompetent for failing to keep proper notes and at worst you appear to be perjuring yourself to save your own skin.

Changing the Chart

Changing the chart is a form of fraud. Never do it. You may think that you can squeeze a note in somewhere that will make your case easier to defend. You may think that you are just taking the trouble at a later date to write things down the way that they happened then and that you would have written such a note at the time if only you hadn't been so busy. You may think that no one will be the wiser. If you think these things, then prepare to be wrong. The game of changing the chart is not a case of "double or nothing." It is a case of "everything or nothing." The likelihood is that you will lose everything. The discovery of such falsification will not only lead to a guilty verdict but may void your malpractice policy and result in suspension of clinical privileges or even loss of medical licensure. Some policies state that any act of fraud or deceit will invalidate the coverage. In other words, you will certainly lose the case, and by invalidating your coverage you will be paying whatever the monetary award to the plaintiff is out of your own pocket. Regulatory agencies, such as the Joint Commission on Accreditation of Healthcare Organizations (JCAHO), have the authority to stop mid-survey and suspend a hospital's accreditation if they find evidence of intentional chart alteration.

How might you get caught at changing the chart? Schutte provides an excellent example.[4] A patient was displeased with the care he had received for an infection that he developed while in a tertiary care hospital. The patient had his wife contact an attorney whom they knew in their hometown about two hours away. The attorney told the couple to say nothing of their concerns but to complete the hospital stay and come home. The patient was then advised to ask his hometown physician to request a copy of the patient's medical records. The director of medical records thought this an understandable request and sent the records to the patient's physician. Several months later, the attorney sent a letter to the hospital demanding a copy of the medical records for consideration of a malpractice suit. This time the director of medical records brought the letter and the chart to the office of the hospital physician so that the hospital physician could review the chart before the records were sent. The physician noticed that there was no note concerning a verbal order he had remembered giving to the nurses for antibiotics. (The nurses, it must be said, had claimed at the time that they never received such a verbal order.) Because the hospital physician was certain he must have given the order, he added such a note to the chart in a place that would correspond with the evening he claimed he gave the order. The rest is obvious, of course. The patient's attorney now had an official copy of the patient's hospital record, mailed by the hospital a week after discharge, in which no such note existed, and a copy from months later with the new note suddenly present. The falsification of records was plain, and the hospital physician's insurer exercised its escape clause for the practice of deceit in the case. The hospital physician paid the settlement out of his own pocket. It is difficult to get new insurance under such conditions.

Pathologists are perhaps protected from altering the chart in that they customarily do not leave notes in a patient's chart. Nevertheless, the penalty for changing the chart is so great that the matter needs to be discussed. Note that the hospital in the story above had a flawed policy of providing the chart to a clinician for review prior to sending a copy of the chart to an attorney who had requested it. The implication of such an action is an invitation to buff the chart. The medical records department could have prevented the falsification by sending a copy of the chart to the attorney at the same time that they notified the hospital physician of the attorney's request for the chart. A copy of the chart as it is when a proper attorney's request is received is what a hospital should be providing. The story told above is the sort of thing that would occur when a chart was thought of as belonging to a physician rather than to a patient, so such an opportunity to review and change the chart would probably not be given to a physician today. Only an unremitting cynic would suppose that the hospital would send a chart to the clinician first to allow the clinician to make a change, and thus deflect all culpability from the hospital to the clinician.

There are times when mistakes are made in a handwritten account. It is appropriate to correct a mistake when it is caught, but there are right and wrong ways to go about correcting an error in a note in the patient's chart. Everyone understands that no one is perfect. If you realize as soon as you write the word "right" that it should have been "left," then you need only draw a line through the incorrect word and write the correct word in an appropriate place (either above or beside the word in error). Trouble can arise when you try to obliterate the incorrect word, either by blacking it out or by whiting it out. Either attempt at obliterating a word will be apparent on the original sheet, and thus either attempt is likely to be discovered later. Mistakenly exchanging "left" for "right," or any other similar error, is an understandable human error. Trying to eradicate any evidence that you ever made an error, however, looks bad, especially if the wrong kidney was removed.

It may be that you discover a few days after making a note that you made an error. Let us again suppose that you mistakenly exchanged "right" for "left". Now that time has passed and new notes have been added following the erroneous word, it is no longer best to draw a line through the incorrect word. Those who have left notes in the interim may have relied upon the erroneous note. The way to correct the mistake is to add a new note that explains and corrects the error. This new note should be written at the end of all the notes already written, and it should be labeled with the date and time of entry (as all notes should) as shown in the following example:

15 March 2003   0815 H

The note I wrote on 13 March 2003 at 1420 H contains an error when it states that the patient's right hand is swollen. The patient's left hand is the hand that is swollen, as all my other notes indicate.

The clinician who added a note to the medical record would not have been guilty of falsifying the document had he added his note at the end and dated it with the date on which he truly wrote the note. Of course, any note that begins "It was not recorded at the time, but I remember that four months ago I called a verbal order to the nursing staff..." is unlikely to convince a jury of your claim. To write a note four months later, and to claim that you are writing it four months later, is not dishonest, merely futile.

Changing documentation in hospitals that have made the transition to the electronic medical record is guaranteed to stand out. The time a note is signed (thus authenticated) is recorded electronically (date, hour, minute, and second). If it is necessary to correct an error in the electronic record, then the clinician must consciously note the date and time of the activities being recorded, otherwise the computer will automatically point a finger at you. An area of difficulty for documentation in the electronic medical record is the electronic capture of informed consent. For example, if a patient receives complete appropriate informed consent and signs the paperwork accordingly, only to have the signed paper routed to a file clerk, who then scans the document into the electronic medical record four days after the procedure, then the computer's automatic capture of date/time for the consent inappropriately reflects that consent was not obtained until after the procedure was done. Documentation that paper consent was collected appropriately requires manual accession of the scanned document—a timely process. Some hospitals have addressed this problem by providing scanners within patient areas where informed consent is regularly required. This helps clarify, electronically, the documentation trail. Having said all this, one of the positive features of the fully electronic medical record is that inappropriate intentional retroactive documentation is virtually impossible.

Losing Pertinent Microscopic Slides

When the malpractice suit concerns an incorrect diagnosis of cancer at frozen section, it has occurred to some pathologists in the past that there would be no evidence for or against the frozen section diagnosis if only the frozen section no longer existed. Glass slides do get lost, but not often. Glass slides are occasionally broken, but not often. If the substance of the malpractice suit is the diagnosis made at frozen section, then you are best served by protecting that slide as though your life depends upon it. Even if the slide was honestly lost, it will look self-serving to a jury's eyes, and it will look ten times more self-serving by the time the plaintiff's attorney has finished badgering you about the lost slide.

Court is but one of the venues in life where you may win the battle and still lose the war.

Because the pertinent glass slides will inevitably be passed from expert to expert on both sides of a malpractice case, the policy of making a simple photocopy of the glass slides as you received them is a clever way to document that the slides were intact when they entered and left your care. You can easily place 50 slides on the copier for a one-page snapshot. You can also use this photocopy to jot a note to yourself ("all slides returned intact 2/2/02"), clipping the shipping receipt to the page. Also, should you later be asked whether you saw a particular slide, you can use your photocopy list to help you answer this question.

Leaving out Information that Does Not Support Your Diagnosis

The practice of any medical discipline is the practice of amassing information, then assessing the information and drawing a conclusion. It is an unusual case that is classic in every feature. A diagnosis may rest upon a half dozen features drawn from the patient's history, physical findings, and laboratory tests. The physician who notes that there is also a feature (or two) that in some way conflicts with his diagnosis is exercising judgment. Physicians are paid to exercise judgment. The physician who ignores a feature or two not in keeping with his diagnosis, however, is either unobservant or else trying to stack the deck in his favor. Later, if the diagnosis proves to be wrong, many people, yourself chief among them, will want to know why you reached the diagnosis you did. Put contradictory information into your reports and mention why you considered the contradiction insufficient to alter the diagnosis. For example, "No psammoma bodies are present in this case, but psammoma bodies are not invariably found in every meningioma."

Rudeness

There is no defense in court for rudeness on the part of a physician. Patients, who are sick, are forgiven of rudeness by the jury. Physicians, who chose to go into medicine knowing that they would be treating sick people, have no excuse for being rude. A jury will have the same sort of affection for a physician who is rude to a patient that the bourgeois held for the aristocracy during the Reign of Terror. Any inconsiderate treatment of a patient by a physician will be brought out in court if the attorney representing the patient can find out about it. If the rudeness was restricted to comments, then the plaintiff's attorney will be dependent upon the testimony of hospital staff, such as nurses, laboratory technicians, etc. This should reiterate the point of why it is important not to lambast the patient to any ears willing to listen when you are slapped with the frustration of a malpractice suit.

Rudeness committed to paper is especially damning of a physician. A patient's medical chart is the repository of reported symptoms and clinical observations related to the patient's health. Notes or comments that amount to potshots at the patient are unprofessional and have no place in a patient's chart. Remember, law in the United States has clearly established that the patient's chart belongs to the patient, so you may assume that the patient will leisurely read every word you have written about him. Be certain all the words written are accurate and defendable. Of course, this does not mean that you can write only nice things about every patient. Some patients behave badly, and a description of that misbehavior is necessary to accurately record the patient's history. But do so objectively, without becoming emotionally involved. For example, if a patient called and spoke to you over the telephone, cursing you about the amount of a bill he received, the following would be a defendable description of what happened:

16 August 2001 1545 H
Mr. Phillips called and demanded to speak to me. When I said hello Mr. Phillips began cursing me for sending him an unreasonable bill for my services concerning his biopsy last month. I told Mr. Phillips I would be happy to discuss the matter with him, provided that both he and I discussed the matter in a civil and professional manner. Mr. Phillips began to shout, and he continued to curse me, whereupon I told him that this conversation was at an end until such time as he could speak politely to me. I then hung up the receiver. Mr. Phillips' speech was slurred and sometimes incoherent throughout the call, and he sounded intoxicated.

The note above records what happened, and it even includes an assessment that the patient was intoxicated at the time. Note that the clinical assessment of intoxication is preceded by the objective observation that the patient's speech was slurred and incoherent. Nowhere in the note does the physician sink to the level of name-calling. If the note above were read aloud in court at a malpractice trial against you, you would have no reason to be ashamed of your behavior. The following note, however, would be harmful to your defense in a malpractice suit:

16 August 2001 1545 H
Mr. Phillips called in a drunken rage, ranting about the bill he received from me. I told him to call back when he was sober and could discuss the matter more intelligently.

The same incident could lead to either of the notes above. In contrast to the first note, however, the second note sounds supercilious and petty. The words chosen by the physician in the second note are more inflammatory, and the second note lacks an objectivity that makes the first note acceptable. Unfortunately, notes more scathing than the second example get left in patient's charts. Surely you know physicians who carefully craft malicious retorts into blistering notes and e-mails. Such a practice is unprofessional as well as a terrible mistake. Do not be guilty of it.

Jokes at a Patient's Expense

Akin to notes that denounce a patient are notes that make a patient the butt of a joke. Again, such a practice is unacceptable. Do not think that you are so clever that your joke will remain a private code that no attorney can break. As an example, an expression sometimes heard on the wards is the phrase "piss poor protoplasm." Surely no physician would write such an expression in the chart, but some physicians do write "PPP" or "P3" in the chart with the thought that no one will break this code. With a malpractice suit potentially worth millions of dollars hanging in the balance, the plaintiff's attorney will be asking you to explain anything he does not understand completely. Remember, too, that the plaintiff's attorney likely has had an expert witness—that is, a physician—review the chart. The physician who reviews the chart was hired by the attorney for his expertise, and that physician may know exactly what some flippant acronym, such as PPP or "BHTM" ("better him than me") stands for. Therefore, do not expect to snow the plaintiff's attorney. One of the maxims of the legal profession is that a good attorney only asks questions to which he already knows the answer. Again, make certain that everything you write down in a note or report is something you would be proud to see attached to your name on the front page of your newspaper.

As an addendum to this point, the foolishness of an inappropriate joke applies to surgeons who send in a frozen section of an accessory spleen with a requisition stating that the specimen is from the pituitary. Some surgeons like to see whether their pathologists are paying attention, but it would be the surgeon who looked a fool in court, should he someday have to explain why he did what he did.

Abbreviations

Medicine is filled with acronyms and abbreviations used to make the writing of cumbersome things quicker. An example is COPD for "chronic obstructive pulmonary disease." Acronyms and abbreviations may have more than one meaning, however. ROM indicates "range of motion" to rheumatologists but means "rupture of membranes" to obstetricians. Usually such distinctions are clear from context. Nevertheless, not everyone reading a chart has a medical background. There exists the possibility that an acronym will be misinterpreted. For example, the patient to whom the chart belongs, may not know the meaning of semistandard acronyms. Any conversation with a patient to explain the distinction between having "SOB" and being an "SOB" will be less amusing in fact than it is in abstract. Of course, COPD is much easier to write than "chronic obstructive pulmonary disease," but the physician using an acronym or other abbreviation in a patient's chart or report would do well to follow the approach taken by medical journals. The first time a concept is introduced in a journal article, it is written out, and then, if the writer wishes to use an acronym subsequently, the full term is followed by the acronym in parentheses. Regardless of acronyms, write out "shortness of breath" when needed, and thereafter use the shorter term "dyspnea."

The Impaired Physician

Because physicians are human, they are susceptible to the thousand natural shocks that flesh is heir to. Some shocks, however, are often associated with impairment, which by definition means that the physician would be unable to render appropriate medical care with skill and safety. A physician may become impaired through little fault of his own due, for example, to a psychiatric disorder such as depression. Or the physician may bear more responsibility for his impairment, such as becoming addicted to alcohol or medication. Whatever the cause, the impairment of a physician tends to develop slowly. The affected physician is often in denial, unwilling to admit that he has a problem. Denial is contagious, and typically the affected physician's family and friends are slow to confront a person who is unwilling to face the truth. It is impossible for friendly colleagues to maintain the sort of emotional distance necessary to recognize the problem in its early stages, so colleagues as well as family are slow to recognize the signs. When people do recognize the signs, the easiest thing to do is to deny the obvious. Denial, however, neither corrects the problem nor helps the physician concerned. Confrontation is difficult and beyond the experience of most physicians. Fortunately, most states have offices with personnel who do have experience in such matters and who can provide help. These offices, often called Physician Health Programs, have various other names, such as Office of Physician Wellness or Office of Physician Assistance. Either the state medical licensing board or the state medical society will know whom to contact at the appropriate office. A list of offices is also available at the Web site of the Federation of State Physician Health Programs (www.fsphp.org).

Physician Health Programs often encourage anonymous calls, knowing how awkward it is to report a colleague, and you may obtain advice and support. Most of these programs are authorized by the regulatory boards to assist physicians in a confidential manner. You can ask if your name can remain confidential before you provide any information. You may be surprised at how the situation is handled and at the good results, for the success rate of this type of intervention by an experienced Physician Health Program director is high. Often the physician is not confronted directly but rather is told that people who know and care about him have expressed credible concerns about possible health issues that could cause impairment. The physician is encouraged to seek thorough evaluation in order to address and resolve these concerns that have been raised. The physician may refuse such an evaluation, but it is then explained that the consequence of refusal is the possibility that the issue may be turned over to the state licensing board for examination (and to the police if suspected drug abuse warrants a criminal investigation). Given this choice, and the assurance that if a thorough evaluation reveals no just cause for concern that the matter will be dropped, most physicians agree to undergo evaluation. Intervention is conducted with respect and support to preserve and assist the potentially affected individual with the aim of obtaining help rather than punishment.

In referring a physician for an evaluation, the Physician Health Programs have learned that referring to an experienced evaluation facility is of paramount importance. In a proper evaluation of the potentially impaired physician, it is not only the physician himself who is questioned. History is also taken from the physician's family, colleagues, and anyone else who may have information and important observations that must be considered in order to make a correct diagnosis. In the case of the chemically dependent physician in denial, it is helpful to that physician to undergo the evaluation process away from his usual environment, usually in an inpatient or residential setting. There are many reasons for this approach: the physician can be observed carefully for withdrawal symptoms, he will be in a secure environment where drugs or alcohol is unavailable, there are usually other patients (perhaps even other physicians) in residence who can support and encourage honesty, and, once removed from his usual environment, the physician's true situation begins to become apparent to him. Furthermore, for addicted physicians, being in a setting with other addicts reduces the shame of addiction, engenders hope, and allows the physician to reduce his denial and realize that he does have a problem.

The good news is that once a physician faces his addiction, he has good reason to hope for improvement in his condition. Help is offered in the form of treatment and long-term aftercare. Physicians have an extraordinarily high success rate from addiction—greater than 90%. Such intervention may well save the physician's practice, home, and life. These programs have proved so successful for physicians impaired by illness or substance abuse that some states have expanded the activities of the Office of Physician Wellness to include physicians with behavioral disorders, sexual misconduct, and inappropriate mechanisms for coping with stress.

Professional Misconduct

If you practice as a member of a group that has been incorporated as a professional corporation, then you are liable for the incompetence or misconduct of a colleague in your group. This point has already been addressed above in the discussion of whom or what entities might be named as defendants in a malpractice suit. There is another way, however, in which you as a physician are liable for the conduct of a colleague, even if you are not yet a partner of the group or do not even practice within a group setting, and that is by failing to report a colleague's professional misconduct. Professional misconduct includes what even you as a physician would consider malpractice, substance abuse, and sexual misconduct. If you know about professional misconduct on the part of a colleague but fail to report that misconduct appropriately, and if a jury can be convinced by the preponderance of evidence presented to it that you knew of the misconduct and failed to report it, then you are liable for your colleague's misconduct. This is no place to be coy or to pretend that some things don't happen, at least not in your group.

The discovery that a colleague, perhaps even a partner, is guilty of professional misconduct will always come as a terrible blow. After all, you thought that you knew this person better than that. You thought that you would have recognized a problem before you asked someone to join your group or department. And now that you have discovered the situation, how will you handle it? If word of this gets out, then how will it reflect upon you or your group, and what sort of liability will your group be subject to?

The person guilty of professional misconduct has made life harder for himself and all those around him. The preceding sentence is true, but notice the subject. The "person guilty of professional misconduct" has made this bed, and the time is coming when he will have to lie in it. Discovering this misconduct thrusts you into an unwelcome situation, but once in, you must do something to change it. Do not be misled; the truth will come out sooner or later. How the truth comes out will determine how it reflects upon you and your group. If it comes out by some means other than you or your group, then you and your group will probably find yourself liable for failure to notify the authorities of your colleague's misconduct. Hard though it may be, for the good of patients, your colleague, and yourself, you must act to end the professional misconduct. Some sort of confrontation will be necessary to end the wrongdoing, and the confrontation must be more than just a simple "Let's not do that again, shall we."

The good news, or at least the best news in a bad situation, is that you do not have to figure out how to handle the discovery of your colleague's professional misconduct *de novo*. We have already discussed resources for helping an impaired physician above. Beyond that, the hospital bylaws will have a peer review protocol for use when needed, such as in a situation that involves criminal misconduct. These bylaws are designed to handle a bad situation as fairly as possible. The bylaws define who the authorities are to whom you must report the misconduct. The bylaws, like the laws that govern our court system, are meant to keep the process of peer review fair and impartial. Furthermore, the bylaws governing peer review are designed to provide the reviewers legal protection for conducting a review while simultaneously affording the person being reviewed the rights of due process.

If you have questions, then by all means discuss the matter with the hospital attorney and the attorney representing your group. Such a discussion does not take place in a confessional, however, so know that by discussing the matter you have released the djinn from the bottle. This admonition is meant not to deter you from reporting misconduct, but to steel you for what will come once you have begun the process of reporting a colleague's professional misconduct. Even though the hospital attorney is not a priest, he does have a professional responsibility to maintain confidentiality.

When the news does spread through the hospital, as it inevitably will, you cannot prevent idle chatter concerning the events. There will always be people who will whisper this or that; the important thing is to give the gossipers no basis for malicious whispering against you and your group.

Criminal Wrongdoing

If a physician is guilty of opiate abuse, then it may be possible to seek treatment without charging the physician with a crime. If, on the other hand, the physician is trafficking opiates, then there are criminal charges that he will have to face. The same is true of physicians guilty of sexual molestation or fraud. This is not to say that the physicians in these examples do not need help but that they have committed criminal acts for which they will be held accountable in criminal court if found guilty.

Criminal wrongdoing can also bring with it charges of civil wrongdoing. One of the axioms of our law is that all criminal offenses have a corresponding civil offense. An example is the criminal wrong of murder and the corresponding civil charge of wrongful death. The burden of proof necessary to find a person guilty of murder is proof that is convincing "beyond a reasonable doubt," whereas for a civil charge of wrongful death the burden of proof is "the preponderance of the evidence." Although unusual, a person might be tried for a murder, for which he is found not guilty, and then tried for the same action—that is, the death of another—in a wrongful death suit. This sometimes happens in high-profile cases. To be tried for wrongful death after being acquitted of murder is not double jeopardy. Double jeopardy occurs if a person is tried a second time on a charge of murder after being acquitted the first time on that same charge of murder. In medicine, if a physician were found guilty of the crime of sexually molesting patients, then he can expect to be sued for the civil offense of malpractice and, since the burden of proof is less for a civil offense, he can expect to be found guilty of malpractice, too.

References

1. Jacobellis v. Ohio, 378 U.S. 184, 197 (1964).
2. Huycke LI, Huycke MM. Characteristics of potential plaintiffs in malpractice litigation. Ann Intern Med 1994;120:792–8.
3. Mackauf SH. Neurologic malpractice: the perspective of a patient's lawyer. Neurol Clinics 1999;17:345–53.
4. Schutte JE. Preventing Medical Malpractice Suits: A Handbook for Doctors and Those Who Work with Them. Seattle: Hogrefe & Huber Publishers, 1995.
5. Bounds JA. Introduction to notification, deposition, and court testimony: a primer for the defendant physician. Neurol Clinics 1999;17:335–43.
6. Fish RM, Ehrhardt ME, Fish B. Malpractice: Managing Your Defense (2nd edition). Oradell, NJ: Medical Economics Books, 1990.

7. Taragin MI, Willett LR, Wilczek AP, et al. The influence of standards of care and severity of injury on the resolution of medical malpractice claims. Ann Intern Med 1992;117:780–4.
8. Lobe TE. Medical Malpractice: A Physician's Guide. New York: McGraw-Hill, 1995.

5
Expert Witness Testimony

As mentioned in Chapter 2, an expert witness has training and experience beyond that of ordinary human experience, and the expert witness is called upon in court to provide the judge and jury the benefit of his special training and experience so that the best possible judgment can be rendered. An expert witness is allowed to give his opinion in court concerning a matter within his area of expertise. In other words, an expert witness is permitted to use his special training and experience to make his own judgment concerning matters that fall within his area of expertise. Having made his judgment, the expert witness may then pass his personal judgment of the situation on to the judge and jury so that they can use his informed opinion to make *their* own decision concerning the guilt of the party accused of committing a criminal or civil wrong. That courts should grant such authority to expert witnesses is, in a way, astonishing. In order for an expert witness to function properly, as a teacher to the court, the court assumes that the privilege granted to an expert witness of offering his opinion is balanced by the responsibility of using his special knowledge to assess each question and situation with equanimity.

Requirements to Be an Expert Witness

What does it take to become an expert witness? If you are a physician, then you are already qualified to be called to court as an expert witness. Any physician can be qualified as an expert witness by virtue of his medical degree and practice. You need not pay for a certificate that names you an expert witness because you have already made that payment in the form of tuition. Companies exist that will claim to certify you as an expert witness in exchange for a fee paid to the company, but there is no need for you as a physician to attend a seminar or take some correspondence course in order to be recognized by courts as an expert witness. If you wish to take a course or seminar to learn how to be an effective expert witness, then that is different and perfectly appropriate.

In addition to a medical degree, the only other attribute that a physician needs to be an expert witness is the willingness to be one. If a fact witness is summoned to court with a subpoena, he *must* go and testify. An expert witness, however, may choose to become involved in a case or not. If you wish to get into the expert witness business, you can. There is always a need for an honest expert witness, and if you prove to be good at testifying before a jury, your name will quickly make the rounds of the attorneys in the area, region, or even nation. Before you get into the business of expert witness testimony, you should assess yourself honestly using five criteria, four of which were listed in the previous chapter.

1. Are you qualified?

Do you have a license to practice medicine? Are you certified by the American Board of Pathology and, if so, in what specialties or subspecialties? Do you belong to appropriate professional organizations? Do you have any publications and, if so, in what areas? All these questions are the means by which attorneys establish to the satisfaction of the lay members of the jury that your professional peers recognize and endorse your particular abilities as a pathologist. Moreover, if you are an academician, you must ask yourself whether you practice pathology as a clinical specialty regularly. It is easy for the opposing attorney to paint you as an inhabitant of the ivory tower who has lost touch with the real world if you are not regularly involved in the activities that are being discussed in the trial in which you are testifying. If you are testifying on a point concerning a surgical specimen, then you should be able to say, honestly, that you regularly practice surgical pathology. Signing out surgical specimens six times per month, or every Tuesday, for example, shows frequent, regular, recurring involvement in the field in question. If your primary work is in your research laboratory and concerns establishing the genetic locus for a certain malignant neoplasm, and if your clinical responsibilities are confined to covering the autopsy service one weekend per month, then you have no business testifying in a case revolving around a surgical specimen. While the researcher in the example just given does have knowledge beyond that of ordinary experience, the researcher's knowledge of the area in question has been fossilized since the day he last practiced surgical pathology.

2. Are you able and willing to devote the time necessary to prepare for the trial?

You will cause harm if you do not give proper time to considering and researching a case that you have accepted. At the least, you will frustrate everyone involved in the case, including yourself. At the worst, you can cause a miscarriage of justice.

3. Have you kept up on the literature in your field?

This question is akin to Question 1; it is a different measure of whether you are really an expert or merely coasting on your laurels. There are several ways to assess whether you are keeping abreast of the literature. Serving on the editorial board of a peer review journal or serving as a reviewer for either a peer review journal or for a national specialty society (e.g., the United States and Canadian Academy of Pathology, the American Society of Clinical Pathologists, or the College of American Pathologists) all indicate a continuing participation in the advancement of medical knowledge. Presenting research, presenting a workshop, or moderating scientific meetings also establishes your involvement in education of both yourself and others.

4. Do you make a good impression on others as a physician?

Traits that mark a good physician in practice are caution rather than recklessness, confidence rather than indecisiveness, and thoughtful humility rather than overbearing pride. A trait that makes a good impression in court is the ability to respond to a question with a straightforward and easily understandable answer. If your answers in court are routinely incomprehensible, then at best the jury will simply ignore your testimony and at worst the judge can exclude your testimony and reprimand you before the jury, which would be embarrassing, to say the least. A physician cowed by being in court makes a poor impression, whether he blusters his way through his testimony or assumes a sullen and defensive posture as if it were he who were on trial. If you cannot answer this question objectively concerning yourself, then perhaps a trusted, straight-shooting friend can tell you the answer.

5. Are you able to maintain equanimity?

If you are to be a good expert witness, then you must understand that, in court, the case you have reviewed is not yours to win or lose. It is the attorneys who must win the case. Any physician who takes the stand determined to make certain the outcome of the trial has completely misjudged his role in the trial. An expert witness should take the stand determined to impart his understanding of the case to the jury, so that the jury can make an informed decision. As part of maintaining equanimity, a physician should recognize the danger of using the retrospectoscope to make himself appear wise after the event. Pulmonary thromboembolus is a good example of a diagnosis that requires some equanimity. The clinical presentation of pulmonary thromboembolus can be notoriously vague. When the patient with vague symptoms dies before completing the sentence "Doc, I feel short of...," the diagnosis suddenly becomes obvious to all. A clinical physician testifying in a malpractice suit stemming from the death in this example must assess the clinical case as though he did not know the outcome in order to give the defendant the benefit of the doubt. Certainly there exist expert witnesses who do compromise their duty and try to testify in such a way as to assure the outcome of a trial; whether they do so for the sake of greed, vengeance, or zealotry, such practice constitutes unethical testimony and will be discussed in more detail in Chapter 7. Here we are discussing what is properly expected of you by courts and what you as an individual should do if you serve as an expert witness.

It is important to assess yourself according to these criteria before you agree to become an expert witness. Question 5 examines your motives for becoming an expert witness. Questions 1 and 3 are exactly the questions you will be asked to establish your qualifications as an expert witness for court. In the case of questions 2, 4, and 5, you will be tested on these points during examination by the attorneys, and you will triumph or fail as an expert witness based on how you handle yourself in interacting with the attorneys. It is far better to take stock of yourself before you ever get into court so that you already know the answers to the four questions above. If the answer to any of the five questions is "no," then you and others are best served by your not becoming an expert witness.

Reasons to Avoid Becoming an Expert Witness

Even if you meet all five of the criteria listed above, there remain reasons to avoid becoming an expert witness. If the requirements of your primary job run counter to the demands of being a good expert witness, then obviously your primary job should come first. If you are shy, then expert witness testimony is probably not for you. The personality of most pathologists is that of someone who prefers to work in the wings rather than on stage. Forensic pathologists, who do regularly testify in court as expert witnesses, are distinct from pathologists as a whole in that forensic pathologists, while enjoying the wings for the most part, are glad of the occasional chance to step onto the stage now and then. When you take the witness stand, you are in the spotlight, and you must be willing to meet the challenge of performing well before a group of strangers in a setting that can become very stressful very quickly. If you are so shy as to dislike that sort of intense attention, then better to avoid it in the first place.

An especially good reason to avoid entering into the expert witness business is if you have something to hide. Specifically, if you have some incident in your past that you would prefer remained secret, then do not get into the business of expert witness testimony. An attorney can enter your name into any Internet search engine and see what might turn up. For more detailed investigations into your life, services abound that will seek out all available public information on you, for a fee. (You can easily find such services yourself by conducting your own Internet search.) Once information has been found that an attorney thinks may prove useful in disarming you in court, then it can come out in court. Unpleasant secrets include any legal settlement or conviction, whether for malpractice, bad debt, failure to pay alimony, domestic violence, sexual abuse, substance abuse, etc. When you take the witness stand, you may be questioned about any record from your past. It is possible that the judge will not allow the attorney who raises the issue to pursue the issue of your past, but the attorney will tell the judge that your integrity is of utmost importance to the case and this secret matter needs to be discussed at length so that the ladies and gentlemen of the jury will understand what sort of integrity you the expert witness have demonstrated in your life. Even if the judge will not allow further questioning, the attorney has already dropped his bomb concerning you for the jury to hear. Attorneys know that a judge might try to stop them from following questioning into some aspect of your past, of course, so an attorney's opening salvo on the topic of your secret will be blunt to ensure the jury gets the point. For example, after your direct examination by the attorney who retained you as an expert witness ends, the attorney may begin his cross-examination as follows.

Cross-examining attorney: Good afternoon, Doctor.

Expert witness: Good afternoon.

Cross-examining attorney: Doctor, you stated a moment ago during your qualification as an expert witness that you are licensed to practice medicine in this state, did you not?

Expert witness: Yes. I am licensed to practice medicine in this state.

Cross-examining attorney: But you failed to mention, didn't you, that you lost your license to practice ten years ago because you became addicted to narcotics, which you were taking from the supply carts at the hospital where you worked at that time?

Attorney who called expert witness: Objection, Your Honor.

Judge: Sustained. Ladies and gentlemen of the jury, forget that you heard the previous question of the attorney representing the plaintiff.

The ladies and gentlemen of the jury will not forget. Even if no further questioning is allowed on this topic, the plaintiff's attorney has achieved his purpose. If further questioning is allowed, then it will be a very long afternoon for the physician expert witness. The only solace possible in such a situation for the physician on the witness stand is knowing that he will never have to go through such an ordeal on the witness stand again because he surely will never again accept another case as an expert witness.

How to Become an Expert Witness

Having decided that you want to try your hand at being an expert witness, how do you announce your interest? It is likely that you know someone who practices law, perhaps socially. At least you know the attorney who represents your group. You can always put the matter to the attorney that you know and ask whether he has heard of anyone looking for an expert medical witness. Another way to make your interest known is to contact the local bar association and ask whether they have any need of a speaker sometime in the future for one of their bar meetings. The bar association probably does need a speaker. If you have a topic, or at least a title, in mind when you call, then it will be easier for the representatives of the bar association to decide whether to invite you. It can be hard to get started because attorneys, like other people, heed Alexander Pope's maxim, "Be not the first by which the new is tried...." Once you get your first chance to present yourself as an expert witness, and provided you prove capable, your name will quickly make the rounds of attorneys in the area and you will begin to get more inquiries for your services.

Accepting or Refusing a Case

When an attorney calls you to consider a case, you should determine two things before accepting the case: what medical theory the attorney wants you to prove and what facts he has to back up that theory. If the theory is unsound or the facts do not support the theory, you have a choice to make. You can either decline the case outright, perhaps telling the attorney why you decline if you wish. The other option is to accept the case and provide a report indicating your reasons why the theory is unsound or the facts do not support the theory. Either way, remember that you have your own professional reputation to consider; you will face a loss of integrity, and no pay is worth such a loss.

If you tell the attorney that the position he proposes is unsound, then the attorney should thank you. He may in fact thank you, but then again he may not. Be prepared for the attorney to berate you or browbeat you for disagreeing with him. You need not take abuse, but know that such *ad hominem* attacks occasionally occur when you dissent from the attorney's party line. Be glad that you did not end up working with such an attorney any more than you did. Also, if you disagree with the attorney, then know that the attorney may try to sweet-talk you, as illustrated by this conversation:

> **Attorney**: I am looking for a physician who will support my idea that my client's hepatitis was caused by his need for pain medications directly due to the back pain that he developed as a result of his job at the factory.
> **Physician**: The sequence of events that you just presented does not make medical sense.
> **Attorney** (*louder and more slowly*): Maybe you didn't hear me, doc. I am looking for a physician who will support my idea.
> **Physician**: Then you need to keep looking.

The attorney never said anything that could be used to prove that he was offering the physician a carrot in the form of money, and he would deny it if asked. The attorney's implication at the time was unmistakable, however. Again, this is the sort of attorney that you want to avoid.

Another circumstance that should prompt you to decline a case is if the case somehow involves a close friend of yours. Not only do you risk your friendship in such cases, but your equanimity will certainly be called into question in court. No matter how fair-minded you may be, the situation is damning, and the jury itself will discredit your testimony. One should always avoid even a semblance of impropriety. Moreover, you risk your friendship.

Expectations of a Good Expert Witness

The British have established a list for their courts of what is expected of an expert witness.[1] Those expectations are as follows:

1. Expert evidence presented to the court should be, and should be seen to be, the independent product of the expert uninfluenced as to form or content by the exigencies of litigation.

2. An expert witness should provide independent assistance to the court by way of objective unbiased opinion in relation to matters within his expertise. An expert witness in the High Court should never assume the role of an advocate.

3. An expert witness should state the facts or assumptions upon which his opinion is based. He should not omit to consider material facts which could detract from his concluded opinion.

4. An expert witness should make it clear when a particular question or issue falls outside his expertise.

5. If an expert's opinion is not properly researched because he considers that insufficient data are available, then this must be stated with an indication that the opinion is no more than provisional. In cases where an expert witness who has prepared a report could not assert that the report contained the truth, the whole truth and nothing but the truth without some qualification, that qualification should be stated in the report.

6. If, after exchange of reports, an expert witness changes his view on a material matter having read the other side's expert's report or for any other reason, such a change of view should be communicated (through legal representatives) to the other side without delay and when appropriate to the court.

7. Where expert evidence refers to photographs, plans, calculations, analyses, measurements, survey reports or other similar documents, these must be provided to the opposite party at the same time as the exchange of reports.

Nor do the requirements of the expert witness testifying in Britain end there. An expert witness testifying in a British court must sign a statement attesting to the truth of the following three statements:

1. I understand that it is the duty of an expert to help the court on the matters within his expertise and that this duty overrides any obligation to the person from whom he has received instructions or by whom he is paid.

2. I have complied with this duty.

3. I believe that the facts I have stated in this report are true and that the opinions I have expressed are correct.

These principles for proper expert witness testimony have not yet been codi-
fied in such a way in the United States. The British principles are sound, however. If every expert witness testifying in the United States took upon himself
the moral obligations of the British principles, then there would be no call for
reform of expert witness testimony to stop unethical testimony.

Equanimity

To reiterate an essential point, a good expert witness approaches and evaluates
each case with equanimity. This point is being repeated because some physicians who should know better fall prey to a subtle loss of equanimity. Notice
that the first three expectations of an expert witness in Britain are related to assuring equanimity. Although you as an expert witness are retained by a side in
the dispute, you yourself are not to be on a side but rather you are to give your
opinion. The temptation may arise to give the sort of opinion wanted, but to
yield to that temptation is a miscarriage of justice; it is the attorneys who are
advocates, not you.[2]

What is the subtle way in which a physician can be led astray in assessing a
legal case with equanimity? As an expert witness, it is your responsibility to
transmit to the jury your understanding of the case, to serve as a teacher concerning the point you have been called to explain. It may be that you have strong
thoughts on what the outcome of the trial should be. If so, then the temptation is
to give not the sort of opinion that the attorney necessarily wants but rather the
sort of opinion that *you* want in order to make certain of the outcome of the trial.
You must keep in mind that it is not *your* responsibility as an expert witness to
win or lose a case. An individual whose responsibility is to win a case is an advocate, and in the United States attorneys, not witnesses, are the advocates of
clients in courts.

Should an expert witness forget his responsibility to maintain equanimity
about a case, then an ethical attorney will remind the witness that he is not to be
an advocate for a side in a trial. Unfortunately, some attorneys are unethical and
succumb to the lure of an expert witness who will agree to take the attorney's
case as an advocate for the attorney's client. A conscientious expert witness is
paid for his time, not his opinion, as we will discuss below. When an unscrupulous expert witness takes on cases with the point of view of an advocate, however, the fee looks more like payment for an opinion, so much so that attorneys
have a term they use to describe an expert witness who takes on legal cases as an
advocate. That term is "whore." When you are asked, as an expert witness, how
often you have testified for the defense and how often for the plaintiff in a civil
case (or for the prosecution in a criminal case), the attorney asking the question
is trying to establish for the jury whether you display equanimity by taking cases
on both sides of an issue or whether you are a zealot with your own agenda.
Zealots for either side can be found for cases that concern malpractice, automobile accidents, or the rights and responsibilities of employers versus laborers.

Perhaps the most charged of all cases is child abuse. Who can defend the deliberate injury of an infant? No one can defend child abuse. In a criminal trial, however, it is not child abuse that is on trial but rather a person who is accused of committing child abuse. A physician who takes up the banner of eradicating child abuse by making it his business to convict anyone accused of child abuse is just as guilty of becoming an advocate in court as is the physician who considers that all childhood injuries are accidental in nature. When a physician decides to take on certain sorts of legal cases with the intention of personally ensuring convictions or acquittals of whomever is accused, then that physician has become an advocate for a cause rather than an unbiased evaluator of information. Notice that the witnesses who become advocates invariably consider themselves right and the advocates for the other side "whores." The truth is that the advocates for both sides are engaged in a fee for guaranteed service transaction, which attorneys long ago recognized as a form of prostitution. Such dogged pursuit of an end makes the expert witness an intellectual vigilante. Both *The Ox-Bow Incident* and *An Enemy of the People* have been written to make clear what happens to people with good intentions who ride the swell of public opinion.

Court allows only two sorts of outcomes, guilty or not guilty. Those physicians who choose to become advocates for a cause will inevitably be pushed to one end or the other of the continuum. Nevertheless, biological systems and medical science rarely deal in absolutes. The truth in medicine is usually somewhere along the continuum, not at either end. The responsibility of being an advocate in court belongs solely to the attorneys, and the responsibility of deciding on the verdict for the defendant belongs solely to the jury.

Keeping Track of Prior Testimony

In the preceding section, mention was made of an expert witness being asked how many times he had testified for plaintiffs and how many times for the defendant physician. Remember that attorneys are trying to settle a disagreement, and because there are two sides to every story it only makes sense that you as an expert would take either side, if you are playing fairly. If you take exclusively one side, then you look (and may well be) biased. Therefore, if you are entering the expert witness business and will be sticking with the expert witness business, then you need to keep track of how often you take cases for each side in civil (or criminal) disputes. A practical problem arises here. It would likely sit ill with your clinical colleagues in town if you made a habit of testifying against them on the side of the plaintiff in a case. The solution to this dilemma is simple. Medical expert witnesses tend to take the side of the defendant physician for cases that are within the region in which they work. To balance this defendant work, the expert witnesses tend to the side of the plaintiff patient in cases removed from the region where they practice medicine. For example, if you live in St. Louis, Missouri, then you would choose to take cases representing the defendant in Missouri and Illinois, but for cases in Texas or Pennsylvania you would choose to work with the attorney representing the patient who is suing for malpractice.

Know that, whatever side you take, in the information age your testimony is more and more likely to be widely available for anyone to review. Do not think that you can claim opposing points of view upon a topic in separate trials without running the risk of being caught and exposed for such duplicity.

Report

If you have been hired as an expert witness, you will need to evaluate the case and communicate your conclusions to the attorney who retained you in a timely manner. The attorney who retains you might ask you to produce a report for him. On the other hand, the attorney might not want a written report because anything written down must be shared with the attorney for the other side according to the rules of discovery. If you are asked to produce a written report, then it should be concise and clear, addressing the following points:

1. **A list of the materials submitted to you for your review.**
    This will help you and the attorney reading the report to know exactly what you have reviewed. It also prevents dispute in court concerning whether you saw some document. Finally, in case some new evidence turns up, it will be clear whether you have seen the new evidence or not.

2. **A list of the questions to be answered.**
    This includes both questions of the attorney and his client and also any questions that you have concerning the case.

3. **A brief recapitulation of the circumstances surrounding the matter in question.**
    There is no need to rewrite the history of the case. This is simply a restatement of the pertinent points in the matter, whether as an outline or in a few paragraphs. Because you are writing this recapitulation of the history, it will naturally contain the points that you consider pertinent, stated in a way that makes sense to you. This summary of the history in your own words will refresh your memory concerning the case quickly when the matter comes to trial three years later, or when the second trial following appeal takes place eight years later.

4. **A list of your conclusions concerning the matter in question.**
    The list should include not only conclusions that would prove helpful to the client of the attorney who has retained you but also conclusions that might be damaging to the client's case. Attorneys hate surprises. A good attorney wants to know of any obstacle to his client's case so that he can prepare for the opposing argument in court. If the obstacle is great enough, it may hasten the end of the case through settlement.

5. **A list of recommendations.**
    This may include recommendations concerning finding additional information or suggested actions in light of your conclusions. Whatever you think would help to make a clearer or stronger case is appropriate. For example, you might recommend electron microscopy in addition to the immunohistochemical stains already done.

Remember that whatever you put in your report will be taken as true by the attorney who hired you, and you will be expected to attest to the truth of the statements and conclusions in your report in court. You should sign and date your report, of course. It might help to think of your report as having the significance of a pathology report—take the same sort of care in wording things correctly.

Finally, it can prove helpful to separate the items in your report under the two headings "Evidence for Consideration" and "Opinions Concerning Evidence." The lists of items provided to you for review and of the questions of the attorney would be "Evidence for Consideration," whereas your interpretation of the evidence and your own questions and recommendations based upon that evidence would be "Opinions." The usefulness of such headings will become clearer later in this chapter in the discussion of being paid for your work as an expert witness.

Competence in Testifying

As implied at the end of the preceding paragraph, the attorney who has retained you will expect that you will be able to testify competently and confidently in court. The art and skills of testifying will be discussed in detail in Chapter 6.

Payment as an Expert Witness

Expert witnesses are entitled to payment for their time spent applying their expertise to a specific case, just as a consultant is entitled to payment for evaluating a patient and offering an opinion about the patient's care. Pathologists are accustomed to being medical consultants, but they are not perhaps accustomed to charging for their consultations in the way that is appropriate for expert witnesses. Pathologists charge for rendering a diagnosis, which includes the time spent in evaluation, supplies used for evaluation, and overhead. Reviewing a specific case personally with the clinician who is caring for the patient, however, is a service that pathologists extend freely as part of their work. Likewise, pathologists freely offer their unique perspective at medical and surgical conferences. In the legal world, however, things are done differently.

What an Expert Witness Is Paid for

Precious little comes without a price attached to it in this world, hence the saying that there is no such thing as a free lunch. Attorneys have taken this truth to heart, and they bill for their time spent working on a case—every minute of it—whether through direct billing of the client at an hourly rate or by taking a case contingent upon receiving a percentage of the client's settlement. This careful accounting for the monetary worth of an attorney's time extends to the consultants an attorney hires and thus to any expert medical witness that an attorney retains. If you agree to take a case as an expert witness, then all the time that you spend working on the case is time for which you are entitled to be paid. This includes time spent in initially reviewing the case, time spent personally preparing for a deposition or for court, time spent meeting with attorneys, and time spent being deposed or testifying in court. It even includes time spent traveling to and from an encounter such as a deposition or court. Always know what it is that you as an expert witness are being paid for. An expert witness should never be paid for his testimony. You as an expert witness are being paid for your time. Thus your opinion, which has not been bought, remains your own. The distinction between being paid for your time and being paid for your testimony is vitally important. You can expect to be asked in court how much you are being paid. That question is common and reasonable, and you will have to answer it. But sometimes, whether as a sneaky trick or simply through careless wording, you will be asked by an attorney how much you are being paid for your testimony. The answer should be a polite yet firm reply that your testimony is not for hire, but that you have been paid for your time spent in considering the case. Payment for your time and the services you have rendered is appropriate. Payment for your testimony is illegal and unethical. Thoughtless confirmation that you have been paid for your testimony is unlikely to send you to jail, but it can damage your integrity in the eyes of the jury.

Setting Expert Witness Fees

The fee that you charge an attorney for your time as an expert witness is up to you, but it should be reasonable. For several reasons, it would be inaccurate to name a specific dollar amount here in the text that would prove useful. For one thing, rates vary from region to region across the United States. For another, inflation will further diminish the usefulness of a stated amount with the passing of time. If you know someone who is already taking cases as an expert witness, then perhaps you can ask your colleague what he charges.

If you have no idea what to charge for your time as an expert witness, then a conservative and safe initial fee is to charge the attorney by the hour for the time that you spend on the case and to set your fee at the level of your average hourly gross earnings. No one should be able to criticize you for setting your fee equal to your hourly wage. A safe place to start, however, may be well below the going rate in your area. Moreover, playing it overly safe may prove too little recompense to make the work that will be required of you worth your while. Following the practices of various other professionals, you could reasonably charge double your hourly wage for time spent on the legal case. Doubling your hourly wage should make sense to the jury. Assuming that you will be working on the case outside of your regular work, you can state that you are charging double for working on your time off just as plumbers or electricians charge double on weekends.

Another approach to setting the rate to charge for your time in considering legal cases was suggested to the author by one pathologist. This pathologist took his first case as an expert witness charging an hourly rate for his time that was equal to his average hourly gross earnings as a pathologist. This pathologist then raised his hourly rate $50 per hour with each successive case that he took as an expert witness. In other words, on his second case he charged his average hourly income plus $50 per hour, on his third case he charged his average plus $100 per hour, and so on. The pathologist who adopted this practice did so with the thought that he would continue to raise his rate in this way until an attorney balked. It may be of interest to learn that the pathologist who follows this course said that he has never yet had an attorney balk at his rate.

One factor to consider in deciding what rate to charge for your time in evaluating a legal case is the impression that your fee makes on attorneys. A high fee indicates to many attorneys that you are worth more. Conversely, a low fee suggests to many attorneys that you must not be very good at what you do. Before you set your fee at thousands of dollars per hour, however, remember that there is some limit to what attorneys are willing to pay. The United States is, after all, a free-market economy, so you can price yourself out of the market. Also, as mentioned above, you can expect to be asked in court how much you have been paid to take this case. If the price is too high, then you risk alienating the members of the jury. The members of the jury should all be upstanding citizens, but they are unlikely to command the sort of salary that a pathologist does. That you would charge as much as you make per hour at your regular job will make sense to the jury. To charge two or three times as much will probably make sense, too, if you explain how you do not wish to give up your free time without being paid extra to do so. To charge twenty times your regular income may strike the jury as exorbitant. Certainly the opposing attorney will tell the jury he thinks such a fee is exorbitant.

However you decide upon the fee that you will charge for your time in a case, you should know that attorneys are willing to pay large fees because the job they are asking you to do is hard work in a specialized area. Reviewing a medical record and offering an opinion may seem easy at first. It may even turn out to be easy at first. Nevertheless, law, like medicine, has plenty of difficult cases. Just as your usual day is filled with routine specimens and a few curve balls, with a knuckleball thrown in every once in a while, so too the review of medical cases for an attorney will consist of some routine work mixed with some odd pitches to keep you on your toes. If you expect that you will feel as though you have earned every penny of your fee by the time the legal matter has been resolved, then you will be less likely to be surprised and frustrated by the vicissitudes of the legal system.

You should also know that your fee comes to you, in some way, from the client of the attorney who paid you, as discussed in the previous chapter. If you are testifying on behalf of the defense in a malpractice suit, then your fee is ultimately being paid by the insurance company that covers the practice of the physician who has been sued. If you are testifying on behalf of the patient plaintiff, then your fee will come out of whatever settlement the patient plaintiff receives, as discussed in Chapter 4. If the patient plaintiff's total award is less than your fee, then your payment will depend upon the integrity of the attorney who retained you. Some attorneys take pride in conducting their business in a professional and upstanding way and would pay the expert witnesses out of their office's assets in such a strait. Others might try to avoid paying you. As already discussed, attorneys will take care to make certain that they accept only cases likely to yield a large monetary award for their clients.

The one way in which you cannot set your fee is to make your fee contingent on the size of the award in a civil suit; such an action is unethical for an expert witness. Attorneys are permitted to set their fees at a percentage of the size of the award, but expert witnesses may not. The reason courts will not allow an expert witness's fee to be contingent upon the outcome of the trial should be clear—it gives the expert witness a vested interest in the outcome of the trial and thus has the potential to taint the expert witness's opinion. (It is acceptable for an attorney to have a vested interest in the outcome of the trial because the attorney's client is paying the attorney to have a vested interest in the outcome of the trial.)

Whatever fee you set for your services, the fee should be agreed upon before you accept the case. Do not hesitate to clarify the charges for your time in the initial phone contact. Agreeing on the fee ensures that everyone understands who is to pay your fee and how much is to be paid. If you know and are familiar with the attorney from having worked together before, an oral agreement is usually sufficient. Otherwise, it is best to get the agreement in writing. Letters exchanged between the attorney and you are sufficient, or else you may use a simple contract. You do not need a complicated contract, and an attorney who represents you will have access to the sort of simple contract you need. (Attorneys call this sort of contract form a "boilerplate.") Whether you use an exchange of letters or a contract, there are a few points that should be covered so that both you and the attorney know what you are agreeing to.

1. You need to have an explicit agreement that you will be paid for your services rendered in the event that the case is settled. Payment should not be contingent upon completion of a trial, especially since few malpractice suits ever go to trial.
2. If you will need to travel to the trial by air and stay in a hotel, you might want to discuss with the attorney having your airplane ticket and

hotel accommodations arranged and paid for by the attorney's office. This will spare you the trouble of personal expense and of billing for the expense. It will be necessary to add a paragraph or item specifically addressing the points of travel, room, and board if they are an issue.

3. If the case that you have accepted as an expert witness will not be going to trial for a long time, then it is reasonable to request payment as services are provided. Alternatively, you may ask for and be paid a retainer.

Have your own attorney look over a contract form that you are going to use before you use it.

There does exist an alternative to working as an expert witness for a fee, and that is to work as an expert witness *pro bono*. To work *pro bono* means to offer your services for free. Why would a physician work on a case for an attorney for free? Some physicians work *pro bono* because of particular passion that they have for the type of cases that they accept, such as child abuse cases. If you take a case *pro bono* out of a sense of zeal and civic duty, then you must be careful that your zeal does not sway your decision. Also, your zeal may be perceived as a bias by the jury, particularly if you are, in fact, biased. Some physicians take cases *pro bono* because they wish to be paid not in coin but with something else, such as a favor. Still other physicians take cases *pro bono* and have their fee donated in their name to a charity of their choice.

Getting Stiffed

Because the money used to pay an expert witness comes from the attorney's client, attorneys have no reason to balk at paying an expert witness compensation for the expert witness's time. Nevertheless, some attorneys do balk at paying physicians for the physician's time. One way is to simply neglect to pay. Another way to avoid paying a physician for his time is to tell the physician that he is being called as a fact witness only.

If an attorney has already hired you as an expert witness, then there should of course be no later talk of your testifying as a fact witness only. The situation being discussed here usually arises when you are called to testify concerning a report that you generated in the course of your usual work—a surgical pathology report, for instance. Recall that a fact witness can be compelled to come to court but that an expert witness may choose whether or not to go to court. As we discussed in Chapter 2, a physician may be called as a fact witness if all that the physician is asked to do is to testify concerning what he did. For example:

Attorney: Did you receive a specimen on October 7, 2000 from a patient named Bill Jones?
Physician: Yes.
Attorney: Did you process that specimen?
Physician: Yes.

Attorney: Will you please read the ladies and gentlemen of the jury what your diagnosis is on the report?
Physician: Squamous cell carcinoma of the lung, moderately differentiated.
Attorney: And is that your signature at the bottom of the report?
Physician: Yes.
Attorney: So you made this diagnosis yourself and signed the report?
Physician: Yes.
Attorney: Thank you, no further questions, Your Honor.

In the exchange above, the pathologist was asked no question that was beyond the ability of most of the people in this country to answer, so the pathologist was questioned by the attorney as a fact witness. With the first question whose answer required the pathologist to answer as a pathologist, such as "What is a squamous cell carcinoma," the pathologist is being asked to use his specially gained expertise, and thus the pathologist is being asked to function as an expert witness. If the attorney insisted that the pathologist was only being called as a fact witness, then with his first call for the pathologist's opinion, the pathologist was being cheated. Unfortunately, this scenario is replayed over and over across the nation. Because the ploy is old, however, the options open to the physician expert witness who is placed in such a position are well-established.

The best option is to talk with the attorney who is calling you as a witness before ever going to trial. Whenever you are served a subpoena to appear in court as a witness, it is wise to call the attorney who sent the subpoena and ask in what capacity you are being asked to testify. Some attorneys seem to think that if they have in hand a report of yours that they did not commission from you personally, then you are obligated to testify as a fact witness, thus saving them money. Provided that you call beforehand, you can discuss with the attorney the difference between what he can expect from you as a fact witness and what he can expect from an expert witness. As a fact witness, you will testify only to what is in your report, that is, your name, the patient's name, the specimen received (as written on the report), and the diagnosis (as written on the report). If that sort of information is all the attorney wants, you can point out that the attorney can get the same result by having someone such as the court reporter simply read your report or by having the report admitted into evidence as an exhibit. If you are being called to court, however, it is likely that the attorney does wish to ask you questions that require your professional evaluation for proper answers. Make it clear to the attorney that you will express no opinions if testifying purely as a fact witness, and thus you will answer no questions concerning what you think, believe, or know related to the case. There will be no reasoning by you as a witness on the stand; the only opinions that will come out in your testimony as a fact witness will be the ones already in your report. The usefulness of heading sections of your report as "Evidence Considered" and "Opinions Concerning Evidence" is that you can show the attorney what it is that you will discuss as a fact witness and what you will not discuss as a fact witness. Some attorneys seem to have difficulty making the distinction between fact and opinion, so headings can help clarify the situation. It can also help the attorney who has been convinced that you should be paid as an expert witness to argue for money to pay you appropriately if he must convince his client or superior.

If you get into court and the attorney still insists that he is only calling you as a fact witness, then a good answer to questions about an opinion in your report is "Yes, that is what it says in my report," as though you are reading the words but cannot speak independently to verify their accuracy. With luck, and some good sense on the part of the attorney, the attorney will realize that your testimony is more useful as a cooperative expert witness than as a reluctant fact witness with an axe to grind. You really should not grind your axe on the attorney in court, but the attorney has no way of knowing for certain that you will not grind your axe on him in court, and few attorneys are willing to take that chance.

Prior to going to court, you may wish to check, or have your personal attorney check, to see whether there is any published agreement between your state bar association and state medical association discussing the ethical boundaries framing professional interactions between members of the two associations. As stated above, this scenario has occurred many times, and it may be covered in such an agreement. In talking with your own attorney, it will be necessary to explain the situation to him. Ask his opinion about how to proceed and how far to push, particularly before going to the next step, which is to appeal to the judge in the case.

If the attorney's questions are fact sorts of questions, as outlined above, then it may be that you are being called purely as a fact witness, and if so you will have to go and testify as such. If you are testifying as a fact witness on your report, then the good news is your time on the stand should be brief, a matter of a few minutes. The attorney's interests and questions, however, may make it clear that he is interested in your testimony as an expert. In that case, if he insists that you will testify for him only as a fact witness and that you will not be reimbursed for your time, then you may have success by telling the attorney that you will not answer further until the judge in the matter hears the basis for your refusal to state opinions and, having heard your basis, then issues an order for you to answer regardless. This exchange with the judge may end up taking place in court and require that you address the judge directly. Remember to address the judge with respect; the judge is not the one mistreating you, and you are appealing to him to take your side in this disagreement with the attorney. Judges usually get the point that the attorney is trying to stiff you, and a few words from a judge can do wonders for loosening an attorney's purse strings. If, however, the judge orders you to testify as an expert witness without pay in this case, then do so. Remember that the judge's word is law in his court, and if you continue to refuse you can be found in contempt of court and spend some time in jail until you learn proper respect.

We have outlined above the steps to take to push the matter of being recognized as an expert witness for expert work as far as it can be pushed. In a specific case, you will have to weigh the costs and benefits to determine how far to push and when it becomes too costly in your time and energy to continue pushing. Again, it would be wise to discuss your specific case with your own attorney. Naturally, the judge and all the attorneys involved in the matter have known reputations and known opinions of their own on certain topics. Even though these reputations and opinions are unknown to you, your attorney may be well aware of them, allowing him to give you handcrafted advice akin to the specifically tailored conversation you have with a clinician at the microscope over a biopsy.

Having agreed to a contract, you can begin your work reviewing the case. With luck, all should go well and you will be paid cheerfully and promptly. Sometimes, however, it becomes difficult to collect your fee, particularly if you waited to be paid until after the trial, and the verdict was against the client who hired you. If the attorney who contacted you agreed in his letter to pay your fee or to guarantee that the fee would be paid, then you may complain to the local bar association or to the medicolegal committee of the county (or perhaps state) medical society. Your complaint should move things along, for no attorney whose livelihood depends on reliable medical witnesses wants a bad reputation among physicians. If the attorney did not guarantee your fee, you can still ask the attorney to use his influence to get his client to pay you. The attorney is usually in a better position to do this than you are.

Despite best efforts on the part of physician expert witnesses, however, it remains true that sometimes an attorney simply will not pay and there proves to be no way to collect the money that you are due. There are occasional bad debts in the expert witness business. Sometimes the best that you can do is to take your lumps, grin, and bear it. At the least, you will know never again to take another case from the attorney who stiffed you. You can also steer other physicians away from that attorney if asked.

References

1. National Justice Compania Naviera SA v. Prudential Assurance Co Ltd., The Ikarian Reefer [1993] 2 Lloyds Rep 68.
2. McAbee GN. Improper expert medical testimony: existing and proposed mechanisms of oversight. J Legal Med 1998;19:257–72.

6
Natural History of a Legal Suit

Preliminary Stages

Your first notice of involvement in a legal matter if you are the defendant in a lawsuit will be a summons. If you are a fact witness, your first notice may be a subpoena. If you are serving as an expert witness, then your first notice was being contacted by an attorney to consider taking the case. Notification of a malpractice suit is discussed in Chapter 4; fact and expert witness distinctions are discussed in Chapters 2 and 5. However you became involved in the case, for you this particular legal battle has begun. In order to be an effective part of the legal proceedings, up to and including a trial, you need to prepare yourself. You prepare yourself by reviewing the case and then by reviewing the case and planning for trial with the attorney that you are working with.

Reviewing the Case with an Attorney

Some people who do not work in law think that it is unethical to review a case with an attorney in order to prepare for a trial, but that thought is no different from saying that it is cheating to take a history from a patient prior to performing a physical exam. It is not unethical to review the case and form a plan for the trial with your attorney; it is essential. Attorneys would say that you have a moral obligation to plan a strategy for the case with your attorney. Remember that our legal system considers that justice is best served by amassing and considering all the evidence and then having that evidence presented as clearly as possible to a jury. The evidence cannot be presented clearly without preparation and planning prior to trial.

Once you have settled on a date to meet with the attorney to review the case, you must first review the case yourself. A methodical approach to case review for expert witnesses is presented in Chapter 5. Although the attorney you are working with may not ask for a report, the discipline necessary to produce a useful report would serve well for a physician reviewing a case. In brief, the steps are to record the following:

1. A list of the materials submitted to you for your review.
2. A list of the questions to be answered.
3. A brief recapitulation of the circumstances surrounding the matter in question.
4. A list of your conclusions concerning the matter in question.
5. A list of recommendations.

Even if your attorney wants no written report from you (and he may not if he is representing you as the defendant in a malpractice suit), having some notes of your own that record items under the five headings above will make your meeting with your attorney go more smoothly. If the attorney were to ask you whether you had seen a certain consult report, then a glance at the report and at your list of materials reviewed would provide a quick answer. You would know, for example, that you had seen the consult report of such a date on the plaintiff patient from a certain pathologist but that the addendum report, from a week later, was unknown to you.

Notes written during your review of the case can help you in another way. Included in your list of questions should be questions that you have of the attorney. Patients often bemoan their inability to remember questions that they wanted to ask while meeting with a physician, and thus physicians recommend that patients jot down questions as they think of them to help the patient remember his questions. Hardly any patient does so, but the suggestion is no less sensible. It makes equally good sense for a physician client of an attorney to jot down his questions for the attorney so that the physician can ask those questions when he meets with the attorney.

If you are serving as an expert witness, it is helpful to the attorney who hired you to provide him with your curriculum vitae when you meet. Do not give him the full thirty pages. All the attorney needs is a single sheet of paper that lists your name, current occupation, education and training, board certification and state medical licenses, membership in professional societies, and any pertinent publications of yours that will fit the room left on that one page.

Teaching and Learning

A good pathologist, or physician for that matter, is a lifelong student of medicine and also an effective teacher. When you meet with the attorney you are working with, it would be ideal if you were able to assume the roles of both student and teacher during the meeting. The attorney has things to say that you need to hear and understand. Likewise, you have special knowledge that can help the attorney do his job more effectively.

The attorney can teach you what to expect as the legal process in which you are involved progresses, whether a settlement is likely or advisable, whether you will be called to testify in a deposition, and how likely a trial is. The attorney can teach you how to conduct yourself—that is, how to dress, how to walk, how to sit, how to keep an amiable poker face—whether in deposition or in court.

(We will go over points on this topic later in this chapter, but listen to the attorney even if you have read this chapter. A good attorney takes no chances and will at the least reinforce points that you already know. Besides, the attorney's points will be tailored to a specific case in a specific courtroom, far better than any book can do.) Finally, the attorney can teach you about the other persons involved in the trial, what the judge is like, what the opposing attorneys are like and how they operate, and which expert witnesses the opposing sides have retained.

You as a pathologist have knowledge that will help the attorney, and it is best if the attorney is as eager to learn from you as you are to learn from him. Serving as a teacher is a role familiar to any pathologist, and slipping into a familiar role can help to put you at ease to some extent. The attorney needs to learn two things from you. First, the attorney needs to learn and understand those points in the case that are favorable to his client's position (if you have been hired as an expert witness) or to you (if you are the attorney's client as the defendant in a malpractice suit). Second, the attorney needs to learn and understand those points that are unfavorable to the case he is representing. Even if the attorney fails to ask you about unfavorable points, you should bring them to his attention. He needs to know, and better to hear it as both of you plan how best to present the medical evidence in the case to the jury than to wait and hear it for the first time in court from a witness for the other side.

Beware of Familiarity

Remember that whenever you meet with an attorney, even an attorney representing you, that the attorney is not a physician. Never assume the familiarity with the attorney that you would with a physician colleague. You may be an expert witness and have come to know and to like this particular attorney, but you would be wise to keep the relationship professional and formal. Never speak in jest about medical matters. Never discuss medical matters that do not pertain to the case at hand with the attorney. The following example illustrates the point.

An attorney just out of law school was dating a fourth-year medical student, so classmates of the medical student came to know the attorney socially. The attorney was a likeable sort of fellow, so a few of the medical students would sometimes invite the attorney to join them when going out for a night on the town. One night, the students began talking about a case that they were familiar with in which a patient's care had been mismanaged and in which the patient had suffered as a result. The attorney quickly asked for a name so that he could contact the patient and offer his services as an attorney to represent the patient in a malpractice suit. The students refused to tell the attorney the name, and that was the end of careless talk and fraternizing with attorneys for those medical students.

Even when the case is your own malpractice suit, the wisest course is to conduct yourself as though everything you say will be repeated publicly before a crowded courtroom whenever you talk with an attorney, even your own. This recommendation may seem to contradict the counsel above to tell an attorney representing you in a malpractice suit the points that are harmful to your case, but there is no contradiction for a specific reason. Concerning your own malpractice suit, it is permissible to tell the attorney points that are damaging because with regard to the malpractice case the attorney has been hired as an advocate to represent you. The attorney would be violating his professional obligation to turn evidence that you give him against you. Evidence concerning something apart from your malpractice suit, however, does not concern a matter for which the attorney must act as an advocate on your behalf, so he can use that information as he wishes.

(The preceding paragraph assumes that the charge of malpractice against you is not for a willful act of negligence on your part. If you were to tell your attorney that the patient suffered because you were too drunk at work to walk across the laboratory and check the results of a test, then the attorney is ethically bound to reveal what he knows to the judge if asked. Let us assume that such an egregious act of malpractice is impossible. A more reasonable situation would be for you to tell the attorney that you considered the frozen section to have an area diagnostic of malignancy but that it is possible that some pathologists would not have interpreted the frozen section as diagnostic of malignancy. That admission to your attorney could not be used against you by the attorney, but it could help him to plan for your defense by anticipating that an expert witness called by the patient's attorney will say that the frozen section was negative for tumor.)

Beware of Resident Teaching

It may be that you practice in a setting where you are obligated to teach resident physicians training in pathology. A chance to see and learn something of the workings of the legal system in the United States would be appropriate for a resident physician, but there are a few things to consider before including a resident in a meeting with an attorney. First, if the trial is your own as a defendant, then you should no more invite a resident to participate in a meeting with your attorney than you should talk about the case with the resident to begin with.

If, on the other hand, you are meeting with an attorney who has retained you as an expert witness, then it may be appropriate for a resident to observe the proceedings between you and the attorney. First ask the attorney's permission to allow the resident to attend the meeting. Attorneys learn their own craft in the same sort of way, so they understand the importance of an apprenticeship and tend to be kindly disposed to such a request. If, however, the case involves malpractice, then the attorney may decline to permit the resident to observe in an effort to protect his client's privacy (that is, the privacy of the physician being sued for malpractice). For this same reason, do not name names when reviewing a case with a resident even if the attorney is willing for the resident to observe.

Having received the attorney's permission, you should tell the resident the essence of the medical matter involved and of your role in the matter before meeting with the attorney. You should make certain to tell the resident that he is to observe only and, after the introductions, to speak only when spoken to and to respond only when a question is directly asked of him.

Residents should be seen and not heard in a meeting with an attorney (or attorneys) for several reasons. One obvious reason that a resident attending a meeting with an attorney should observe the proceedings silently and hold questions until after the end is because it is not the resident's time and expertise that the attorney is paying for, it is yours. Another reason that residents should keep silent grows out of the way in which medicine is taught in the United States, where medical students are trained to know answers and to sound confident in giving an answer. That confidence is what distinguishes a fourth-year student from a third-year student, hence the saw that a fourth-year student is sometimes wrong but never in doubt. One problem for a resident, who was but recently a medical student, is that medical students are taught that "I don't know" is an unacceptable answer. It would be more accurate to teach students that an immediate appeal to "I don't know" is an unacceptable answer and that it will take years of experience before a student has earned the right to give "I don't know" as an answer. Nevertheless, "I don't know" is the correct answer in some circumstances. Residents still lack the tempering that comes from handling cases that defy explanation, and residents also lack the sage humility that accompanies this sort of tempering. In other words, residents have the potential to combine youthful enthusiasm with inexperience. The possibility of harm being done by medical students is minimized because students realize that they know virtually nothing. Residents, though, have begun to learn a thing or two, which gives them confidence. By the time that a physician in training has reached residency, he has begun to grow accustomed to the debate of medical matters in settings such as a morbidity and mortality conference, and he may be willing to chime in with his opinion. What residents forget is that everyone attending a morbidity and mortality conference is a physician, and thus everyone at the conference has the training necessary to judge for himself whether a comment is appropriate or outlandish. The attorney with whom you are meeting does not have medical training, so he cannot discern any difference between the opinion of the pathologist that he has retained (that is, you) and the opinion of the resident. No difference in accuracy of diagnosis, no difference in likelihood of occurrence, no difference in certainty of being correct will be apparent to the attorney. This can prove awkward at best, as the following scenario illustrates.

During review of a civil lawsuit brought against a car manufacturer for wrongful death in a traffic accident, the attorney asked the expert witness whom he had retained to what extent the airbag may have contributed to the injuries suffered by the decedent. The expert witness (an attending physician with 20 years of experience) gave his opinion that the airbag had not especially contributed to the injuries, along with some reasons to support his opinion. The resident then spoke up to say that he had done a rotation in emergency medicine a year and a half ago in which he saw a patient with similar injuries who had been injured by the airbag and that it was important to consider whether the airbag had an internal tether or not before making a conclusion.

In this scenario, the resident has undermined the expert witness in two ways. The resident has contradicted the expert's opinion, and he has, by mentioning his own experience with the latest technology while still a medical student, given the impression that the attending physician is out of touch with current thought. It may be that the attending physician is out of touch, but provided that the attorney has chosen his expert witness carefully, it is more likely that the resident physician does not know as much about this case as either the attorney or the attending physician who is reviewing the case as an expert witness. In this case, the resident did not know that the attorney and physician had already discussed the airbag question over the telephone the week before, so there was no need for them to go into some of the details that they had already discussed, such as the presence of an internal tether. An interruption like the one above should not cause any miscarriage of justice, but it will derail the thoughts of both the attorney and the expert physician witness. It takes longer than you may think to restore the conversation to its proper track after an interruption like that.

The author tells any resident invited to observe a meeting with an attorney that there is to be no interruption, even if what the author says is flat wrong. After all, it is the author's opinion that is being sought, and it is the author's responsibility to get the facts straight. Residents are told that even if what the author says is wrong, they are not to make that error known until after the attorney has left. If the author is wrong, then it is and remains the author's responsibility to straighten things out with the attorney, not the resident's.

The observation of the legal system need not be restricted to meetings with attorneys. Residents may observe depositions and go to court, if their schedule permits. The same rules apply, and it is always polite to ask the attorneys involved if a resident may observe the deposition. There is no need to ask permission for a resident to attend a case being tried in court because court is a public forum in almost all cases.

Reviewing the Case Yourself

You must review the medical record of the case involved prior to testifying, whether that testimony be in deposition or in trial. If you have been hired as an expert witness, you must also review your own report. The material needs to be fresh in your mind. You are allowed to take the medical chart with you onto the witness stand (and you should take the chart, or at least your report), but you should have to look at the chart for only a few things or if you are asked about a minor point. It makes a bad impression on the jury if you must fumble through the chart to answer every question. The opposing attorney will quickly pick up on your lack of preparation if you must look up every answer, and not only will he attack more strongly when asking you questions in his turn, but he may well try to embarrass you by asking some simple question such as whether the patient in question was a man or a woman. If you must look up the sex of the patient, the opposing attorney will be able to point that out to the jury. If you at least know the sex, the opposing attorney can still comment "Well, at least that is one fact in this case that you didn't have to look up here on the witness stand," Either way, the jury will be amused at your expense. When reviewing a case prior to testifying, you would also do well to review a textbook or two on the medical problem that will be discussed. It never hurts to search the medical literature for any pertinent articles. If you are testifying as an expert witness, then more is expected of you and you might need to dig still deeper into the literature if that might help your case. Presumably, as an expert witness you already did your homework in the medical literature when reviewing the case, so a search done the week before testifying would be for any pertinent articles published in the year or two or three from the time you took the case until the time for you to testify concerning the case.

Deposition

What Is a Deposition?

A deposition is a legal proceeding in which a witness testifies under oath. A deposition always precedes the trial and takes place outside the courtroom. The testimony is recorded, either in writing or by a videotape recording, so that it may be read (or replayed) in court as a substitute for your personal appearance in the trial. In effect, a deposition is *your* portion of the trial, without any trimmings such as other witnesses, judge, or jury. A deposition can be taken from a witness at any location mutually agreeable to the witness, the attorneys representing each side, and to the court reporter who will record your testimony. A deposition is a formal legal proceeding, and the word even sounds imposing, but it can prove a benefit to the physician witness.

Attorneys may choose to depose a witness prior to trial for various reasons. Some state laws require that witnesses in certain types of trials (such as murder trials) give sworn testimony before the trial begins. This testimony may be in the form of a preliminary hearing or as a deposition. In civil trials, an expert witness may be retained from another state, and the attorneys may decide that a deposition is the best way to elicit the expert witness's testimony because of potential conflicts between the schedules of the trial and of the expert witness. In that case, the attorneys all come to the expert witness rather than the expert witness going to the attorneys. This seems expensive. If, however, the expert witness is charging hundreds of dollars per hour of his time, then the cost of three attorneys flying to the expert and taking up two hours of the expert's time may be little different from the cost of flying the expert witness to the trial for two or three days. Other factors may enter into the decision to depose as well. A cross-country deposition in January can look especially attractive to attorneys if the attorneys are in Cleveland and the expert witness lives in San Diego. A third reason for a deposition is if the attorneys are unsure of the witness and wish to pin down the expert witness's statements and opinions concerning the case. We have already discussed that a good expert witness will consider the case and draw his conclusions and then tell his story clearly and consistently to the attorneys he speaks with from the first conversation until the trial is over and the appeals are exhausted. Some attorneys, however, wish either to have a trial run at examining a witness with whom they are unfamiliar or else they lack faith that a witness will stick by his story until the witness formally testifies on the subject. By testifying in a deposition, an expert witness has formally stated his positions in a way that is legally binding upon him. Prior to testifying, an expert witness could, without any legal repercussion, say one thing and then reverse himself upon testifying. (Although reversing yourself in such a way might be without legal repercussions, it is not without repercussions.) Still, it is clear that some attorneys are simply uncomfortable with trusting that a witness will speak truthfully regardless of the setting in which he speaks. If you had suffered the shock in court of having a witness reverse himself while on the witness stand, as many attorneys have, then you would probably understand why so many attorneys feel more comfortable deposing their witnesses prior to trial.

Advantages of a Deposition

Convenience

Regardless of why a deposition is being conducted, the deposition should be scheduled at the convenience of all parties who will attend, including you. It can be in your office or at one of the attorney's offices. The witness being deposed is, in a way, an invited guest to this legal proceeding, so the attorneys will generally defer to the witness's choice if the witness has a preference on the venue for the deposition. If you have a conference room available in your office, then your office is probably the most convenient place for you to be deposed. You can expect anywhere from two to four attorneys and one court reporter to be present, so the room for the deposition should hold a half dozen people comfortably. Everyone attending the deposition will have some sort of notes either to refer to or take, so there should be a table around which everyone may sit comfortably and spread out their papers. If you own or rent your office, then there should be no reason that you cannot hold a deposition in your office if you wish. If you are provided an office, as may be true for those who practice academic pathology, then the pathology department or hospital may have a policy concerning whether you can be deposed in their office space. After all, if you are being paid for your time as an expert witness and none of that money is going to the owner of the office space, then the owner may take exception to your use of the space to earn extracurricular income. Presumably you have requested and received approval to take on legal cases for review as an expert witness, but if hospital policy forbids you to pursue your extracurricular activities while on the job, then you will need to be deposed elsewhere, such as in an attorney's office. (On the bright side, you can charge for the time you spend driving to and from the deposition.)

Fair to All Sides

Sometimes as an expert witness an attorney will call and ask you a few questions about a case. After you answer the questions, the attorney will ask you to please help him by signing a statement that he will have typed and sent to you concerning the answers that you just gave over the telephone. The attorney invariably states that this is just a small matter that will help him and will save you the expert from the inconvenience of a deposition. Remember that one of the hallmarks of the American legal system is that if one side gets something then every side gets that same something. It is unnecessary to have a conference call whenever any attorney calls, but something written down should be available to all sides. Provided that you wrote a report, then all sides should have a copy of your report. The author is less certain that all sides will receive a copy of such a signed statement, however, and it can set off an avalanche of calls and similar requests from the other attorneys involved in the case. Rather than sign any such statement, the author always insists that if his word is not good enough over the telephone, then the fairest way to pin him down in his statements legally is through a deposition, where all sides will be represented. The attorney who has made the request for a specially signed statement usually grumbles and offers various reasons why the author should do things in the way that the attorney asks, but the author holds firm, always emphasizing his intention that the matter be done in a way that is fair to all parties. This insistence on a deposition will impress upon all the attorneys involved that you as an expert witness are playing by the rules and win you some respect, albeit grudgingly from the one whose request was thwarted. It is important to be fair and to have a reputation for fairness among attorneys if you are going to make a habit of testifying as an expert witness.

Conduct at Deposition

A deposition looks much less formal than court. The proceeding is probably in your own office suite. The attorneys may show up in knit shirts and loafers. If the deposition is written, then there is no reason you cannot attend in scrubs. Although it may seem casual, do not be lulled into thinking that a deposition is an informal proceeding. A witness who is being deposed is testifying, and the statements you make to the attorneys in deposition are as binding as if you were in a crowded courtroom before a judge and jury.

A deposition serves attorneys by allowing each side to take your sworn statements prior to the trial. It may help to think of a deposition as the bidding round in a game of contract bridge. After bidding is completed, everyone at the table should have a fair idea of the cards in everyone else's hand. The playing of the cards corresponds with the trial, where it is revealed which player is the most clever user of the knowledge gained during the bidding. As discussed in the previous paragraph, following the deposition, each attorney will know what you are now bound to say later in court. Knowing what you will say, each attorney can then adjust his strategy accordingly. One attorney may need to work on an argument to rebut, or contradict, your statements. The other may decide you are a particularly strong witness for his side and shuffle the order of appearance of his witnesses to move you into a starring role. Conversely, some weakness of yours may be apparent to an opposing attorney at the deposition, and he will now be able to plot how best to exploit that weakness to serve his client.

A deposition seems different from court while you are being deposed because some of the principal players in a trial are absent. There is no judge, so if an attorney has an objection during the deposition he will say so, and then you will go ahead and answer the question as if no objection were raised. Later, at the trial, the judge will review the deposition, and if he sustains the objection, then your answer will be edited out of what the jury hears. If your written deposition is accepted in place of your testimony during the trial, your words will be read aloud to the jury by someone sitting in the witness stand. Any subtle tone of voice used by you during the deposition will be lost, and any medical jargon is likely to be mangled, so it is more important than ever to say what you mean and to keep it in laymen's terms. If your testimony was videotaped, then the jury will watch you give your deposition on a television monitor. For this reason, if giving a videotape deposition, look into the camera as though it were the jury when you answer so that you will be looking at the jury when they watch your deposition. Try not to use your hands. You can learn how to be more effective testifying on camera by watching television newscasts. The jury will see you in the same way that you see the news anchor, so do what the anchor does. One hint is to avoid wearing a white dress shirt or blouse. Wear instead an unassuming colored shirt, such as blue oxford cloth, or a colored top. The white of a dress shirt will glare on the television screen when the tape is replayed. In a similar vein, be mindful that the videotape will be seen later, perhaps months later, and try to avoid clothing that looks especially seasonal, such as a heavy woolen jacket or a summery tie.

Despite the informal setting and tone prior to and following the sworn testimony, remember that you are always a sheepish physician among wolves. Convey no meaningful information about the case to the plaintiff's attorney during the informal times (either before the deposition begins, during a break, or after the deposition ends). Be polite when not testifying on the record and speak polite nothings. Follow the rules of etiquette. Assume that the attorneys are fishing for information that they can use against you. Now more than ever it is not the time to joke about medical matters.

If you change the substance of your statements when you later testify in court, you can be sure that one attorney will refer back to your statements made under oath in the deposition. That is why you must stick to the matter being discussed during the deposition, always maintaining a serious and professional manner. Furthermore, if the attorneys have a copy of your transcribed deposition when in court at the trial, then you need to have a copy, too. The wise witness always asks for a copy of his deposition before testifying in the trial. It is essential to review your deposition before you testify. Review will help you keep your statements consistent, and it will also protect you from the attorney who twists a statement you made in deposition and asks you to agree with that twisted statement during the trial, as in the following case.

During a trial in which a family was suing the decedent's employer for wrongful death due to exposure to harmful chemicals, the expert witness (a pathologist) was asked by the attorney representing the family what the pathologist had found at autopsy. The pathologist said that he had found marked emphysema. The plaintiff's attorney then asked the pathologist whether he remembered testifying earlier in a deposition. The pathologist replied that he did remember testifying in a deposition. The attorney then asked whether the pathologist recalled saying that the physical findings at autopsy indicated that the decedent had evidence of a malignant neoplasm. The pathologist replied that he would be happy to read exactly what he said concerning a malignant neoplasm from his copy of the transcript of the deposition, beginning at the top of page 17, as follows

> **Plaintiff's attorney**: What did you notice first about the decedent at autopsy?
>
> **Pathologist**: The decedent was gaunt, with the remains measuring 72 inches in length and weighing 136 pounds.
>
> **Plaintiff's attorney**: What sorts of things could cause the decedent to be so thin?
>
> **Pathologist**: Several things, among them chronic illnesses such as tuberculosis or a malignant neoplasm, neither of which was present at autopsy, and also chronic obstructive pulmonary disease, which was present at autopsy."

The attorney in this example gambled by violating the legal maxim of never asking a question in court to which the attorney does not already know the answer. Sometimes gambles are worth taking, and here the attorney worded the question to make it as easy as possible for the pathologist to agree with his misrepresentation of the pathologist's statement in deposition. Had the pathologist not reviewed his deposition, then he might have had a vague memory of saying "malignant neoplasm' and perhaps been tempted to agree. Barring the mistake of agreeing, the pathologist might have become nervous or bewildered and gone on to be an ineffective witness. The pathologist had reviewed his deposition, however, so not only was he confident in his memory of what he said but could quickly direct the attorneys and the judge (each of whom had a copy of the transcript) to the proper page, so that all would serve as mute (but expressive) witness to the accuracy of what the pathologist read before the jury. In this particular case the expressions were that the plaintiff's attorney looked stricken, because he now appeared foolish before the jury for apparently forgetting what he himself had asked the pathologist at the deposition. The opposing attorney looked delighted, and the judge gave the pathologist a look of approval for handling the situation so well. It is gratifying to call an attorney's bluff in court, but be sure not to look smug about winning that particular round or you will throw away everything you just gained. Some triumphs are best enjoyed quietly, behind an expression that seems oblivious to the implications of what just transpired.

In general, you should not change the substance of your statements at all because your initial interpretation of the case should have been correct. If necessary, you *can* substantially change a statement that you made in deposition during the trial, but you must have a good reason for doing so and be ready to give it. The following case illustrates the point.

A pathologist investigated a death in which an individual had been shot and also run over by a car. In the autopsy report, available to attorneys for both sides in a murder trial, the pathologist said that he thought the gunshot wound of the head that the decedent received was the sole cause of his death. The pathologist also noticed and recorded the tire mark on the decedent's chest, but he thought that the tire mark occurred after death, and therefore the pathologist did not attribute the death to the chest injury. One week before the trial, the pathologist was told by the prosecuting attorney that a suspect, who was turning evidence against the other suspects in exchange for a lesser sentence, stated that the decedent had lived for an hour or two after he was shot in the head. Therefore, the suspects had thrown him out of the trunk of their car and run over him to kill him. Quick study and consultation by the pathologist made it clear that the decedent need not necessarily have died quickly from the gunshot wound of the head. The defense attorneys were apprised of this substantial change in the interpretation of the case by the prosecuting attorney, and each defense attorney quickly arranged a meeting to review the case with the pathologist. In court the pathologist testified that death could have been caused by being run over by a car in addition to the gunshot wound. The defense attorneys wanted to know why the pathologist changed his mind on such an important issue. The pathologist replied that he had been provided with additional and new history concerning the circumstances surrounding death. The pathologist had to consider such information, and having considered it, found it credible. Therefore, the pathologist changed his opinion. The defense attorneys did not like it, even if they could acknowledge intellectually that the new interpretation was correct, and the pathologist underwent about three times the usual grilling, returning again and again to the original diagnosis and why the pathologist could not have made the correct diagnosis in the first place.

Do not make a habit of changing your mind concerning the crux of the case. It will not be much fun for you, and if you do it with any frequency you will quickly lose all credibility. As an addendum to the case history above, only the suspect who pled guilty was punished for the murder. Both the defendants who chose to stand trial were found not guilty of any charge by the jury.

Outcome of a Deposition

A deposition may prove especially beneficial to you as a physician witness. Sometimes your deposition will allow each side in a civil suit to come to a settlement now that neither side has any illusions about what your opinions and positions are in the matter. Sometimes the attorneys representing each side will be satisfied by your deposition and will enter it into trial rather than call you personally into court. In either case, you will be saved the time and the adventure of testifying in the matter again. Do not count on getting out of the trial, however, any more than you should count on having no cases while you are on call. If even one of the attorneys involved in the case decides that he wants you to appear in person to testify in the trial, then you will be testifying in the trial.

Trial

If the case is not ended by a settlement that is mutually agreeable to all the parties in the dispute, then the case will go to trial so that the dispute can be settled with either a judge or (more commonly) a jury serving as the arbiter. Much work leads up to a trial, but the trial itself begins when the jury is selected. A trial is really a simple proceeding consisting of three phases: jury selection and instruction, the presentation of evidence, and jury deliberation.

Jury Selection

The process of jury selection is described in Chapter 2. All phases of a trial are important, and selecting a jury is part of a trial, even though most laymen do not consider jury selection when they speak of a trial. In the same way, most laymen (and physicians, for that matter) consider the examination that occurs in a morgue "an autopsy," even though an autopsy begins with review of the patient's chart and ends some days or weeks later when all the microscope slides and laboratory tests have been considered and the report proofread and signed. If you are on trial as a defendant, then one responsibility of the attorney representing you will be to make sure that the jury chosen is composed of members willing to consider that you might be innocent of all the charges that have been brought against you. If you were on trial for murder, then you would not want the jury to be composed only of relatives of the man who was killed. Likewise, a physician on trial for malpractice does not want the jury to be composed of twelve individuals who bear grudges for wrongs they have suffered at the hands of the medical profession. Chapter 2 discusses how the attorney representing you will try to choose fair-minded jurors and how he can remove biased jurors from the pool, that is, from the group of potential jurors. Because jury selection is part of the trial, the defendant has the right to be present, and Chapter 2 relates how an attorney may get a defendant physician to help with jury selection.

As an aside, what can you do if you as a physician are called to jury duty? You can show up for jury duty, of course, but if you wish to try to get out of jury duty, then you have two choices. You can call the telephone number on the summons to jury duty and ask to speak to the office of the judge presiding over jury duty at the time you have been called (known as the presiding or organizing judge). When you speak with the judge's office, explain your position and tell what commitment prevents you from reporting for jury duty as scheduled. It is likely that you will be excused for that week, but your name will be enrolled on a later jury duty summons in a few months, and eventually you will have to report to court. The other option is to report to jury duty on Monday morning (be sure to take something to do such as paperwork or reading) and tell the person to whom you report that you need to speak with the presiding judge when possible about why you are unable to serve at this time. Your name will be recorded and at some point later in the day you may present your request for dismissal to the presiding judge. It is likely that the judge will excuse you. The advantage of reporting to jury duty to explain why you cannot serve is that you have, in fact, reported to jury duty, so if excused by the presiding judge your name will not be placed on the list of jurors to be called in a few months.

Presentation of Evidence

Evidence in a trial is presented in three phases.

1. The attorney for each side makes his opening statement. The first statement comes from the attorney representing the party who initiated the lawsuit (that is, by the plaintiff in a civil case and by the prosecuting attorney in a criminal case). The attorney representing the defendant will then give his opening statement. Each attorney will briefly recap his client's version of the story and then tell the jury what sort of information will be presented by witnesses to corroborate his client's version of the story.

2. Each side presents evidence and calls witnesses to testify. The testimony comes from witnesses. The side that initiated the suit will go first, calling its witnesses. As each of this first group of witnesses fin-

ishes being questioned ("examined" in legal parlance) by the attorney who called him, he will then be cross-examined by the attorney for the defendant. After the plaintiff or state has called all its witnesses, the defendant's attorney may then call witnesses. After the defendant's attorney examines each of his witnesses, the plaintiff's attorney or prosecuting attorney may cross-examine each witness for the defense. The point of all this examining and cross-examining is to fulfill the aim of providing the opportunity for each side to challenge the veracity of what is being said by the witnesses testifying for the other side.

3. The attorney for each side makes his closing statement. Again, the first statement comes from the attorney representing the party who initiated the lawsuit, followed by the closing statement of the attorney representing the defendant. Each attorney will recap his client's version of the case and remind the jury what evidence and testimony he presented to corroborate his client's story. The jury will be exhorted by each attorney to do the only right and just thing that can be done, which is to decide in his client's favor.

Notice that the format for a trial is nothing more than the age-old guide to speechmaking—"tell 'em what it is that you're going to tell 'em, tell 'em, and then tell 'em what it was that you just told 'em." The structure of evidence presentation to the jury is reminiscent of a baseball game in which each side takes turns presenting witnesses to give evidence.

Jury Deliberation

Once the closing statements are completed, the judge will instruct the jury about the level of certainty necessary to convict the defendant ("the preponderance of the evidence" in a civil case, evidence establishing guilt "beyond reasonable doubt" in a criminal case). The judge will tell the jury what verdict they can reach if they find the defendant guilty. (No jury can convict a defendant of more than he is charged with, but they can convict him of less. In other words, if the defendant is charged with "murder," then the jury can convict him of murder or of the lesser charge of manslaughter. The jury cannot convict a man charged with "murder" of "capital murder.") The jury will retire, discuss the case, and return when they reach a consensus, known as a verdict. If the defendant is found guilty, then the next step is sentencing. State law determines whether the jury or judge does the sentencing. In some cases the jury will have the duty of recommending a sentence to the judge, but often it is the judge who will assign the sentence, which is another reason to make certain that you never anger or irritate the judge. Regardless of who does the sentencing, the sentence may be temporal (time in jail) or financial (money owed by the defendant to others). If you are the defendant found guilty of malpractice, then hold on tightly and continue to look at the foreman who is reading the charge, then at the judge when the judge begins speaking. It may be that you will have an appeal, and by conducting yourself professionally you will better your chances of succeeding. Collapsing publicly will not help your cause. There will be time for collapsing later in private with the ones who love you. Devastating though the blow is, being found guilty of malpractice is not a death sentence. Being guilty of malpractice will probably be a life-changing event, but it is not a death sentence, either literally or professionally.

If the verdict is "not guilty," then the defendant is released from the charge and, by the prohibition against double jeopardy in the United States, the defendant can never be tried on that same charge for that same case again. If you are the defendant in a malpractice suit, and if you are found "not guilty," then you have every cause to be elated (if you are innocent) or at least relieved (if you got away with something). You should maintain your professional decorum, however, because you are still a professional in a professional setting. A relieved and grateful look to your spouse or a quietly mouthed "Thank you, God" are reasonable, but you should not jump up and pump your fist in the air or exclaim "Yes! Yes! Yes! I knew I was right." The only professionals who publicly exult in their triumphs are athletes, and it is usually unbecoming even then. If you need more reason to practice restraint than simple professionalism, then remember that it is possible that a newspaper or television reporter is present in the courtroom, and any such show on your part will be newsworthy.

Mistrials

If the jury cannot reach a consensus, then it is a "hung jury" (hung on some point that they cannot agree upon) and a mistrial is declared. A mistrial means that a new trial will be necessary, and that means that the whole process must start all over again. The whole process will not start all over again, however, for at least months if not a year. If you are the defendant in a malpractice suit that ends in a mistrial, then about the best you can say is that you have not yet been found guilty. Nevertheless, the sword is still suspended over your head, and will be until the months pass before another trial can be scheduled. Even expert witnesses who are not defendants dislike a mistrial because now they will have to read another document, the transcript of the evidence presented in the mistrial, and keep that additional information in their heads at the next trial.

However much you dislike being part of a mistrial as a physician, attorneys dislike mistrials at least as much as you do and probably more. A mistrial need not necessarily lead to another trial if (and only if) the parties agree to settle. If you are being sued for malpractice, you may be tempted to settle to get the thing over with and to avoid the stress of another trial, but listen to the counsel of your attorney before settling just to end the matter. A mistrial was not play-acting, and the attorneys for each side will have observed how things went and will have reassessed the position of their client, given that the jury could not agree on a verdict.

Trial Dates

Just because a trial is scheduled to begin on a certain date does not mean that it will begin on that date. Trials are frequently postponed and rescheduled for a later date. This postponement is particularly common in civil trials, so expect it. A judge's docket, or the list of cases to be heard in a courtroom in a given week, is always overbooked, just as airlines oversell seats on an airplane. Overbooking the docket is how the judge assures his courtroom will not sit idle. Cases are routinely postponed (or "continued," to use the legal term) at the request of attorneys for either side for various reasons up to the moment the trial begins. One side may have produced new evidence that the other side now wants to consider. One side may have a case of greater legal importance scheduled to be tried at the same time in a different court. (A murder trial takes precedence over a malpractice suit, for example.) Someone connected with the case (judge, attorney, witness, plaintiff, or defendant) may have to undergo surgery or else have a death in the family.

If you are an expert witness in the case and you know that you are going to be out of town for a business trip, then let the attorney you are working with know so that he can avoid having the trial during the time you will be gone. It is up to the judge to allow a trial on his docket to be continued. There are judges who occasionally decide to make you stay in town for the case and, if so, then you will have to stay—that burden is something that you assumed when you accepted the case as an expert witness. Ask your attorney about the reputation of the judge in your case about trips. Generally, if you are going on a professional trip, such as a professional meeting, you will be allowed to go and the case will be rescheduled. It is better to avoid the confrontation and inform the attorney of your travel plans as soon as you know when you will be away so that the attorney can keep the trial from being put on that week's docket in the first place.

The subpoena you receive will state that you are to be in court at 9:00 AM on Monday morning of the week of the trial. No witness ever testifies first thing Monday morning. On Monday the jury selection begins, and that usually takes all day. Why then does every witness get that Monday morning date on their subpoena? Because some witnesses are unreliable about showing up, especially witnesses in criminal trials. Once an unreliable witness shows up the attorney knows that *that* unreliable witness is there, and if necessary the witness can be forced to stay (in a jail cell) to ensure that he is present to testify when his time comes. If the unreliable witness does not show up then the police have a day to go and find him. You as a physician witness enjoy the privilege of being a reliable professional. On either the Friday before or on the Monday morning of the trial, you should call the office of the attorney that you are working with to make certain that the trial is in fact taking place that week as scheduled. As a professional, you are entitled to be treated as one, so when you contact the attorney who sent the subpoena arrange an approximate day and time for you to show up to give your testimony. The attorney will then call to confirm when it is time for you to come. You can still expect some wait in court even after taking these measures. It might frustrate you less if you expect that at least half of a working day will be consumed by court.

If you have never been to the courthouse, it is a good idea to arrive early or make a special trip a few days before to learn the layout of the place. At the least, ask the attorney for the number of the courtroom so that you can find it. If you do not know how to get to the courthouse from your office, you need to get directions so that you do not get lost on the way, and remember to ask about parking, which is at a premium around a courthouse. If you are present as a defendant, then all the more reason to get to court on time. Prosaic as it might sound, be sure to go to the restroom before you enter the courtroom. Once you as a witness are on the stand you will be there until both sides release you, and that can be a long time. As a defendant you will be attending the trial each day. The judge will order a break, called a recess, periodically throughout the day so that everyone in the court room may relieve themselves (and snack or smoke or make a quick telephone call or whatever else they choose to do in their twenty minutes).

Testifying

On Giving a Good Performance

Now that the background on court and trial proceedings is in place, it is time to discuss the art of testifying. Earlier we spoke of the theatrical nature of a court. In a very real sense, the testimony of every witness is a performance. The truth is the truth, of course, but how a person conveys the truth makes all the difference in the world. For example, there are many ways to answer a question in the affirmative. Saying "Yeah, sure" is a very different answer from pausing for a half moment and then stating "Absolutely" with the ring of conviction in your voice.

Many people, including physicians, are nervous about testifying. Nervousness is a good symptom. It is appropriate to be nervous when testifying, just as great actors are nervous before and while they perform. That nervousness heightens your senses and lends your testimony an edge that will impress itself upon the jury. Without that nervousness, your performance will be flat. The nervousness also leads to a heightened awareness of the sort that one has around the times of special events, such as a graduation or marriage. A heightened sense of awareness is very useful when testifying. Rather than be crippled by nervousness, anticipate nervousness and work within it to give your best performance as you testify.

Your performance begins as you enter the room. The jury will begin to size you up as soon as they see you. Your appearance should be professional, neat, clean, and conservative. "Clothes make the man," they say, and you want your attire to be in keeping with what the jury expects from you. You do not want to be remembered as either a disheveled, absent-minded professor or as a plain slob. Nor do you wish to be remembered as a dandy, so let a simple wedding band suffice for jewelry and save the cufflinks or solitaire diamond stud earring for another place. Ask the attorney for advice if you are unsure what is acceptable where you will be testifying. Remember, when the jury deliberates, you want them to remember what you said, not what you wore. For men, no worn and cracked shoes, no plaid blazers, no loud golf socks, and no loud or overly trendy ties are acceptable. Men should dress in a conservative business suit that is neat and clean and not outrageously expensive. Women also should dress professionally in conservative business attire. However capable a woman might be of pulling it off elsewhere, court is no place for a decolletage or a skirt so short as to raise eyebrows. Juries include female jurors (females are usually in the majority on the jury, it so happens), and those female jurors will be the female witness's harshest critics concerning the appropriateness of her attire. A good rule of thumb for men or women is to wear the sort of outfit that you would wear to interview for a job that you very much want.

Men need one additional bit of advice at this point, and it concerns bow ties. As a sometime bow tie wearer, the author is fond of all the virtues of a bow tie, and he realizes that some men, particularly pediatricians, wear bow ties exclusively. Nevertheless, you must know that many people distrust something about a bow tie, and thus about the man that wears it. You do not want the jury to distrust you. I do not say never wear a bow tie, but be certain that you have the negligent panache necessary to pull it off. If you have any doubt, wear a regular tie to court, as I always do.

The jury continues to assess your character and ability as you walk toward the witness stand. Do so at a regular, steady pace that shows you are confident in yourself and ready to enter the fray. You will be nervous, but do not let it show by running or dawdling toward the witness stand. At some point, you will be sworn in. The place within the court where you will be sworn in and the person who will swear you in vary with the judge. You might ask the attorney how witnesses are sworn in that particular judge's court, but as long as you are walking steadily and looking around to see what is happening, then things should go well. The judge or a bailiff usually will be trying to get your attention to tell you what to do and where to stand or sit before being sworn in. Look squarely in the eye of whomever swears you in, think about the words no matter how many times you have heard them before, and answer "I do" with a clear voice that indicates you care about telling the truth and that the truth you have to tell concerns important information about this case. A trial is very boring for a jury, and anyone who looks like he has an important story to tell and who wants to tell it will command the attention of the jurors. A bored and disinterested "I do" will tell the jury that you would really rather be someplace else, and the jury will daydream through your testimony.

Incidentally, it is not only the jury that is assessing you as you enter the courtroom. Both your own attorney and the opposing attorney are studying you to see what you are made of and how you will likely behave in the crucible of court. As the saying goes, you never get a second chance to make a good first impression, and making a good impression can not only help you but even protect you. Assuming that you are entering court as an expert witness, then you begin to establish rapport with the jury as you enter court. If the opposing attorney sees that you have established a good rapport with the jury and that you are so careful in your actions as to have learned the proper etiquette of court, then he will be less able to attack you upon the witness stand. If, on the other hand, you have impressed everyone with your boorish behavior within the first two minutes, then you yourself have declared that it is open season for taking shots at you. Even as a nontestifying defendant in a malpractice case, the impression you make in court will be assessed by the attorney defending you. If you look and act guilty because you are so nervous, then the attorney defending you may decide that you will make such a bad impression in court that you would be better off to settle the case than to proceed. You may be afraid as the defendant in a malpractice suit, but you must summon all your skill as a physician for looking cool under fire. Not cold and icy, but cool.

A physician who is new to testifying may be disoriented by the newness and strangeness of the experience so that he no longer feels in charge, but in fact he is in charge in a very important way—nobody else in the room knows as much about his specialty as he does. The truth is that the attorneys are as afraid of you as you are of them, particularly if you have never testified for them before. Attorneys hate ugly surprises in court, and if you have never testified before these attorneys then every attorney considers that you have the potential to create an ugly surprise for him. Each attorney is striving to achieve a goal, and if unfamiliar with you they will feel their way carefully. The attorneys may test your mettle, just as the surgeons tested you when you began working in the hospital. (With time and experience in working together, this sort of testing will fall by the wayside as the attorneys spread the word to other attorneys about what to expect from you.)

On Testifying

Qualifying Yourself as an Expert Witness

After you have been sworn in and seated yourself, the attorney who has called you as a witness will ask you to state your name. Simply reply with your name, leaving out any degrees or titles. The attorney will then continue with his direct examination. If you are a fact witness, the attorney will ask you questions concerning the matter that you witnessed or participated in. If you are an expert witness, you will be asked to qualify yourself—that is, to tell the court what training and experience you have that qualify you to claim to be an expert in your particular area. You may have a 30-page curriculum vitae, but all that is needed is a brief history of your training and a list of the positions you have held since the completion of your residency. Following is an example of how a surgical pathologist would qualify himself to the court in a way that gets the point across without presenting the jury enough information to recommend him for tenure. (The corresponding qualification for a laboratory director in clinical pathology should be clear enough):

> **Attorney**: What training and experience do you have that qualify you to practice as a surgical pathologist?
>
> **Expert**: A pathologist is a medical doctor. I got my M.D. at _____ Medical School, graduating in 1975. Following graduation, I chose to specialize in pathology. Pathology is a specialty area in medicine that concerns itself with determining how a patient has come to be sick. In surgical pathology, this determination is made by examining some tissue or an organ, such as an appendix, removed during an operation. A pathology residency is 4 to 5 years in length, and I did my residency training at _____ Hospital. At the end of my residency, I decided to take an additional year of intensive training in surgical pathology, and I took this additional training at _____ Medical Center. At the completion of my training, I was hired as an assistant professor of surgical pathology at _____ University Hospital, where I worked for 9 years. I was then hired by _____ Medical Center to serve as the Director of Surgical Pathology, and I have served there as Director of Surgical Pathology up until the present.

The attorney for the other side will then have an opportunity to challenge your qualifications. He may or may not. He is more likely to challenge if you are new to the field of testifying. If you are a proven player known to the judge and all the attorneys, then there is no point in wasting the time. As soon as the attorney who called you asks the judge to admit you as an expert witness and the judge agrees to do so, you will have been qualified as an expert witness in the case for which you are testifying.

If you are an established player in the field of expert witness testimony, then the opposing attorney may tell the judge that he and his client recognize you as an expert in your area and that they stipulate that you are an expert; that is, they will accept you as an expert witness in this case without challenge, obviating any need for you to tell the jury your qualifications. Oftentimes the attorney who called you will tell the judge that he would like the jury to hear a brief synopsis of your qualifications anyway, which the judge will usually allow. There are two reasons that an attorney will have you tell about your training and experience anyway. One is to impress upon the jury that you are the genuine article, not some two-bit "expert" who replied to a want ad. The other reason is that the attorney will use the minute or two that your qualification spiel lasts to gather his notes and thoughts before he proceeds with the meat of your examination. Occasionally, however, the attorney who calls you will accept the opposing side's offer to stipulate that you are an expert and proceed directly to examining you.

Direct Examination

After qualifying yourself as an expert witness, the direct examination begins in earnest. This portion of testimony should be easy because the attorney who called you wants the jury to hear what you have to say. How do you best get the information across to the jury? Because you are a pathologist, you are familiar with teaching small groups of people in conferences, so use that experience to help you teach this group of twelve laymen. Prepare for your testimony as you would for a conference. Do your homework. Make yourself familiar with the case and with the points you want the jury to take away. There should be no more than two or three points. For example, the points may be that a Pap smear read as normal showed a cluster of malignant cells within a thick area, that knowing the malignant cells were present would be expected to have changed the course of treatment for this patient, and that Thin-preps™ were not yet available for general use at the time the slide was made. For a hemolytic transfusion reaction, the points are a little more complicated, but not much:

1. In a crossmatch (the standard test for compatibility between the patient and the blood cells that he will be given), no antibody (similar to a bullet that the body's immune system forms to lyse or kill abnormal cells) was detected in the plaintiff patient during the pretransfusion antibody screen. Thus all testing before the blood was given indicated that the blood was safe for transfusion.
2. After receiving that specific unit of blood, the patient's body began producing antibodies (immune system bullets now targeting the foreign transfused blood cells). These antibodies lysed or "popped" the transfused blood cells, something doctors call a "hemolytic transfusion reaction."
3. This delayed hemolytic transfusion reaction is never predictable the first time it happens, but a second reaction can be prevented if the blood bank keeps a "transfusion history" on this patient.

Whatever the points that you need to make as an expert witness, think of ways to make the complicated medical aspects clear to laymen by way of example or by using a model. Assemble your ideas in effective order. Have in mind the points you want to make, and then string those points together as you are questioned. Do not memorize your testimony. It is unlikely that you are a good enough actor to make your spiel sound spontaneous, and it is even more unlikely that the questions you get will come in the order that you have memorized. A sharp cross-examiner will spot a memorized statement and ask unrelated questions to get you so far off track that you will become hopelessly lost and flounder your way to mediocrity on the witness stand.

The rapport that you establish with the jury is critical. That rapport began when you entered the room. It grows as you testify. You should sit up straight and give the attorney asking the questions your careful and respectful attention. If the answer to the question is short, then address the attorney. If the answer is long, address the jury. Look at the jurors as you talk, and catch their eye if you can. Let them know that you have nothing to hide. Speak clearly, and use understandable words. The jury knows that you are a physician, and they expect you to use a few medical terms. Your ability to easily pronounce and correctly use a few medical terms reassures the jury that you are truly a physician in a way that hearing about your education cannot. Therefore, give the jury a *few* medical terms, and then gradually revert to using laymen's terms. For example:

> **Attorney**: What did you see when you reviewed the microscope slide of the lump from the breast?
>
> **Witness**: On the microscope slide was a portion of breast tissue that showed ductal carcinoma *in situ* with a microscopic focus of invasion. That is the medical diagnosis, but what it means is that there was cancer in the lump from the breast. For the most part the cancer was still inside the duct in which it arose, but in a tiny spot the cancer had broken out of the duct and begun to spread into the breast tissue.
>
> **Attorney**: And what is a duct?
>
> **Witness**: A duct in the body serves the same purpose as the ducts in a heating or cooling system in a building—to carry something from one place to another. In the breast the ducts are tubular structures that carry milk from the glands where the milk is produced to the nipple. Most of the ducts in the breast are no larger in diameter than a human hair.

In other words, address the jury as you would address a patient you like to whom you need to explain a particular medical matter. Not only is that approach effective, but it helps to take you out of the unfamiliar territory of the witness stand and returns you to your familiar role as a teacher.

Once you establish a good rapport with the jury, you will have accomplished two things. You will best assure that the jury will pay attention to your testimony, and you will also have taken a step in protecting yourself from particularly vicious attack. The truth is that the jury wants to like a physician witness even before that witness enters the room because even today a physician is still considered a professional, productive member of society with a respected title. You will throw away your advantage if your behavior on the stand is suspicious, curt, condescending, or belligerent. Such rude behavior will turn the jury against you. Attorneys know all this, and they usually will try to discredit you only if you have already begun to establish a poor rapport. The attorney who tries to attack a witness that the jury likes will be turning the jury against himself, something he dare not do.

Keep your answers to questions as brief as possible. Brevity comes hard to many physicians. Physicians are trained to be educators, hence our title of "Doctor," and thus the knowledgeable, compassionate physician has a tendency to answer and without persuasion proceed to explain, a tendency that can prove disastrous in the judicial setting. In testifying, as in architecture, less is more, and restraint makes for a better witness. Restraint also limits the risk of opening an area for prolonged cross-examination, because legally no topic can be discussed during cross-examination that was not first broached during direct examination. Contrast the following exchange:

> **Attorney**: Are you certain that the pathology slides of this patient showed a malignant lymphoma?
> **Witness**: Yes.

with this second example:

> **Attorney**: Are you certain that the pathology slides of this patient showed a malignant lymphoma?
> **Witness**: Well, I'm as sure as I can be.

The witness in the second scenario has, by sounding less than certain, opened up an avenue for discussion during cross-examination that will take a long time to explore. (What do you mean "As sure as you can be"? What would make you more sure? When do you know that a lymphoma is real, and when are you only making an educated guess? How often do you "guess" at the proper diagnosis?) Pathologists have a reputation for hedging, and there is a time and place to hedge. If for some reason you really are unsure whether the slides of the malignant lymphoma are the slides of the patient in question, then you need to transmit to the jury exactly what your level of uncertainty is, particularly since the possible mix-up will probably be the focus of the malpractice suit. Or, if you are unsure that the lymph node is malignant, then you need to transmit to the jury exactly what makes a diagnosis one way or the other difficult in this case. Unfortunately, some pathologists become so accustomed to using a hedge as a crutch that they hedge every time they speak. Hedging every statement that you make in court would be just as inappropriate as telling a surgeon that your frozen section diagnosis is "probably negative for tumor."

If you have gone over the questions that the attorney who has retained you will be asking of you in court (as you should have) and if you have prepared by reviewing the case, then you will have a fair idea of what your direct examination will be like and things should go well. To reiterate, it is appropriate for a physician expert witness to have reviewed the medical findings with the attorney who retained him and for the physician and attorney together to determine how best to get this information across to the jury. No matter how familiar you are with what the attorney is going to ask, however, let him ask and let him finish the question before you start to answer. Otherwise it will look as though you have been tutored by the attorney in what to say. You want the jury to know that these are *your* answers. If the question is one that should require a moment's consideration to answer properly, then take that moment before you answer. You will not even be acting if you actually reconsider the question and the pertinent facts in the case before you answer.

In answering the questions of either attorney, it is a good idea to form the habit of pausing a half second before you answer. That gives the opposing attor-

ney the opportunity to object if he wishes. That slight pause is good courtsman-
ship, particularly when you are being cross-examined; it might save you from
having to answer a difficult question. If an objection is raised, then you should
keep silent until the judge says "Sustained" or "Overruled." If the objection is
sustained, then you are not to answer the question, and the attorney who asked it
must either try to get at the answer with some other question or else let the matter go. If the objection is overruled, then you are to go ahead and answer the
question.

If at any time you do not understand the question posed to you, then ask the
attorney to repeat it. Attorneys know what they want to elicit from you, but usually the specific wording of the question is improvised. Sometimes the question
gets convoluted before the attorney finally comes to the end of it. If you did not
understand exactly what was being asked, then it is likely that some of the jury
did not either, and in any case you should not guess at the attorney's meaning. If
you still do not understand even the second time around, then say that you do
not understand the question, with perhaps some suggestion to the attorney of
what is confusing you. You do not want to look like a smart aleck, so make certain that your voice is one of sincerity and not sarcasm when you ask the attorney to repeat the question. If the question brought on an objection, then the legal
wrangling of the judge with the attorneys that may follow can last several minutes. Often the legal wrangling ends with the judge saying "Overruled" and the
attorney who asked the question turning to you and saying, "Please answer the
question." In that case, regardless of how clear the question was, you will do
well to ask the attorney to repeat the question so that everyone involved in the
case will remember what you are being asked before you answer.

Returning for a moment to the rapport that you as an expert witness establish
with the jury, it is not necessarily a sign for alarm while testifying if you do not
command the rapt attention of every juror for the entire time. Even during a trial
for murder, it is surprisingly common to see that at least one juror has dozed off
during your testimony. If all twelve doze off, then you have a problem, but
judges seem to allow a juror or two to take a nap without interruption. One word
of caution about catching the eyes of the jury—know that it is possible for a
juror whose eye you catch to wink back at you. This is disconcerting to say the
least, and it can derail your train of thought in a way that no opposing attorney
can. Make certain when you catch a juror's eye that you do not gaze too long, or
longingly.

Cross-Examination

When the attorney who began questioning you says, "No further questions, Your
Honor," there will be a pause, and then the attorney for the opposing side will
rise. Cross-examination has begun. During direct examination, you have been
making compelling arguments in favor of the side represented by the attorney
who retained you. Nevertheless, "There are two sides to every story," and the
opposing attorney represents the other side of the story. The purpose of cross-

examination is to take the teeth out of whatever argument you just made. Teeth can be extracted in several ways, with or without anesthesia. If you are sloppy in your pathology, then your conclusions can be attacked. Probably you are very careful in your pathology, so if it is vital for the cross-examining attorney's case to discredit your conclusions and testimony, then the attorney must use other means. Some of the other means are ploys, and we will outline some ploys below. First, however, it is useful for you as a witness to realize that the cross-examining attorney will almost certainly question you until you concede at least one point in his favor. (Otherwise, it does not look as though the opposing attorney is doing his job.) Consider what point the attorney wants you to concede when it comes, and then fight or capitulate as appropriate.

For example, malpractice has been charged by the relatives of a man who died of adenocarcinoma of the lung. The relatives consider that, had the tumor been detected the first time the patient was seen, he would have received treatment and survived. Instead, the bronchoscopy specimens were all non-diagnostic. The patient missed his 3 month follow-up visit and returned 15 months later with metastatic adenocarcinoma of the lung. You have been asked to review the case by the attorney for the defendant. We begin in the midst of cross-examination.

>**Attorney**: A few moments ago, during your examination by Mr. _____, you said that the cytology preparation you reviewed was not diagnostic for carcinoma, did you not?
>
>**Expert**: I said "No definite malignant cells detected."
>
>**Attorney**: Malignant cells could have been present, but you did not detect them?
>
>**Expert**: That is correct.
>
>**Attorney**: Why did you not detect them?
>
>**Expert**: The preparation did have some slightly abnormal cells, but the cells were present within a setting of intense inflammation, that is, there were many white blood cells present, the kind of cells that fight infection. An infection in the airways of the lung could cause cells to look slightly abnormal as the ones on the slide did. Because I could not distinguish between the abnormal appearance caused by infection and that caused by some types of cancer, I said that "no definite malignant cells were detected" on the slide.
>
>**Attorney**: But those abnormal cells on that slide could have been malignant, couldn't they?
>
>**Expert**: They could have been.
>
>**Attorney**: No further questions, Your Honor.

Here both the expert witness and the attorney may take pride in a job well done. The attorney has tried to leave the impression with the jury that the cells on the slide were malignant all along. The pathologist witness has reiterated that he knew that the cells might be malignant, but the setting called for caution so he used caution. The attorney got what he wanted, and there was no harm in letting him have it because the pathologist never said that the cells on the slide could not possibly be malignant. As an expert witness, you need only state your position a time or two and then give the attorney what he wants. The attorney who called you to testify can go over the point again on his re-direct examination if he thinks it necessary. The jury will have gotten the point.

In contrast to the previous example, what the attorney wants in the following case is not in keeping with what the pathologist witness is saying, so as a witness you do not give an inch.

Attorney: A few moments ago, during your examination by Mr. _____, you said that the cytology preparation you reviewed was diagnostic for adenocarcinoma, did you not?

Expert: Yes.

Attorney: Couldn't the cells that you find suspicious have really been reactive, as my client thought?

Expert: No, sir.

Attorney: Why not?

Expert: Because the appearance of the nuclei of the cells we are discussing was so abnormal, as I showed earlier in the diagram when I was comparing the cells in question with normal cells.

Attorney: But couldn't something other than cancer cause that abnormal appearance?

Expert: No.

Attorney: But medicine is a big field, and unusual things happen sometimes, don't they?

Expert: Certainly.

Attorney: So it is conceivable that some other rare condition occurred that mimicked cancer in this case, isn't it?

Expert: The abnormal appearance of those particular cells is specific for one thing and one thing only, and that is cancer.

Attorney: But there are other conditions which...

Opposing attorney: Objection, Your Honor. The witness has already answered this question.

Judge: Objection sustained. You may proceed with some other line of questioning.

Attorney: (*Riffles through notes, then*) No further questions, Your Honor.

Notice that the attorney tries to minimize the pathologist's interpretation of the cells as malignant by wording his question, "Couldn't the cells that you find suspicious..." rather than "Couldn't the cells that you find malignant...." Even so, a simple and unyielding "No" is the best answer. Attorneys are somewhat like clinicians. Both have an answer that they want from the pathologist, and if you do not give either one the answer that he wants, then he will try to trick it out of you. (Clinician: That lung biopsy has to be malignant; the patient has a 5 cm mass with an enlarged hilum. Pathologist: Nevertheless, the portion that you biopsied is all here under glass and is fibrous tissue, nothing more.) Either way, all you have to do is stand your ground. If the attorney in the exchange above is bent on discrediting your testimony, he will have to do it by discrediting *you*. That leads to the discussion of ploys.

Legal Ploys Used by Attorneys

Attorneys have a reputation for being tricky, for using words to trap witnesses into making a mistake or contradicting their earlier statements. There are a few tricks in the attorney's armamentarium, just as physicians have a few tricks for certain situations with patients. Here are some ploys with proper responses.

Ad hominem *Attack*

The sign: The opposing attorney is rude to you, to the point of provoking you to anger and a sharp retort.

The trick: The attorney is trying to discredit you with the jury by making you either flinch under pressure or else lose your temper.

The solution: *Never* lose your cool on the witness stand. Never. This tactic of attorneys is probably more common than any other, so common in fact that it even has its own name. An *ad hominem* attack, literally an attack "to the man" himself, is a personal attack upon the witness rather than upon the testimony of the witness. Attorneys use an *ad hominem* attack in several different circumstances depending on what the attorney is trying to accomplish. It may be that the attacking attorney is trying to browbeat you, the witness, in order to show the jury that you are a coward or that you are unsure of yourself, and thus your opinions are worthless. Sometimes attending physicians who are accustomed to terrorizing students and residents find the tables turned upon them in court by an attorney, where the attending physician promptly caves in under the pressure in an unfamiliar setting. (One problem of reaping what you sow is that you usually reap it at the worst possible time.)

Another outcome that the attacking attorney may wish to provoke from the witness is a shouting match, which the attorney can then twist to his advantage. An unusually cool and unflappable pathologist once fell into this trap.

After enduring some unjustified barbs and taunts, the pathologist snapped back at the attorney. The attacking attorney then turned to the jury and said, with poisonous sweetness, "I'm sorry, doctor. None of us has had the opportunity and benefit of all your education, so I suppose none of us is good enough to ask a simple question out of ignorance without having you put us in our place. No further questions, doctor." The pathologist knew that he had fallen into the trap, and that knowledge is a bitter taste for the drive back to your office.

When an *ad hominem* attack occurs, it can be handled in several ways. The attorney who called you as a witness may object to the judge concerning such behavior. The judge himself may interpose and remind the rude attorney that you are a guest of the court, and that as a guest you are to be treated with respect. Or it may be that the attack will be allowed to proceed. The attack may continue because the attorney probably would not have attacked if he knew that the judge would reprimand him. Even if no one intercedes on your behalf, you must answer all questions politely and evenly. It may help you maintain your composure to remember that an *ad hominem* attack only occurs when the medical evidence you have presented is damaging to the side of the attacking attorney and that your medical evidence cannot be challenged with any hope of success. Therefore the attorney's only hope is to discredit your character. Your best retribution is in denying the attacking attorney the anger or uncertainty that he wants from you. The longer that you the witness are able to give polite responses and hold firm to your position, the more the attacking attorney will draw the ire of the jury upon himself. The important point is to recognize the *ad hominem* attack for what it is because that knowledge will provide you the detachment necessary to thwart the attorney's purpose.

Sometimes *gentle* humor can defuse the situation in an *ad hominem* attack, but humor is a dangerous weapon in court and should only be used sparingly. No matter how clever you are, remember that the wielding of words is the attorney's trade. In an exchange of wit you are likely to come out the poorer. Any humor you choose to use while testifying should not be condescending in nature, such as a put-down.

The Garden Path

The sign: The opposing attorney compliments you on your vast medical knowledge and begins to move the questions into a medical area outside your own specialty. ("Doctor, isn't what the surgeon did in this case unusual?")

The trick: You are being led out of your area of expertise. If you do not recognize that you are being led out of your area, you will soon be in over your head.

The solution: Reply that you really cannot answer that question as the field lies outside your area of expertise. By saying this you are saying that in this matter you have no more knowledge than the average individual, and you have disqualified yourself as an expert in something in which you are not expert. If the question concerns something common to all medicine, then it is perfectly appropriate for you to answer it. For example, a physician's training is sufficient in medical school to allow a physician of any specialty to state, "Provided that a patient is not intoxicated and that there is not some other mitigating circumstance, then a broken bone is usually very painful." A pathologist witness should excuse himself from questions that move into orthopedics.

As a related note to this discussion, beware of assuming that you know more about some field than does the attorney if the field is not your area of expertise.

It is true that most attorneys dislike science, but there are attorneys who have scientific backgrounds, even M.D. degrees. Resist the temptation to show off in an area outside your specialty, or you may find yourself being grilled on both sides before the attorney is done with you.

Misleading Questions

The sign: The opposing attorney demands that you answer the following question or questions "yes" or "no."

The trick: Somewhere in the list will be a question whose answer requires an explanation in order to be clear.

The solution: In this circumstance you may appeal to the judge and say, "Your Honor, that question concerns a complicated matter that requires some explanation. I fear that if I answer that question simply "yes" or "no" without an explanation then I will mislead the jury." The judge will allow you to explain because you swore to tell the truth, not to mislead.

Authoritative Texts

The sign: The opposing attorney holds aloft *Gray's Anatomy* or some other textbook or journal and asks whether you consider it authoritative or standard.

The trick: If you say yes, you will soon be quoted a section out of context or be undergoing a pop quiz on the contents of page 317.

The solution: Say that you do not recognize any textbook as authoritative. If pressed about why you would not consider such a cornerstone of medical training authoritative, say that no one book or article takes into consideration the clinical picture presented in this case.

Hired Gun

The sign: The attorney asks you how much money you have been paid for your testimony as an expert witness.

The trick: If you say the dollar amount, it sounds as though your testimony is bought.

The solution: Say, "I'm not being paid anything for my testimony. I have been paid for my time, my professional knowledge, my services in studying the medical facts in the case, and for my medical opinions based on those facts." If asked to give the dollar amount, then do; trying to hide it will make it look like you have something to hide.

Insinuation of Wrongdoing

The sign: The attorney asks whether you have discussed this case with anyone.

The trick: An attempt to fluster you and make you think you did something wrong.

The solution: Say "Yes." If asked with whom, tell with whom. If then asked, "You discussed the testimony you would give in court, didn't you?" reply "We discussed the medical matters involved and how we could most clearly present the information to the jury."

Going on Memory Alone

The sign: The attorney demands that you answer the following question without looking at your notes.

The trick: You might not remember the detail that is asked or else be flustered by the request.

The solution: You are perfectly within your right to look at your notes before answering. Simply say that you prefer to look at your notes. If the attorney persists in his demand, then the opposing attorney will probably object. You should be able to look at your notes. This particular ploy may be brought out if you have been looking at your notes constantly, and the attorney may only want to point out to the jury that you cannot remember a thing that is not written down. Reviewing the case before testifying will often prevent this sort of request.

Two-Part Questions

The sign: The attorney asks you a two-part question.

The trick: One answer is "yes" and one "no." The attorney is hoping you will only give one of the answers, usually the latter.

The solution: Answer each question in turn. (Actually, the opposing attorney may well object because the two-part question is not permitted in court for this very reason. In a similar way, the spitball is illegal in baseball, but that doesn't mean pitchers never throw one.) If the attorney does not object, you still separate the questions and answer each question in turn.

Sowing Enmity

The sign: The attorney tells you that your opinion in a complicated matter is at odds with the opinion of Dr. _____ and asks whether you are implying that Dr. _____ does not know what he is doing.

The trick: It is for the jury to decide whether Dr. _____ knows what he is doing.

The solution: Say that Dr. _____ is certainly competent but that this is a complicated medical matter that is open to interpretation, and your opinion is as you have stated it. Dr. _____'s opinion is such and such, and in this instance you happen to disagree. Remember that you are not there to see that your opinion prevails; you are there to provide your opinion. It is the jury's job to sort it out. (If you really think that Dr. _____'s opinion is due to incompetence, then leave out the sentence on competence and avoid disparaging him on the stand.)

In court it is always appropriate to answer "I don't know" if you do not. This point should be easy for pathologists, given our reputation for hedging. If you need to hedge or to say "I don't know," then do so succinctly. In a paraphrase of E. B. White from *The Elements of Style*, when in court you should "hedge in a straightforward manner." Juries respect candor and honesty, and they will respect you more as a witness for showing your honesty than for pretending that you know every detail of the whole discipline of medicine. The jury and attorneys already realize that you know more medicine than they will ever know.

7
Unethical Expert Witness Testimony

It is a regrettable truth that some practitioners of medicine are corrupt. Some unscrupulous physicians forsake the practice of sound medicine for new careers as suppliers of pain medications. Other physicians are willing to testify to unsound medicine in court as expert witnesses. What constitutes unethical expert witness testimony, and what can be done about it?

Ethical Expert Witness Testimony

Naturally, in any complicated medical case, two conscientious physicians may consider the evidence and arrive at two separate, conflicting opinions about the case. Given that circumstance, the American legal system would actually welcome the testimony of each expert witness. If there is just cause for diverse interpretation, then the jury needs to hear the conflicting opinions in order to render an informed and rational verdict. It would be morally wrong to try to hide one expert witness's opinion in order to preserve some sort of artificially determined "united front."

Unethical Expert Witness Testimony

Unethical expert witness testimony is not the carefully considered difference of opinion concerning the interpretation of a complex medical case. Unethical testimony occurs when the expert witness lies, when he willfully fails to take into account all the circumstances involved in the case, or when his medical conclusions are outside the realm of accepted scientific method and practice.

Lying

Lying while testifying under oath in a court of law has its own name—perjury. The lie may be blatant, such as claiming that the frozen section control was inexplicably lost when the loss was not only explicable but intentional. Perjury also occurs whenever an expert witness falsely claims experience and training that qualify him as an expert. An obvious example of falsifying training would be to claim to be board certified when one is not certified by any medical board. Either of the lies above, when discovered, will ruin the expert witness or malpractice defendant who told it.

In addition to the two obvious forms of lying mentioned above, there is a third, more subtle form of perjury. False claims of experience also include inflating the number of cases that you claim to have performed. It is wrong to claim that you have personally grossed in over 20,000 mastectomy specimens in your career by counting the work of all residents in the training program that you oversee. If you signed the case, then you may reasonably count it as one case with which you have experience, but even then the proper course would be to claim the case as one with which you had experience in microscopic diagnosis, not in dissecting.

The claim of an expert witness to have done more cases than is true occurs over and over. Why would someone make an egregious overstatement concerning the volume of work done in his career? In some cases, the pathologist who makes such an inflated claim seems unsure of himself in court, particularly if the other side has its own expert in pathology. The inflated claim is made to try to convince everyone that the expert who claims superhuman experience is superior to the expert retained by the other side. In such cases, the person in court who seems most in need of being impressed is the expert who makes the outrageous claim. A second reason that a pathologist may make an unreasonably elevated claim has more to do with a failure to understand his place in the process. Simply put, some pathologists have trouble distinguishing themselves from the laboratory they direct. It is perfectly appropriate to say that the laboratory you direct processes 50,000 specimens per year. To claim that you yourself process 50,000 specimens per year is wrong.

Whatever the reason that a witness may exaggerate his experience, there is no need to exaggerate. A jury will be amply convinced of your experience if you have grossed in 1,000 mastectomy specimens, or even 600. Claiming ten times your total is wrong because it is a lie, but it is also silly because you are gilding a lily.

Willful Failure to Consider Pertinent Medical Evidence

Failure to consider all the facts available in a case is unethical. An example from forensic pathology should clarify this point.

A pediatrician specializing in neonatology is asked to serve as an expert witness in a child abuse case. The decedent was three months old and was born six weeks prematurely. Autopsy showed a healing fracture callus of the left clavicle. The pediatrician would be correct to say that fracture of a clavicle is an occasional complication of vaginal birth. If the history and findings in this case include contusions on the scalp, cerebral edema, and the statements of a friend of the parents that he saw the father take the child into an adjoining room and then heard the father strike the child repeatedly while shouting "Stop crying, stop crying," then the pediatrician gives unethical testimony when he chooses to ignore this other information, stating that the only possible explanation for the clavicular fracture is the process of childbirth and that the scalp contusions probably represent forceps marks.

You may think this example far-fetched, but unethical testimony of this sort is neither exaggerated nor impossible.[1]

Quackery

In measurement, precision has to do with reproducibility. In the science of medicine, a precise diagnosis made by one physician should be reproducible by another physician; that is, the second physician, given the same facts available to the first physician, should come to the same diagnosis or, if the case is particularly subtle, at least the same short list of differential diagnoses. Beware of any witness who says that his conclusions are radically different because he uses techniques superior to, but unaccepted by, the ordinary practitioners of medicine in the world. It is true that genuine medical breakthroughs, such as hand washing, were once decried by all physicians save for a lone man of vision. Charlatans who claim to get unique results because of their unorthodox techniques invariably say that they are from the same mold as the lone men of vision. Usually the man who claims that he has special abilities is no more sincere than the wizard of Oz, and, like the wizard, he insists that we pay no attention to the lack of substance.

It should be easy for attorneys to spot a charlatan; he is the one who, by means of his special techniques, always tells the attorney exactly what the attorney wants to hear. It is appropriate to ask for details concerning the case, and it is even appropriate to ask the attorney who contacts you what he believes to be the truth of the matter being tried in court. But if you begin jotting down what the attorney says so that you can work toward that specific end while evaluating the case, you have abandoned equanimity for partisanship. Attorneys call expert witnesses who practice partisanship "whores" for a reason. The article by Chadwick and Krous cited above gives examples of this sort of unethical testimony, also.[1]

Mechanisms for Handling Unethical Testimony

In Court

How is unethical testimony in court handled? There are two approaches now, one recent and one established.

As mentioned in Chapter 2, the result of the 1993 ruling in Daubert v. Merrell Dow Pharmaceuticals, Inc is that judges now have the authority (and to some extent the responsibility) to make certain that the scientific testimony being presented in their courts is valid.[2] A portion of Daubert v. Merrell Dow states that the "following parameters (are) relevant, but not controlling, in determining validity, reliability, and subsequent admissibility into court of scientific methods or theories: whether the methods or theories have been (or can be) tested, their known or potential error rate, publication or peer review, and their widespread acceptance within a relative scientific community."[3] This ruling gives judges the authority to dismiss testimony even before it is offered if the judge finds review of the expert witness's report suspect for validity or reliability. The use of such authority is described in the section on the role of the judge in Chapter 2.

Having the judge allow or disallow testimony in court is a new approach to the evaluation of the validity of an expert witness's testimony. The older, established approach is to test the testimony of each witness within the framework of the adversarial trial system. Because a trial is an adversarial proceeding, every witness who testifies is subject to having his testimony challenged. The cross-examining attorney who has done his preparation will be ready to question the witness concerning any lie or omission of truth about his credentials. The witness will have to justify ignoring important medical points in the case or drawing conclusions outside the realm of accepted scientific method and practice. Since the cross-examining attorney is no expert in medicine, he will look to the expert witness who is working with him for help in dissecting the credentials and conclusions of the unethical expert. If one is opposed to exposing a professional colleague's shortcomings in this way, then it would be better not to enter the fray as an expert witness.

Assuming that you are willing to play the game of court, how then would you evaluate the integrity of the pathologist expert witness who will be testifying for the other side if asked to do so by the attorney who hired you? Remember that each side in a trial must discover its evidence to the other side, that is, provide the other side access to all the information it has. To evaluate the opposing expert you should ask for a copy of the opposing expert's curriculum vitae, a list of the cases in which he has testified (including who retained him in each case and what the medical issue was in each case), and a copy of his report on the case under consideration, assuming that a report exists.

Check the facts listed on the curriculum vitae to make certain that all information listed is correct. Look for missing gaps of time such as years unaccounted for between two positions. Remember that the CV may be worded to hide irregularities. For example, the statement "1979–81, federally financed research" could be a carefully worded admission that the individual was receiving welfare aid while out of work. If something is vague or makes no sense, alert the attorney with whom you are working and tell him what troubles you about the opposing expert's CV.

The attorney you are working with will probably have beaten you to the next step, but you need to see in what sort of cases the opposing expert has testified. If, for example, the opposing expert has been called and testified twice for the defense and 97 times for the plaintiff's counsel, then you have a clear indication of the opposing expert's bias. (You as an expert should be careful to balance the sides you represent, aiming for a 50/50 split without being obsessive about it.) Look for previous cases the opposing expert has testified in that are similar in thrust to the current case. If you have concerns of unethical testimony, discuss with the attorney you are working with the possibility of acquiring transcripts of the opposing expert's testimony in those similar cases. Read his testimony from the previous trial and compare the cases to each other. Again, medical diagnosis is largely scientific, so a given set of circumstances determines a predictable result. If the opposing expert had previously testified in four similar cases and in each case he made statements consistent with his testimony in the other cases, then that argues for an ethical witness. If, on the other hand, the opposing expert says one thing in one trial and in the three other trials drew the completely opposite conclusion, then the possibility exists that the opposing expert is changing his story to suit some need other than the need for accurate diagnosis. A related means of assessing the opposing expert's integrity is to compare what he has testified to in court to any articles he may have published on the same topic. As with conflicting testimony, if in his publications the opposing expert has argued for a certain diagnostic criterion and then in court testified that the certain criterion is unimportant, then he is being inconsistent and unethical. Either he needs to clean up his act in court, or journal editors need to start rejecting his manuscripts.

Finally, if a report on the present case is available, then compare the opposing expert's report on the current case with his stance in his publications and in previous testimony. It may be that you disagree with the approach to diagnosis taken by the opposing expert, but as long as he is consistent and his approach is defendable, his testimony is likely to be ethical. As we have said before, medicine is a complex discipline, and it is acceptable for two capable and honest pathologists to disagree in their interpretation. In searching for indications of unethical conduct, you are looking for a pattern of behavior that is, to use the vernacular, sleazy.

Once in court, you may be allowed to sit with the attorney you are working with while the opposing expert testifies, just as the opposing expert may be allowed to hear your testimony and advise the questioning attorney concerning questions to ask you. If you hear the opposing expert's testimony, then consider what he is saying and alert your attorney to any egregious lies, willful failure to consider all the evidence, or quackery spoken by the witness.

Willful failure to consider all the evidence and quackery can be easy to spot. Let us return to the discussion of wildly exaggerated claims for experience. Suppose the opposing expert claims to have personally dissected and submitted 20,000 mastectomy specimens in his career. Once you hear a number, evaluate it. Think through the claim of grossing that many specimens in your career. If a pathologist has been practicing for 20 years, the claim would require grossing 1,000 mastectomy specimens per year. Assuming a busy working year of 300 days (5 days per week x 50 weeks per year plus weekend coverage every other weekend), 1,000 mastectomy specimens in one year would require that you personally receive an average of over three mastectomy specimens per day, every day. Breaking an expert witness's claim down in this way makes the validity of the claim much easier to assess whenever you hear a claim made. A few calculations will reveal the absurdity of an outrageous claim in a way that the opposing attorney, and the jury, will understand.

One other point is worth mentioning as a word of caution. A clever expert witness may be very careful to keep his practices in court quiet if his diagnoses are questionable at best and unethical at worst. As stated above, even attorneys call a witness for hire who will say whatever the attorney wants a "whore," but the fact remains that prostitutes do not go hungry for lack of business. Some physicians who have a prominent national reputation for excellence in their work and research are still willing to practice unethical medicine in court. These physicians have their reputation to consider, however. Generally someone with a national reputation is from an academic center in a large city. To hide their tracks, these physician witnesses will take cases from the hinterlands, where news of their work will never make it beyond the local newspaper with a circulation of 5,000. The surest way to evaluate this situation is to make yourself familiar with the opposing expert's body of written work and compare it to transcripts of his testimony in court. If he is consistent throughout his work and his testimony, then he is probably doing his most honest work. If he says "yes" at national meetings and "no" in Pine Fork, then you need to flush him out in court. The good news is that the people of Pine Fork who are on the jury do not give tuppence for the opposing expert's national reputation if they can be made to see that he is a humbug. In fact, the jury will resent having a big shot try to take them for a fool.

It will be the job of an attorney, not you as an expert witness, to cross-examine a witness that is giving unethical testimony. To reveal unethical testimony or fraudulent credentials to the jury, the attorney must ask the expert witness questions that will show that the witness has either falsified information or is speaking out of both sides of his mouth. You must believe that the judge and jury need to understand when unethical expert witness testimony occurs. A dishonest witness has no place in a court of law.

Out of Court

Unethical expert witness testimony is a blot on the practice of medicine. What then can be done by the medical community to prevent unethical testimony from reaching the courtroom? The answer at present is that little is done. For one thing, mechanisms for redressing the matter within the medical community are nearly nonexistent. Many solutions have been suggested, however, and some have even been implemented.

Some have suggested that a medical license be necessary to testify in a state (Massachusetts requires this, for example).[4] This practice would make expert medical witnesses subject to discipline by the state licensing board. The effectiveness of this approach is suspect, however. Whatever your opinion on whether testimony constitutes the practice of medicine, in some states, such as Missouri, courts have ruled that expert medical witness testimony is not the practice of medicine. Such a ruling might have proved expedient for the legal system in a given case, but one consequence of this interpretation is to shield a physician from discipline by a medical licensing board purely for testimony given in court, for even loss of a medical license would not be sufficient to stop a physician from giving expert medical witness testimony in a state that legally does not recognize medical testimony as the practice of medicine.

A particularly lawyerly response to the problem of unethical medical testimony is for expert witnesses to be subject to civil suits.[4] A variation of this approach is to hold academic institutions accountable for the testimony of their faculty members, perhaps because the institutions have deeper pockets for monetary damages than does an individual.

Guha has suggested requiring certification of potential expert witnesses according to national standards developed jointly by the medical and legal fields.[5] If you wish, this approach amounts to postgraduate training in legal medicine and case review akin to fellowship training in a subspecialty of medicine. Would such training last for an entire year? The implementation of this suggestion implies, perhaps, the formation of a new medical specialty board with legal and medical representatives overseeing certification. Who will determine who is admitted into the practice of expert witness testimony? As it stands, a physician can practice medicine without being certified by a specialty board, provided that he has a license to practice medicine. Could one also, under this plan, testify without the imprimatur of board certification in Testimony Medicine? If so, then how has this approach remedied the present situation? As an alternative, Guha also suggests holding two-day courses on the topic of expert witness testimony similar to ACLS certification review.[5]

The American Medical Association (AMA) has spoken concerning the practice of expert witness testimony. The AMA Council on Ethical and Judicial Affairs has set forth the following opinions:

- As a citizen and as a professional with special training and experience, the physician has an ethical obligation to assist with the administration of justice.
- The medical witness must not become an advocate or a partisan in the legal proceeding.
- The medical witness should be adequately prepared and should testify honestly and truthfully.
- The attorney for the party who calls the physician as a witness should be informed of all favorable and unfavorable information developed by the physician's evaluation of the case.
- It is unethical for a physician to accept compensation that is contingent upon the outcome of the litigation.

In 1997, the House of Delegates of the American Medical Association (AMA) adopted Resolution 221. Resolution 221 called upon the AMA to adopt a policy that expert witness testimony be considered the practice of medicine subject to peer review. The resolution also requested that the AMA study mechanisms by which such peer review could be conducted.

In response to Resolution 221, a committee studied the implications of having the AMA consider expert witness testimony the practice of medicine subject to peer review. The committee presented its findings in a report.[6] Report 18-I-98 highlights the important role of medical societies and licensing boards in maintaining the integrity of physicians who provide expert witness testimony. It suggests that this role be carefully defined after first discussing some of the inherent difficulties, both conceptual and practical, in conducting peer review of physicians who provide expert witness testimony. The obstacles to peer review of expert witness testimony found by the committee are great—such review would be time-consuming, expensive, and duplicate the work of an adversarial trial. Nor is it clear what authority a state licensing board might have over one who was found guilty of unethical testimony by a review board. The report recommends that the AMA work with state licensing boards to develop effective disciplinary measures for physicians who provide fraudulent testimony and suggests further study in collaboration with interested organizations. According to the AMA, Hillsborough County, Florida (Tampa), and San Diego County, California, have instituted boards to review the testimony within courts in their systems. So far, the accomplishment of each of these review boards is existence.

There are legal reasons why licensing boards and medical societies are unlikely to do more than decry the practice of unethical expert witness testimony. The institutions can be guilty of restraint of trade and intimidating witnesses, especially if the institution turns out to be wrong, and thus the institutions would be liable to the individual in civil court.[7] Furthermore, however good the intentions of a group that initiates a campaign to clean up unethical medical testimony, there lie the makings of a star chamber. Thus it remains unclear what steps, if any, the medical profession will take to review the testimony of medical expert witnesses. More medical testimony takes place than one might imagine.

According to the Federal Judicial Center, physicians and other medical experts represent the largest proportion of expert witnesses appearing in federal courts, testifying in at least half of all federal civil trials. Similar data are not available from state courts.

Despite the pessimistic tone of the preceding paragraphs, some hope remains. Perhaps the AMA encompasses too diverse a group to effect change. The American Association of Neurological Surgeons, which has unusually great concerns about unethical medical testimony, has taken the lead in flushing out unethical expert witnesses within its specialty. The professional conduct program of the AANS investigates claims of misconduct by AANS members. The Professional Conduct Committee addresses complaints received by the Association. Complaints found to be lacking in substance are recommended to the Association's Board of Directors for dismissal. Complaints that warrant further investigation lead to a hearing with due process for all parties involved, including legal counsel if desired. After evidence in a case deemed worthy of a hearing has been presented, the committee determines whether professional misconduct has occurred and, if so, what penalty to recommend to the Association's Board of Directors. The penalties include censure, suspension of membership, or expulsion from the AANS. The AANS also maintains a library of transcripts from depositions and trials given by neurosurgical expert witnesses. These files are available for a fee to either AANS members or to an attorney representing an AANS member. The testimony of an individual can thus be checked for the soundness and consistency of his medical opinions from case to case. The American Association of Neurological Surgeons has refused to be bullied by the threat of lawsuits against them for investigating unethical testimony, and their program has successfully withstood three court challenges against it.[8,9]

Conclusion

The adversarial trial process is designed to flush out incorrect testimony; that it sometimes fails to do so is an unfortunate truth. Attorneys are naturally loathe to give up control of their system, just as physicians do not willingly relinquish control of medical practice. Remember that the expert witness system as currently practiced costs attorneys nothing; the pay for expert witnesses comes either from the insurance company (or other corporation) that the defense attorney represents or out of the award to the plaintiff that the plaintiff's attorney represents. Therefore, there is no financial incentive for attorneys to redress the present system, and in a land devoted to economic pressures for correction, what effective force is there for redress? As long as the present system remains in place, playing the expert witness game will include looking for signs of unethical claims by the expert representing the other side, even for neurosurgeons.

References

1. Chadwick DL, Krous HF. Irresponsible testimony by medical experts in cases involving the physical abuse and neglect of children. Child Maltreatment 1997;2(4):313–21.
2. Daubert v Merrell Dow Pharmaceuticals, Inc, 113 SCt 2786 (1993).
3. McAbee GN. United States Supreme Court rules on expert testimony. Pediatrics 1995;95:934–6.
4. Committee on Medical Liability. Guidelines for expert witness testimony in medical malpractice litigation. Pediatrics 2002;109(5):974–9.
5. Guha SJ. Fixing medical malpractice: one doctor's perspective of a non-system in need of national standardization. N C Med J 2000;61:227–30.
6. American Medical Association. Board of Trustees Report 18-I-98.
7. Crane M. How do expert witnesses get away with lying? Med Econ 1999;76(1): 152–64.
8. Pelton RM. Professing professional conduct: AANS raises the bar for expert testimony. AANS Bull 2002;11(1):7–13.
9. Pelton RM. Questions and answers follow-up: professing professional conduct. AANS Bull 2002;11(2):32–3.

8
Quality Assurance and Record Keeping

Properly conducted programs in quality control and quality assurance improve the practice of pathology and are, of course, required for accreditation of a pathology laboratory. The laws governing quality control and quality assurance in hospitals vary greatly from state to state, and thus only general points will be discussed here.

Definitions and Requirements

Quality control and quality assurance are related but distinct. Quality control is something physical done to monitor an individual testing process during the analytic phase only. Quality control is subject to statistical analysis of mean and variance. The physical assessment that is quality control differs from quality assurance, which is a process of continual review of the policies and procedures for each area of laboratory testing to identify potential problems and areas for improvement.

In order to be accredited, hospitals, as well as pathology laboratories, must maintain records of their efforts to maintain and improve quality of service. A hospital will have a department named Joint Commission Regulatory Affairs or Department of Quality Assurance, or the hospital will at least contract with an agency to provide such an administrative service. This department will oversee the details necessary to pass an accreditation inspection, such as the maintenance of procedure manuals and quality assurance documentation. For accreditation, quality assurance documentation must be maintained for at least three years.

Importance of Quality Assurance to a Hospital

Hospitals have reason to require departments to maintain a quality assurance program beyond the simple need for accreditation, and that is the legal concept of negligent entrustment. Negligent entrustment occurs whenever a third party may be sued because the third party should have known that the negligent person was unfit to perform the task that led to the negligent injury. In the medical environment, negligent entrustment allows a plaintiff patient to sue a hospital, a practice group, or even nonmembers of a practice group because each entity should have recognized the incompetence of the physician who committed malpractice. An example would be a physician with an obvious and known addiction practicing medicine even when intoxicated. A quality assurance program *that is enforced* is how the hospital and the group document that each was checking regularly and had no reason to believe that the physician charged with negligence or misconduct was unqualified to have medical staff privileges or to practice as a member of the group.[1]

Overlap of Quality Assurance and Risk Management

Sometimes quality assurance programs and risk management will both examine the same case. Any hospital case that merits investigation because of a lapse in the quality of care may be of interest, or even concern, to the Department of Risk Management as well. State laws differ on the degree to which information generated in a quality assurance program is discoverable, that is, to what extent attorneys can use their power of subpoena to gain access to quality assurance records. Most states consider quality assurance documents privileged, reasoning that the public good that comes from having an active quality assurance program should not be deterred by forcing hospitals to air the findings of a quality assurance investigation for the benefit of a single citizen (and his attorney) for a single malpractice suit. Nevertheless, some state courts have, in individual cases, ordered that quality assurance documents pertaining to the case in question be opened and admitted into court. The damper that such public exposure of a quality assurance investigation would put on subsequent quality assurance investigations within the entire state is obvious. The legal precedents within your own state are either known by the attorneys in your hospital risk management department or can be found by the attorneys in risk management.

Shortcomings of Quality Assurance Programs

Traditional mechanisms for quality assurance are often ineffective for two reasons. Firstly, the work of quality assurance is often done in an ad hoc way, depending upon a data collection system based on anecdotes. Any system based solely on anecdotes or recalled cases is subject to bias. Bias is avoided by incorporating a random method of choosing cases for quality assurance review. This is not to say that a case remembered as being worthy of review should not be reviewed. Rather, a set number of cases randomly chosen (whether by a roll of dice, cutting cards, or using some computer algorithm) should be reviewed in addition to cases that merit specific attention. If you as a group already incorporate cases randomly chosen for review, then you have already seen how those random cases bring to light problems that were not apparent before.

The second way in which quality assurance programs within medicine are often ineffective is that the system of review is unduly influenced by the actions of popular (or politically powerful) personalities. Every group has such personalities, and it is unlikely that such people will be effectively regulated. The solution to this dilemma is difficult, particularly if the personalities are not amenable to being regulated. Know, however, that if the politics of your situation makes this particular dilemma insurmountable, that there is always the potential that a situation will arise that will force the issue, so prepare for such an occurrence as best you can.

Record Keeping

Discussion of quality assurance documentation for accreditation leads naturally to the discussion of record keeping in general. How long should a record be kept? There are requirements, such as three years in order to be accredited. There are guidelines, such as the College of American Pathologists's guidelines for tissue retention. Beyond those guidelines and requirements, however, there is another consideration for the length of time a document should be retained. The *purpose* of a particular document determines the length of time you will wish to retain a document beyond what is required for accreditation. Remember that a document may serve more than one purpose, and the period of retention will be whichever purpose dictates the longest time for having the document available. If, for example, the document relates not only to quality assurance, but also to medical malpractice, then you may wish to keep the document until the statute of limitations for medical malpractice in your state expires. As discussed in Chapter 4, the statute of limitations varies from state to state, including the point at which the clock starts. Some states consider that the clock starts when the event occurs, others that the clock does not begin until the patient becomes aware of the occurrence of the event. If, on the other hand, the purpose of a record is to document poor performance by an employee, then that purpose will determine how long you need to keep the document.

Obviously the laws governing an individual state play a role in quality assurance, from the length of time records must be maintained to the likelihood that quality assurance records will be exposed in court. To assess your own situation in your own state, it is best to talk with the people in your hospital who are familiar with accreditation and with risk management, perhaps at one of your regular quality assurance meetings.

Reference

1. Richards EP, Rathbun KC. Medical Risk Management: Preventive Legal Strategies for Health Care Providers. Rockville, MD: Aspen Systems Corp., 1983.

9
When the Time Comes to Be an Activist: Interacting with the Legislature

Gregory J. Davis

"It's not your obligation to complete the task, but neither are you free to abstain from it."

—Rabbi Tarfon, *Pirkei Avot*, Sayings of the Ancestors

As members of a representative democracy, it is incumbent upon us as citizens and as physicians to be well-informed about, and interactive with, our communities, both large and small. Many issues with great impact upon our daily and long-term practices are debated within our state legislatures and by the U.S. Congress. Medical malpractice, tort reform, education, budgets, crime, the environment, beginning and end-of-life concerns, medical research, Medicaid, and Medicare are but a few of the issues currently being considered by legislatures across the nation. We as physicians have an ethical obligation to attempt to constructively influence legislation that will affect the quality of the health care offered our patients.

A common complaint that state representatives and senators have is that they do not hear from their constituents or that they only hear after-the-fact complaints. Being available to his or her constituents is an expected portion of a legislator's duty, and it is our duty in turn to communicate in a timely fashion with them regarding issues affecting our practices.

General Overview of the Legislative Process

Before we delve into constructive ways in which one might interact with one's legislator, it may be helpful to outline the general legislative process itself, describing in brief how an idea becomes a bill and then perhaps becomes law.

Please keep in mind that the following is a generic overview and that specifics will vary from state to state.

While anyone may draft a bill, usually only members of the legislature may introduce legislation and thereby become its sponsor. The official legislative process begins when the bill is referred to a committee and is then made available to the public in printed form. Bills are then usually referred to standing committees according to rules of procedure, then placed on the committee's calendar and perhaps referred to a subcommittee. If the committee does not act upon the bill, it is effectively killed. If the subcommittee considers the bill, hearings often provide an opportunity to record the views of public officials, experts, supporters, and opponents of the legislation. When hearings are completed, the subcommittee may "mark up," or modify, the bill. If the subcommittee votes not to report the bill back to the committee, the bill is at that moment dead.

After receiving a report from its subcommittee, the committee may conduct further study, or it votes on the subcommittee's findings and recommends further modification. The full committee then votes on its recommendations to the full House or Senate in a procedure known as "ordering a bill reported." The committee chair then will instruct staff to prepare a written report on the bill, describing the intent and scope of legislation with its impact upon existing laws and programs. The bill is then placed on the House or Senate calendar for debate.

When the bill reaches the Senate or House floor, procedures and rules govern the format of the debate, including decorum and time allowed for discussion. After the debate and approval of any amendments, the bill is then passed or defeated by the members present and voting. Should the House or Senate pass the bill, it is then referred to the other chamber, where it usually follows a similar path through committees and floor action. This second chamber may approve the bill as received from the other chamber, or it may elect to reject, ignore, or change the bill. If only minor changes are made to the bill by the second chamber, the bill often goes back to the first chamber for concurrence; however, if the action of the second chamber substantively alters the bill, a joint committee will be formed to reconcile the differences between the House and Senate versions. If the joint committee cannot reconcile the differences, the bill dies. If an agreement is reached, both chambers must approve the report of the joint committee. After approval of the bill by both the House and Senate, the bill is sent to the Governor, for signature into state law, or President, for signature into federal law.

Staying Current with Legislation

The most efficient way to be up-to-date with legislation and the stance of individual legislators on particular bills affecting one's practice is to be a Fellow of the College of American Pathologists (www.cap.org). The College is the principal organization of board-certified pathologists, and its primary mission is to represent the interests of patients, the public, and pathologists by fostering excellence in the practice of pathology and laboratory medicine worldwide. The College offers Action Alerts by facsimile or e-mail to its members, as do many county and state medical societies as well as the American Medical Association.

The most personal way to keep in touch, if you cultivate the luxury, is to develop a professional relationship with the legislators who represent you. An established relationship will serve not only to provide you warning of potential legislation that may affect your practice but also help assure that you have an ear that considers your views when a bill is being debated and voted upon. Lobbyists do such work, but provided that you yourself are willing and capable of getting involved in a personal way in legislation, you will be that much more certain that your voice is heard.

Communicating with Your Legislators

Telephone Calls

When making telephone calls to legislative offices, the caller should remember the old public speaking aphorism, "Short and sweet is hard to beat." One should be concise, polite, and exact. Before the call, write down the key talking points you wish to discuss. Note your own position, rationale, and, importantly, the action you wish the legislator to take. This last point is important, as many legislators complain that they receive many phone calls, after which they hang up not knowing what the caller actually wanted. Plan for a maximum of three minutes on the phone.

During the call, identify yourself and your constituent connections with the legislator. If you live in the legislator's district, give your home address; if your office is in the district, give your work address. Ask to speak with the lawmaker, but do not be put off or offended if you speak with a Legislative Assistant (Legislative Director) instead of the legislator himself, as the legislator is, like you, often quite busy. Often the Legislative Assistant will actually know more about the issue under discussion. Briefly state the purpose of the call, and ask the lawmaker to support your position. If the legislator already does so, thank him. If the legislator is undecided or opposed to your position, ask why and address the legislator's concerns. Be polite, concise, and do not argue or assume an antagonistic attitude. Make notes, recording the name of the person with whom you spoke, thanking them for taking the call and forwarding your concerns to the legislator. After the call, follow up with a letter recapitulating your stance and thanking the person who took your call, as well as the legislator, for considering your position.

Facsimiles and E-mail

Even with the wonders of electronic technology, and even given that most law-makers' offices have a fax machine and e-mail capacity, such communications are much less effective than telephone calls with their personal interactions or, better yet, personal letters. Faxes and e-mails tend to become lost in the shuffle of the voluminous communiqués received in a busy office. If your legislator or staff member requests information via such media, however, feel free to communicate in such fashion.

Personal Letters

The letter is the most popular and well-received means of communication with a legislator's office; it is most effective in communicating your ideas and concerns. When addressing correspondence, adhere to the following salutations:

To a Senator:

The Honorable (full name)
Address

Dear Senator:

To a Representative:

The Honorable (Full Name)
Address

Dear Representative

Note that when writing to a Chair of a Committee or the Speaker of the House, the proper salutation is:

Dear Mr. Chairman or Madam Chairwoman

or   Dear Mr./Madam Speaker

The following suggestions will assist you in presenting your views.

- Use personal stationery.
- Note in a subject line which issue or bill you are addressing.
- Be concise: do you support or oppose the bill.
- Be timely, as letters arriving after a vote are of no use.
- Provide concrete and reliable information on the impact of the legislation.
- Brevity is best: one-page letters have a better chance of being closely read.

- Follow up: if the legislator does as you request, write a thank you letter, but, on the other hand, don't become a "pen pal" by writing so often that your letters become annoyances.

Meeting with Your Legislators

Planning the Meeting

Of all forms of communication, the personal meeting is the best for conveying one's ideas. The first step to the meeting is contacting the legislator's personal or scheduling secretary. Unless you already know the legislator, it is best to do so in writing and in doing so explain who you are and why you wish to meet. Follow up after the letter is sent with a telephone call to the secretary. Again, do not be put off if you are scheduled to meet with a legislative assistant rather than the lawmaker himself.

During the meeting, it is important to know your issue and related facts well. Be careful not to overwhelm the legislator or assistant with too many people or issues: go alone or at most with one or two others, and concentrate upon one major issue with only a few talking points. Be prompt, preferably a few minutes early, but also be patient, as many legislators have cramped schedules with multiple daily exigencies. Be "political" in the constructive connotations of the word: articulate the ways that what you are requesting will be beneficial to the legislator's constituents. If you are able, describe how your group might be of assistance to the legislator. It is important to be responsive, providing additional information and answering the legislator's questions. Remember that the point of your meeting is discussion, implicit in which is an exchange of ideas. Keep an open mind, and do not lecture or antagonize the legislator, as doing so will cause loss of any opportunity for rapport. Be firm but courteous and open to the legislator's questions, concerns, and opinions. Leave the legislator with a brief, one-page outline of your issue, and give him the courtesy and acknowledgment of a thank you letter upon your return home.

Common Errors in Interacting with Legislators

- Assuming the legislator knows all there is to know about an issue. Legislators deal with a staggering number of bills each session. Most legislators will know most about bills they sponsored themselves, those with which their committee is involved, and those that their constituents have asked them to support or oppose.
- Coming to the meeting without the facts. Most legislators want to know the facts about the issue and will expect you to inform them. Never guess, never wing it; if you don't know an answer to a question, state as much and promise to find the answer and follow up.

- Not acknowledging that there are two (if not more) sides to an issue. The legislator will have visits from those that oppose your stance.
- Denigrating the other side. Name-calling and jejune behavior will win neither friends nor influence in the legislature. If your issue won't stand on its own merit, foul language won't help, and besides, some of the legislator's friends may be on that other side.
- Expecting the legislator to immediately commit to your cause. Most politicians are, to paraphrase Nikos Kazantzakis's Zorba the Greek, like all clever people and grocers: they weigh everything. Allow the lawmaker to consider all sides of the argument before taking a position.
- Burning bridges. All battles do not end in victory, and it is important politically to live to fight another day. Working with legislators is a long-term effort, and there will be other engaging struggles in the future.
- Failing to say thank you. In our human hierarchy of needs, acknowledgment ranks right up there with food and shelter. A note thanking the legislator for meeting with you is always remembered fondly.
- Being a "one-hit wonder." Follow up is important. While you do not wish to deluge the legislator with correspondence (i.e., don't be a "pen pal"), do keep in touch on occasion to let the lawmaker know that your interest has not waned. Stay informed of your issue so that you in turn can communicate your concerns.

Conclusion

As a citizen in a participatory democracy and physician concerned for your patients, it is imperative that you stay informed about issues affecting your practice and the delivery of health care to your patients. As our Oath of Hippocrates mandates, by doing so we will honor our commitment to practice medicine with conscience and dignity while keeping the health and life of our patients our highest priority.

Sources

1. College of American Pathologists. Available from http://www.cap.org.
2. Lexington Medical Society. Available from http://www.lexingtondoctors.org.
3. Kentucky Medical Association. Available from http://www.kyma.org.
4. American Medical Association. Available from http://www.ama-assn.org.

10
Legal Implications for the Information Age

The practice of medicine has always depended upon effective communication. The quality of patient care is highest when the patient and physician freely communicate with each other and when attending and consulting physicians freely communicate among themselves. Today patients have an unprecedented ability to educate themselves concerning their health and health care. Any patient with Internet access can search the Medline, seek an explanation of the content of medical reports (including pathology reports), explore the practice history and licensure of his physicians, or look into the feasibility of bringing a malpractice suit. Meanwhile, the nature of the physician–consultant physician relationship is also changing because of telemedicine.

The changes in communication brought by the electronic age will be incorporated into the practice of medicine. This chapter addresses, in a superficial way, some changes wrought by the ease and speed with which large amounts of medical information can be transferred. The topics mentioned are still evolving, but some principles will remain true regardless of the course that electronic medicine takes.

Health Information Portability and Accountability Act

The Health Information Portability and Accountability Act, commonly known by its acronym HIPAA, is the federal response to a sense that each patient is the owner of his own health information (Public Law 104-191, 104th Congress). Because of congressional concern about the privacy and security of medical information concerning patients, HIPAA is intended and designed to guard the privacy and security of patient information in the era of electronic data transmission. Furthermore, HIPAA also is intended to establish coding standards for the interchange of electronic data and identifiers that will be uniform throughout the nation. Without the overarching federal authority of HIPAA, the standards for data exchange would be determined by each state, resulting in a patchwork quilt. Therefore, HIPAA now mandates a minimum federal standard for all institutions that are in some way involved in health care or research.

Each medical center will hold training classes concerning HIPAA for its staff, and this book is not intended to duplicate such information. Nevertheless, one point bears mention concerning each patient's right to review his medical record. HIPAA specifically states that an individual patient has no access to his medical record for civil or criminal actions. Does this mean that a patient contemplating a malpractice suit cannot gain access to his chart? No, it does not, and in any case it is the patient's attorney who gains access to the patient's chart for review in a potential malpractice suit through a subpoena. The purpose of the HIPAA restriction on a patient's access to his medical record is seen most clearly in a child being treated for child abuse. Here the parents, who will almost certainly be suspects in addition to being the legal custodians of the patient, may not gain access to the medical record of their child so that they can review the medical record prior to being questioned in the criminal investigation of child abuse. Moreover, the parents cannot bring a civil suit requiring that they be allowed to see their child's record. The attorney who would represent the parents against the criminal charge of child abuse will be given access to the child's medical record according to the rules of discovery, but the parents cannot stymie the criminal investigation by demanding their right to see their ward's medical record.

Finally, HIPAA changes nothing about one important aspect of a malpractice suit. A patient who brings a malpractice suit against a physician still waives his right of privacy concerning his medical record.

Telemedicine

The Internet has opened new avenues of medical interaction and information exchange. The marketing of these changes is sometimes known as telemedicine. Some specialties, notably radiology, have explored the possibilities of telemedicine more than have others.[1] In pathology, it is easy enough to attach a video feed to a microscope and transmit images for consultation on difficult surgical cases, and the raw data from some tests from the clinical laboratory can be transmitted more easily still.

Advantages and Disadvantages

Telemedicine has two obvious advantages—the speed with which consultation can occur and the access to highly trained specialists for rural patients. These advantages are pitted against the disadvantages of cost required to install and maintain the necessary infrastructure, the quality of the image that is transmitted, and changes in the practice of how health care is delivered. With respect to the changes in health care delivery, the specific change is to the need for specialists in every locale. Providing remote access to subspecialty consultation for rural patients is likely to make subspecialists all the more scarce outside of the

big cities. Some physicians perceive telemedicine as a threat and so have lob-
bied for legislation within their own state to restrict the practice of telemedicine.
Those in favor of telemedicine have their own lobbying to do.

With respect to the quality of the image transmitted, the disadvantage is especially clear. There is no need to consult on an obvious case, and a subtle case
calls for the consultant to have all the resolution available to the physician consulting him. Loss of resolution in a digital photograph, compounded with loss in
display on a monitor, will hamper telepathology until digital technology exceeds
the resolution of the human eye.

Legal Matters

Telemedicine is new, and untested waters are always a breeding ground for
questions and concerns about legal rules for fair play, especially since the craft-
ing of laws and the practice of law depend partly on precedent. Heretofore a
patient and his service provider were probably within the same building, but
with telemedicine a patient can be separated from a pathologist by several states,
raising legal questions concerning licensure, malpractice, information security,
and image storage and retention.

Licensure

The erosion of boundaries that telemedicine makes possible is in conflict with
the political interests of states and practitioners within a state to both protect
their business within the region and to control the practice of medicine within
the region. In telemedicine, the matter at stake is where exactly the practice of
medicine takes place in an encounter in which the patient is in one state and the
consultant in another. Some have argued that in telemedicine the practice of
medicine occurs in the state where the physician is. This view has not held sway
in state courts, which, after all, will inevitably be in the state where the patient
is. (There is, of course, no constraint on the practice of telemedicine within a
state.)

The tenth amendment to the Constitution grants states the powers that are not
reserved by the federal government. Because there is no general federal licensure for the practice of medicine, states oversee licensure. There is no indication
that the federal government will alter the way in which a license to practice
medicine is granted within the United States.

One could obtain a license to practice medicine in every state where one
would practice telemedicine. Obtaining a license to practice in every state is
expensive and time-consuming, however. Each license comes with its own demand for continuing medical education documentation, which varies from state
to state. Some states require a personal interview and test for licensure, and in
any case states will require documentation of good standing in all other states of

licensure, which becomes onerous in a geometric progression. Several options have therefore been proposed for handling licensure in a telemedicine market.

Consulting exceptions—already established in most states. Here a consulting physician is not required to have a state license for the state from which he was consulted, but neither was the consultant allowed to have an office in the state from which the consultation arose. Technically these exceptions would apply to telemedicine, but the laws were enacted for the relatively infrequent occurrence of consultation out of state as occurred decades ago. The regular and continuing nature of telepathology violates the spirit in which the consulting exception laws were passed.

Endorsement—A state grants a license based on the licensure of the practitioner in a state with equally stringent requirements for licensure. The licensing state may request additional documentation from the consultant before endorsing him.

Mutual recognition—In this system, several licensing agencies (that is, several states) would enter into an agreement to legally accept the license from any of the states participating in the agreement. All states in the agreement would have to agree on policies regarding licensure and medical practice, and then a physician with a license to practice in any one state could practice in all the states participating in the agreement. The European Community and Australia practice mutual recognition.

Reciprocity—Reciprocity allows one state to grant subjects of other states certain privileges on the condition that its own subjects will be granted those same privileges in the corresponding state. Obviously the states must once again agree, but reciprocity precludes further review of the credentials of each individual practitioner.

Registration—A physician licensed to practice in one state would inform another state of his wish to practice part-time or in some limited way within that other state while submitting to the legal authority and jurisdiction of that other state. Although the physician would not have to meet the licensing requirements of a state in which he registered, he would be held accountable for any breach of professional conduct.

Limited licensure—Here the scope of the physician's practice would be limited within the state where a limited license was held. As a condition for limited licensure, the physician would have to hold a full license to practice medicine in at least one state.

National licensure—A national standard for the practice of medicine throughout the United States would be established. Each state would have to incorporate the national standard into its state law. Practitioners would still have to get an individual state license, but the shared standard would facilitate the administrative process.

The College of American Pathologists has recommended that physicians obtain a license to practice medicine in each state in which the patient presents for diagnosis.[2]

Finally, state licensure is not the only form of accreditation that a physician practicing telemedicine will have to maintain. A hospital, for example, may require its physicians to perform a minimum number or percentage of their procedures within that hospital, lest the hospital provide office space to a physician who is earning his keep "abroad" via telemedicine.

Malpractice and Liability

The advent of telemedicine has both benefits and risks for malpractice liability. The benefits are the involvement of two or more physicians in the evaluation of a given case (particularly a difficult case) and the decreased time from biopsy to final report. Two risks exist for the pathologist practicing telepathology. One has already been mentioned, namely an error in diagnosis due to the poorness of the quality of the image on which the diagnosis was made. The second risk is the potential for a plaintiff patient to win a larger award against the defendant physicians. Remember that the entire area is new legally, so the laws and precedents are still being established. There exists the potential that a plaintiff patient's attorney could consider the laws governing malpractice in each of the states where the telemedicine consulting business is practiced, looking for a state most favorable to the plaintiff–patient's suit. Not only would the patient's attorney consider which state had the highest cap, if any, for a malpractice award but also the tendency of the juries in each state for making awards, both in size and frequency. Having chosen the optimal state, the patient's attorney would then file a malpractice suit against the defendant physician in that state. The indication that courts consider that the practice of medicine occurred where the patient was may well prevent such shopping, however.

Information Privacy, Confidentiality, and Security

The ease with which information can be shared not only makes telemedicine possible but also makes possible the misuse of patient information. This potential misuse is much of what HIPAA is intended to address and was discussed in the first section of this chapter. The principles of HIPAA indicate that when specific patient information is sent electronically, it should be kept as secure as possible, including encryption and the use of a safe server.

Image Storage, Retention, and Manipulation

Accreditation in pathology requires that certain materials must be held for certain times before being discarded. The time for retention of electronic images remains to be established. This is perhaps more urgent in radiology departments that have gone entirely to digital systems than in pathology, but any practice that includes consultation based on digital images must capture and retain the digital images in some way for some period of time. If the image is used for a microscopic diagnosis, then holding the image for the same time as holding the original item from which the digital image was made seems appropriate, until such time as guidelines are established.

Some individuals have expressed concern about the ease with which digital images can be altered, but legally this is less compelling than it may seem. In fact, attorneys are little concerned about the digital manipulation of images. Attorneys are little concerned because in a trial it is individuals who attest to the appearance of the image as a fair and accurate representation of what the lesion looked like at the time the physician saw it, regardless of whether the image is a conventional or digital photograph.

The concern over the potential manipulation of digital photographs is not related to the digital nature of the photographs. After all, the technology for manipulating conventional photographs has existed for years. It is the new ease of manipulation that is of concern to some.

Unfortunately, there seems to be no shortage of dishonest men. What pathologists will have to begin to consider is the possibility that a digital photomicrograph shown as an exhibit in a trial may have been altered to show something that was not on the original slide, such as dysplastic nuclei on a cervical Pap smear when the smear itself was diagnosed as "drying artifact, no dysplasia detected."

On the other hand, digital manipulation or enhancement may help in the diagnosis of certain conditions. As mentioned in Chapter 7, beware of the pathologist who claims that he has a secret technique that allows him to diagnose malignancy with absolute accuracy in a setting where no one else can; such a claim carries with it the echo of the quacks and snake oil, and it is certainly void of the reproducibility that sound science requires.

Fraud and Abuse

Any medical venture that involves Medicare, Medicaid, or third-party reimbursement must adhere to state and federal laws concerning referrals and kickbacks, and that requirement will extend to telemedicine as well. The Medicare–Medicaid Patient Protection Act makes it illegal to offer, solicit, or pay anything of value in return for a referral for services provided to Medicare, Medicaid, or state program patients. Federal law prohibits any referral by a physician in which the physician has ownership or financial interest or receives compensation. Physicians entering telemedicine ventures must carefully consider these restrictions before referring a case to another physician linked to the network.

Antitrust

Antitrust regulations are intended to prevent practices that create unfair competition among providers. One allegation of antitrust could be made by a rural practitioner who resents the infringement on his trade by a telemedicine network. Another, less obvious antitrust charge could be made by the government concerning providers in a community who share a database, where the accusation could be made that shared information led to price fixing.

E-mail

The advantages of e-mail have made it a popular means of sending and receiving messages. The ease of sending a message carries with it a risk, however. Who has not hit "send" only to realize that the message is going not to the intended recipient but instead to everyone on the listserver? Such a mistake may prove to be either humorous or awkward. Considering the ease with which e-mail can end up in the wrong hands, it would be wise to consider your e-mail correspondence as having the same sort of privacy as is enjoyed by a postcard. True, no one should read a postcard not sent to them, but who will be the wiser? Any thoughts you wish to remain private should be transmitted by word of mouth, whether in person or over the telephone. Things written down have a way of persisting, and even a casual reader of newspapers knows that e-mail messages can be used to provide evidence during an investigation.

A particular boon of e-mail to physicians is the creation of listservers, where physicians with similar interests can send and receive e-mails that are shared with all. Sometimes the e-mails concern cases, sometimes administrative matters, and sometimes queries for addresses of colleagues with whom the sender has lost touch. HIPAA requirements for maintaining patient confidentiality apply to e-mail and thus to the practice of querying colleagues about a problematic case through a listserver. HIPAA requires that identifying patient information be removed from a document made public, such as a journal article, and this also would apply to e-mail. A case is considered void of identifying features if the following items are absent from the document.

1. Name
2. All pertinent geographic subdivisions smaller than a state, including street address, city, county, precinct, and zip code
3. All dates (except year) directly related to an individual, including birthday, admission date, discharge date, and death date
4. Telephone numbers
5. Facsimile numbers
6. E-mail addresses
7. Social security numbers
8. Medical record numbers
9. Health plan beneficiary numbers
10. Account numbers
11. Certificate/license numbers

12. Vehicle identifiers and serial numbers, including license plate numbers
13. Device identifiers and serial numbers
14. Web site URLs
15. Internet Protocol address numbers
16. Biometric identifiers, including finger and voice prints
17. Full-face photographic images and any comparable images
18. Any other unique identifying number, characteristic, or code

Common sense should enable a useful case scenario to be composed that avoids the sorts of specific personal details listed above. An e-mail that begins "Attached are two representative images of a soft tissue mass removed from a 4-year-old female..." is reasonable, whereas "Attached are two representative images, identified by their case and patient numbers, of a soft tissue mass removed from a 4-year-old female (born 14 August 1999)..." is not.

References

1. Norris TG. Telemedicine and teleradiology. Radiol Technol 1999;71:139–63.
2. College of American Pathologists. State legislative issues brief 2000 (August) [online] [cited 2003 May 29]; Available from http://www.cap.org/html/advocacy/instates/teleiss.html.

Glossary of Legal Terms

Ad hominem Latin, literally "to the man." A tactic sometimes used by an attorney in order to try to discredit a witness. The attorney attacks the witness verbally, hoping to get the witness to either cringe or counterattack. The attorney will then point out to the jury what a coward or jerk the witness is, depending on the witness's response. The correct response of the witness is to maintain a professional manner and to refuse to stoop to the attorney's level. Not only is such professionalism correct, it should also be satisfying since by refusing to fall into the attorney's trap the witness is actually discrediting the attorney.

Adversarial trial system The method of achieving justice in the United States. The principle that a dispute is settled most fairly by having each side present its evidence publicly, in the presence of the one accused, in a forum where the opposing side can then vigorously challenge the merit, or even truth, of the evidence just presented.

Appellate The adjectival form of "appeal." An appellate court is a court where appeals are heard.

Attorney A professionally trained advocate for a side in a legal dispute. Since the attorney is his client's advocate, he must abide by his client's wishes regarding making or accepting offers of settlement.

Bailiff The sergeant at arms in a courtroom who enforces order; he may also swear in witnesses.

Chain of custody A written record of where and in whose custody an item has been since it was discovered. Also known as *chain of evidence.*

Civil trial A trial in which an irreconcilable dispute between two or more parties is resolved by binding arbitration. No crime has been committed. The party who brings charges against the accused must convince the jury that the "preponderance of the evidence" supports his accusation against the accused.

Continued	A legal term meaning "postponed," as in "This case has been continued until next year."
Court reporter	The stenographer who records the words of the trial. The reporter usually sits near the witness and types on a small machine from which a spool of white receipt tape emanates. The reporter appreciates a witness with a strong, clear voice. If you are new to the reporter, it would be a good idea to slip the reporter your business card as you leave. Make a note on the card for the reporter to call you if the reporter has questions about spelling or what you said. They will appreciate your thoughtfulness, although they rarely call.
Criminal trial	A trial in which the person suspected of committing a crime is tried. The state must provide evidence that establishes the suspect's guilt "beyond reasonable doubt."
Defendant	The accused in either a civil or criminal trial.
Deposition	A sworn written statement or videotape recording of someone's testimony that may be read or played in court as a substitute for the appearance of that person in the trial.
Discovery	The requirement that both sides in a legal case have access to all the available information well in advance of the trial.
Docket	A list of law cases to be heard or tried in a courtroom.
Double jeopardy	The process of trying an individual for a charge a second time after the individual was found not guilty of that same charge in that same incident the first time. Double jeopardy is not allowed in the United States.
Due process	The right of an individual charged with violating the law to be served notice of that charge and to be heard concerning that charge. From due process derives the right to be present at your own trial, the right to question your accusers, and the right to have legal counsel in that trial.
Expert witness	Any individual who has training or experience beyond that of everyday experience who agrees to testify in a legal proceeding based on that training and expertise.

Fact witness
Any individual who saw, heard, or was otherwise directly involved in the matter that is being disputed in court. In a medical case, a fact witness is one who actually saw the patient, either as the attending physician, as a consultant, or as part of the support staff. Any procedure done or any notes or reports generated by the physician will likely be the major reason for the testimony. Should the physician's opinion about the case be sought to any significant extent, the physician has gone from being a fact witness to an expert witness. Fact witnesses are also known as evidentiary or material witnesses.

Informed consent
Consent of a patient to undergo a procedure after the risks and benefits of the procedure are explained to the patient and understood by the patient. Life-threatening emergencies requiring immediate action require no informed consent, but otherwise the performance of a procedure without the patient's consent can be construed legally as assault.

Judge
The sole authority in the courtroom. The judge presides over the case, settles disputes between the attorneys concerning points of law, and instructs the jury in its responsibilities. If the defendant is found guilty, the judge will determine the sentence. Most judges are kindly disposed to physicians who have been called to testify because the physician is a professional. If you get a judge who is belligerent, you must grin and bear it; the jury takes its lead from the judge, and if you are rude back to a judge the jury will remember it and probably penalize you for it.

Jury
A panel of citizens, usually twelve in number with one or two alternates (in case a juror must be dismissed from the trial before the trial ends). The members of a jury are your peers as human beings. They will want to hear what you have to say. Although they are silent, they hold great power in the trial, so address them with deference and respect. They will relate your testimony, even your expert testimony, to their everyday experience to make their decision. Thus it behooves you to use everyday sorts of words and examples.

Mistrial
A trial rendered invalid by some error, such as a disqualification of a witness or juror. A mistrial also occurs if the jury cannot agree on a verdict, making the trial inconclusive.

Negligent entrustment   The legal concept that a third party may be sued because the third party should have known that the negligent person was unfit to perform the task that led to the negligent injury. This allows a plaintiff patient to sue a hospital, a practice group, or even nonmembers of a practice group because each corporate entity should have recognized the incompetence of the physician who committed the alleged malpractice.

Notice   The written document by which an individual is notified that he has been sued in civil court. Also known as a *summons*.

Objection   During a trial, a formal protest to the judge by one attorney that the other attorney's action violates the principles by which a trial is conducted. The judge must then decide which attorney will have his way. If the objection is accepted by the judge, he will say "Sustained," and the attorney about whom the objection was raised will have to abandon that question of the witness. If the objection is rejected by the judge, he will say "Overruled," and the question about which the objection was raised may be asked of the witness.

Perjury   Occurs when a witness forswears his oath to tell the truth. In other words, perjury is lying while testifying. Perjury can occur either by commission (telling a lie) or omission (failing to provide information that has been called for).

Plaintiff   A person or party suing a defendant in civil court. In the case of a charge of malpractice, the plaintiff is the legal term applied to the patient who believes he has been wronged.

Pool   The group of citizens selected by lot to report for jury duty. A jury of twelve will be chosen from a larger pool of citizens. Different states have different laws governing how its citizens are called to report to jury duty. In times past, jury pools were drawn from the list of registered voters. Because an adult could shirk jury duty by not registering to vote, some states now draw their jury pool from registered drivers.

Preliminary hearing   A legal proceeding that precedes a trial. In a preliminary hearing, each side in the dispute will present a portion of its evidence before a judge so that the judge can rule whether sufficient evidence exists to warrant a trial. Rarely does the judge rule that there is insufficient evidence to warrant a trial. Both sides use the preliminary hearing to assess what the other side has. You may think of the preliminary hearing (or "prelim," as attorneys call it for short) as the bidding round in a game of contract bridge. The trial is the actual playing of the cards.

Pro bono

Legal work done for free, whether by an attorney for his client or by an expert witness for an attorney.

Recess

A break in the trial (for lunch or a smoke or so that everyone may relieve themselves). If you have exhibits to show, then you may be asked to set them up during the recess.

Subpoena

The written notice to a witness that he is required to come to court at a certain time to testify in a case. Failure to comply with a subpoena is subject to whatever penalty the judge sees fit to impose, including fines and jail.

Summons

The written document by which an individual is notified that he has been sued in civil court. Also known as a *notice*.

Tort

The legal concept that a person who has suffered as the result of another's actions is entitled to compensation for that suffering, so that the guilty party will suffer for his misdeeds. "Tort" is from the Latin word *tortus*, meaning "wrong."

Transcript

A written record of what was said in a legal proceeding. If a transcript of prior testimony by you is available, then review it before testifying again.

Verdict

The decision reached by a jury in a case. A verdict may be either "guilty" (of the charge brought against the defendant or of a lesser charge) or "not guilty." The verdict is "not guilty" rather than "innocent" because the legal system acknowledges that neither it nor the jury is omniscient.

Witness

A person who gives evidence under oath or affirmation in a court or in a judicial inquiry.

Index